jazz

ON THE RIVER

William Howland Kenney

The University of Chicago Press
Chicago and London

William Howland Kenney is professor of history and American studies at Kent State University. Among his books are *Recorded Music in American Life: The Phonograph and Popular Memory, 1890–1945* (1999) and *Chicago Jazz: A Cultural History, 1904–1930* (1993).

The University of Chicago Press, Chicago 60637
The University of Chicago Press, Ltd., London
© 2005 by The University of Chicago
All rights reserved. Published 2005
Printed in the United States of America

14 13 12 11 10 09 08 07 06 05   1 2 3 4 5

Part of chapter 4 was originally published as "Just before Miles: Jazz in St. Louis, 1926–1944," in *Miles Davis and American Culture*, ed. Gerald Early (St. Louis: Missouri Historical Society Press, 2001), 24–39. © 2001 by the Missouri Historical Society Press, St. Louis. Reprinted with permission.

ISBN: 0-226-43733-7 (cloth)

Library of Congress Cataloging-in-Publication Data

Kenney, William Howland.
    Jazz on the river / William Howland Kenney.
        p.   cm.
    Includes bibliographical references and index.
    ISBN 0-226-43733-7 (cloth : alk. paper)
    1. Jazz—History and criticism. 2. Rivers—United States—Songs and music—History and criticism. I. Title.
ML3508.K45 2005
781.65'0976—dc22

                                                                    2004015751

⊗ The paper used in this publication meets the minimum requirements of the American National Standard for Information Sciences—Permanence of Paper for Printed Library Materials, ANSI Z39.48-1992.

For
Françoise Massardier-Kenney

Contents

Acknowledgments   *ix*

Introduction   Playing Changes: Music, Movement, and
the Performance of Power on "America's River Nile"   *1*

Chapter 1   "Masters of the River": Streckfus Steamers, Inc., and
the "Swan Complex"   *12*

Chapter 2   Fate Marable, Musical Professionalism, and
the Great Migration   *37*

Chapter 3   Groovin' on the River: Louis Armstrong and
Riverboat Culture   *64*

Chapter 4   From Beale Street to Market Street: Music and Movement
Through Memphis and St. Louis   *88*

Chapter 5   "Blue River": Bix Beiderbecke and Jess Stacy
on the Mississippi   *115*

Chapter 6   Steamin' to the End of the Line: Jazz On, Along, and
Beyond the Ohio River   *141*

Epilogue   The Decline and Fall of Excursion Boat Jazz in St. Louis   *171*

Appendix A: Excursion Boat Musicians   *179*

Appendix B: River Songs and Tunes   *184*

Notes   *193*

Index   *213*

Jazz on the River

Acknowledgments

Summer breakfasts with Françoise Massardier-Kenney gave me a most agreeable opportunity to talk about whatever aspects of this project I was raving about, helping me formulate ideas that would find their way into the manuscript. Any of the weaker notions that emerged from my fevered brain were met by her polite but acute criticisms, while those made of more powerful stuff received her measured encouragement. When I got lost in the conversion from one word processing program to another, she stepped in to banish those maddening hidden formats. That was an act of pure kindness.

My special thanks to Dean Joe Danks of the College of Arts and Sciences at Kent State University for his unflinching support of my work and of interdisciplinary studies in a time of budgetary crisis in public higher education. I am equally indebted to the National Endowment for the Humanities for the one-year Grant to University Teachers that allowed me to travel to several archives along the Mississippi River. Just when I most needed it, the Missouri Historical Society provided a one-month research fellowship to scour its wonderful collections. The considerable geographical scope of this project made that help indispensable. Kent State's Office of Research and Graduate Studies approved additional financial assistance that permitted my return to the archives on several occasions.

Douglas Mitchell, executive editor for history at the University of Chicago Press, extended his bracing support in setting this project in motion and in seeing it into print.

Bruce Raeburn, curator of the William Ransom Hogan Jazz Archive at Tulane University in New Orleans, Louisiana, inspired my growing interest in riverboat jazz with his excellent Web site "Riverboats and Jazz." He kindly shared with me many of his ideas about these topics while also sharing some of his Web site photos and arranging an occasion for me to speak about my work at Tulane University's Mississippi Basin Seminar. The initial idea for this approach to the history of jazz came while attending one of Gerald Early's scholarly conferences on the black heartland at Washington University. His concepts of an interurban and interstate African American network stretching through the Mississippi valley has served as the foundation of my thinking. John Waide, archivist of the University Archives in the Pope Pius XII Library at St. Louis University, greatly assisted my work in the Judge Nathan B. Young Collection. Eugene Redmond took me on an insightful introductory tour of East St. Louis, Illinois. Steve Bolhafner of the News Research Division of the *St. Louis Post-Dispatch* guided my research into the newspaper's clipping files.

In Davenport, Iowa, Eunice Schlichting, chief curator of the Putnam Museum of History and Natural Sciences, organized two outstanding seminars on Bix Beiderbecke and generously shared the fruits of her own research on music in Davenport. She also put me in touch with researcher Craig Kline, who graciously shared summaries of his work on African Americans and music in the Quad Cities area.

Robert O'Meally generously organized two occasions for me to speak at Columbia University about my evolving interpretations of riverboat jazz. Thanks to Mark Tebeau and James Borchert of Cleveland State University and the Thomas Campbell Seminar on the City for providing me with an opportunity to speak about riverboat jazz. Similarly, I extend my thanks to Jeffrey Jackson of Rhodes College in Memphis for inviting me to speak at Rhodes while on a research tip to Memphis.

Phil Cartwright interviewed the St. Louis ragtime musician, composer, and sheet music collector Trebor Tichenor in my stead and greatly assisted me in a joint interview of Fate Marable's children Fate Marable Jr. and Isadora Sandidge Marable. Our thanks to the Marables for their kindness and assistance. David Chevan extended permission to quote from one of his insightful manuscripts about Fate Marable Sr. The jazz musician Eric Sager offered some especially perceptive insights into the riverboat jazz scene in St. Louis. Eugene Miller kindly supplied copies of historical recordings from St. Louis. Thanks to Peter Fry, chair of the English Department at Western Reserve Academy, for a choice quotation from Ralph Ellison's *Invisible Man*.

Several musicians and scholars read portions of this book. I thank Bill Fuller for his hard work and insightful criticisms and Charles Hersch, Victor Greene, Ken Bindas, and Burton Peretti for their criticisms of various sections and for their encouragement.

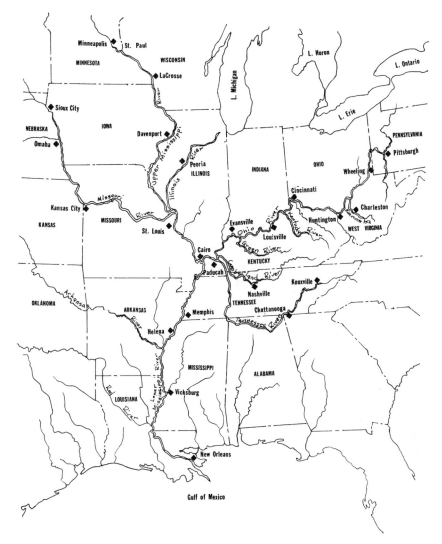

Map of the Mississippi and Ohio Rivers. (Reprinted, by permission, from Alan Bates and Clarke Hawley, *Moonlight at 8:30: The Excursion Boat Story* [Louisville, Ky.: Alan Bates and Clarke Hawley, 1994], i.)

Introduction

Playing Changes: Music, Movement, and the Performance of Power on "America's River Nile"

> In his inmost recesses, the human being is sharing the destiny of water which flows. Water is truly the transitory element. . . . The being dedicated to water is a being in flux.
>
> —Gaston Bachelard, *Water and Dreams*

Just after World War I, the musical style called jazz began a water-borne journey outward from New Orleans, that "exotic oasis of romance and forbidden delights,"[1] the only subtropical city in the United States, the capital port of the Mississippi River. Steam-driven boats that sold harbor excursions in New Orleans during the winter months began, for the first time in any organized way, to leave town during the summer months to "tramp" the Mississippi and Ohio rivers, bringing an exotic new music labeled riverboat jazz to the nation's inland waterways. To tourist and excursion boat entrepreneurs promoting the late night scene in New Orleans during World War I, this seemed a promising and significant mobile stage from which to spread northward the exotic sounds of the Crescent City. Rather than waiting about for those upriver to make their way down to the city as tourists, some New Orleans musicians could now act as emissaries to spread their exciting sounds up into the Mississippi, Missouri, and Ohio River valleys. A much wider spectrum of Americans could now begin listening and dancing to this music while marveling at its musicians, the music, and their own slightly hypnotized fascination with both.[2] Out in the "fresh" river air, under the sun or the moon and stars, jazz's energy set into motion stirring waves of sound on the country's most famous rivers. The players and their music melded with historical and cultural interpretations of our greatest rivers, of riverboats, of race, and of American

1

sectionalism and with the ongoing cultural construction of racial and national identity in the United States.

The great Mississippi River, navigable for most of its 1,944 miles from St. Paul, Minnesota, to New Orleans, Louisiana, offered a new and richly suggestive musical context in which to portray American national identity. The Mississippi, the Ohio, the Missouri, and their tributaries had carried the nineteenth-century tide of violin and banjo players on flatboats, keelboats, and rafts, peopling the huge area served by the river network. The great era of American steamboats, which lasted from Robert Fulton's 1815 invention to 1870, did much to build a system of national trade and commerce. The railroads, however, proved able to move far more produce faster and more efficiently than did the old steamers, driving most of them out of business. In 1907, John Streckfus, the son of a German immigrant, had the idea of attracting passengers by inviting a hot ragtime band on board his new excursion boat.[3]

Long-distance travel changed New Orleans jazz. What came to be known as riverboat jazz took the form of "hot dance music" played by a relatively large ten-to-twelve-man combination of musicians from the Crescent City and points north on imposing wooden excursion boats. In major river cities such as Memphis, Tennessee, Helena, Arkansas, Cape Girardeau and St. Louis, Missouri, and Davenport, Iowa, as well as the myriad smaller river towns, Americans learned to associate a relatively short pleasure cruise with great dance music. Jazz on the river introduced fundamental changes in instrumentation, repertoire, and style to the small-ensemble New Orleans styles, making them far more accessible to broader popular audiences. This music endured for two generations, greatly sustained by jazz recordings, which began to appear in 1917, if not by riverboat jazz recordings, which were to be few. Riverboat jazz never entirely disappeared from the steadily declining number of riverboats, but the years from 1917 to 1945 saw its pinnacle.

After nearly thirty years of outstanding success, riverboat jazz became the swan song of the great steamboat gothic paddle wheelers, the likes of which fewer and fewer living Americans ever got to see. The diesel-powered barge replaced the ornate steamboat gothic after World War II. While it lasted, riverboat jazz seemed a particularly resonant development, a reminder to the nation of New Orleans's street parades by day and of its dance halls by night.

But the great inland waterways added plenty of their own particular mystique to jazz. In every culture, water and rivers have been imagined to be fountains of youth, immortality, and knowledge. "A hero's journey through unknown and dangerous waters is one of the greatest metaphors in literature, art, myth, and dreams. Personal growth was the expected result from a sea voyage, a few continents discovered along the way." A river journey within the United States emphasized the recovery of something, someone, or a part of oneself, an attempt to restore harmony and wholeness.[4] All of these themes worked their ways into the early twentieth-century invention of commercial river cruises and riverboat jazz.

The excursion boats and their music resonated with other historic themes, as well. Riverboat jazz popularized one especially gifted young musician who was made its figurehead. In 1919, America's grisly "Red Summer," a season of unprecedented racial violence,[5] a young African American cornetist from New Orleans, Louis Armstrong, became a modern musical herald bringing the glad tidings of his original music to restless black and white youth in the Mississippi valley. He, the many famous jazz musicians who followed him, and large numbers of oppressed African Americans left the South, setting out, in what came to be called the Great Migration, to find greater freedom, increased economic opportunity, and wider experience of the world. The excitement of music and movement seemed to promise great things and to suggest a new way of life and greater sense of wholeness within it. Some highly regarded musicians of jazz's first half-century—Warren "Baby" Dodds, Henry "Red"

The steamer *St. Paul,* the largest and most popular of the Streckfus excursion vessels. (Photo courtesy of the Jones Steamboat Collection, Special Collections Division, Howard-Tilton Memorial Library, Tulane University.)

Allen, Jess Stacy, Zutty Singleton, Leon "Bix" Beiderbecke, Harold "Shorty" Baker, Boyd Atkins, Earl Bostic, James Blanton, Eugene Sedric, Tab Smith, and Clark Terry—followed in Armstrong's wake. These musicians and many more largely unknown to history tested their mettle on hundreds of short, arduous voyages of recollection, adventure, and discovery on America's inland waterways. Some, such as the St. Louis trumpeters Charles Creath and Dewey Jackson, the drummer and vocalist Floyd Campbell, the reed man Thornton Blue, and the pianist Burroughs Lovingood did not gain much national fame. They did, however, earn high regard from the fans and fellow musicians who heard them on the Mississippi.

The very young German American musician Bix Beiderbecke also became an enduring symbol of riverine jazz aesthetics and culture. Like Armstrong, Beiderbecke imagined that jazz on the Mississippi River excursion boats might be his passport to a greater freedom and also might help fill a void in his erratic young life. Neither he nor Armstrong ever recorded with their riverboat orchestras, but, during their careers, they did record outstanding jazz interpretations of river and levee themes that still serve as musical reminders of the Mississippi Valley between the world wars. Armstrong best caught the rugged excitement and hot anticipation in voyages of discovery; Beiderbecke's ringing majesty best carried the bittersweet mixture of anticipation and regret associated with voyages of discovery.

The combination of the new jazz music with the ancient mystique of water and of the greatest rivers of the United States introduced a powerful, popular, and emotionally complex experience of the promise of American life. Dancing to the exotic sounds of live jazz on the majestic Mississippi and Ohio rivers helped create a dream-filled threshold experience of life's possibilities, an apprehension of a mysterious, renewing interval that left passengers of that time powerfully and unaccountably moved.[6] Jazz-influenced dance music seemed somehow very seductive when sounded and heard in motion, creating a sensational siren song at the close of World War I only to fade slowly away after World War II. Riverboat jazz expressed an unsettled, exploratory musical sensibility for its radically unsettled times. The idea of riverboat jazz subsequently lived on through the revival of traditional jazz after World War II.

As long as we have believed that jazz musicians played only in obscure, smoke-filled inner-city clubs and bars, we have thought them absent without leave from the public arena of civic life in the United States. Although substantial numbers of Americans went to listen to them in downtown clubs, only a few writers brought such experiences to the level of public discourse. This book argues that the illusion of absence stems from the instinctive desire of most customers and riverboat passengers to keep their jazz experience "im-

plicit," to make it a powerful but illicit "trip" that they preferred not to analyze. As a result, it has been possible to think that jazz and those who played it
must have been somewhere else whenever the proud public narratives called
American history were being made.

This has been a significant misunderstanding. Like the enduring cultural
stereotype of the "baaad black man," so the pop terms "jazz" and "jazzman,"
too, long served to erase any serious investigation of their social, cultural,
and historical construction. The scholarly movement that analyzed ragtime and
jazz only from a musicological perspective perpetuated the mystery of the
African American vernacular musician and white America's unexamined fascination with him. From 1918 to 1950, jazz and hot dance music touched on,
albeit from opposing perspectives, black and white people's shared need to
feel themselves in motion through space, time, and culture and to express in
music and dance their sense of excitement, anticipation, and apprehension of
movement, migration, and changing race relations. African American jazz
musicians expressed in bright, exciting, and always enigmatic music their own
hopes that the Great Migration from the rural South to northern industrial
cities would bring greater freedom and economic opportunity.

At the same time, jazz, that exciting enigma, fascinated many white people
who felt apprehensive about the Great Migration's impact on the social order
of the United States. Riverboat jazz and hot dance music along Mississippi
and Ohio rivers helped white Americans approach in an oblique manner
underlying social and cultural changes that were too deep and too heavily
laden with pain, guilt, and fear for most citizens to discuss openly. Early jazz
was stimulated by, responded to, and trumpeted with bright optimism the social transformations of its time.

This examination of jazz on the river therefore explores an important liminal groove in America's history, analyzing how and why a major style of the
past emerged, why it moved its listeners into such stubbornly unexamined
realms of experience, and why that generation's jazz became increasingly out
of touch with changing times. The chapters that follow attempt to re-create
the shared emotions and the particular cultural and musical sensibilities of
riverboats and river cities in order to better reveal the social, cultural, historical, and musical processes involved in riverboat jazz.

The Mississippi and the Ohio rivers formed enormous topographical in-
terstices in the land. Much to the frustration of many American citizens, the
Big Muddy, the longest and most powerful river in America, ran north-south
rather than east-west or west-east, obliging our nation's builders to construct
bridges to assure a national continuity of economic and political purpose. But
some midwesterners preferred to live their lives on the water, cruising up and

down the major river valleys in modified old wooden riverboats, instead of joining the nation's gasoline-and-coal-powered march westward. Hundreds of thousands of twentieth-century tourists liked to imagine themselves errant adventurers, fun-loving "pirates" who turned their backs on all that land-locked striving. The riverboat experience, a commercialized reworking of Tom Sawyer, Becky, and Huck Finn, carried these Americans away into stirring dreams of water-borne adventure and errant discovery. Riverboat passengers danced their dreams.

The historical importance and the undeniable might of the Mississippi and the Ohio deeply influenced the jazz that animated those ornate and slow-moving vessels. Although excursion boats steamed out of and back into the same port on two-to-four-hour daily tourist trips, passengers, in their imaginations, at least, "floated" all the way downriver to New Orleans or up to Minneapolis–St. Paul. The shimmering, roiling, fascinating waters of the Mississippi led the mind's eye toward the paths of the country's nineteenth-century expansion and sectional conflict. The promoters' publicity and lectures linked excursions to simplified and romanticized historical commentaries and to literary interpretations of the Mississippi, the South, the North, the Confederacy, and the Union. Riverboat jazz, like many a historical interpretation, became a palimpsest, a message that concealed upsetting social, political, and economic realities of black life and American race relations. The music professed an interpretation of the national might of the United States, one that encouraged white Americans to relax and act out their dreams of a release from labor's daily grind.

At the same time, jazz, riverboat jazz, and the Mississippi itself allowed passengers to steam right on by without investigating too closely what they instinctively knew to be the dangerous shoals of sectional and racial tensions. The musical excursions united a long-struggling country in an unspoken understanding that seemed to allow everyone involved to have a good time. The rivers and their old-fashioned boats seemed to flow past and beyond the sites of America's shattered historical dreams, reassuring everyone with their majestic and fluid motion. When perceived from the middle of the Mississippi River, North peacefully coexisted with South, Confederate gray with Union blue, and whites with blacks. Riverboat jazz reaffirmed confidence in the United States.

Boats, crews, passengers, and jazz musicians performed in a national spectacle—a parade and celebration of national power and confidence—one that fit the moods of a country beset by war, social change, and economic depression and one that has largely disappeared from the major rivers in the United States. Bridge after bridge has permitted trains and cars to pass over but prevented the tall stacks of riverboats of late nineteenth-century proportions from passing underneath. The British writer Jonathan Raban, who as a child had so admired George Caleb Bingham's paintings of sunny hilarity on the Mississippi, had trouble as an adult actually finding the Mississippi River under all the bridges, overpasses, underpasses, and buildings in Minneapolis–St. Paul.[7] These days, only a few citizens would think to beat the heat by taking the river breezes. Air conditioners provide ample refrigerated relief at home and at work. The persistent use of our rivers for industrial sewage disposal has fouled the waters and the breezes above them. The vagaries of the weather, levees, and current-borne silt rendered long stretches of the rivers too shallow to float boats of any appreciable draft. Locks solved this problem while reducing the river's romance.

Despite the many problems of making a living from a nineteenth-century technology, the excursion boats enjoyed enormous popularity for more than thirty-five years in the twentieth century. The music called riverboat jazz played a pivotal role in that success. The "mile-wide" Mississippi was often too broad for passengers to see much of anything pointed out to them. Without music, the glistening water and bright skies could mesmerize those who sat down on the rocking chairs scattered along the veranda-like decks. The boats moved so slowly, vistas seemed so vast, and the chunking rhythms of the paddle wheels were so tranquilizing that imaginations slowed, turning torporously inward toward sleep and the edges of depression. Music's dynamic movement got people up off their chairs and into each others' arms, the imagined adventure of errant discoveries expressed in breathless anticipation of physical intimacy in smoothly coordinated dance movements. Excursion-boat escapades would have seemed disappointing had they not included hot dance music played by groups of young black or young white musicians.

Riverboat jazz touched powerful emotions and sensibilities beneath the surfaces of public life. Music, particularly hot dance music, provided the psychological experience of a powerful, transporting motion that carried mind and spirit beyond the limited social and geographical loops of the commercial excursions. As the German musicologist Victor Zuckerkandl so compellingly explains, each musical note possesses a dynamic quality, "a direction, a pointing . . . in the direction of its will, going toward the expected next tone; our hearing does not remain with the tone, it reaches through it and beyond it, pure betweenness, pure passing over."[8] So, too, intense rhythms and constantly shifting harmonic progressions pulled passengers into adventurous musical trips of the sort that Walter Donaldson evoked in his popular 1920s song "Changes," in which a jazz musician slips furtively but skillfully through "beautiful changes in different keys, beautiful changes in harmony": "First he changes into C, changes into D, changes into E, as easy as the weatherman. Now he's getting kind of cold, getting kind of hot, Baby, I forgot, he's the talk of Dixieland."[9]

Waves of musical meter interacted in tension and continuous adjustment with dynamically sounded notes to produce a kinesis of hot dance rhythms on the river, a new experience of time.[10] Dance music added its waves of sound and motion to those of the river currents and to the steamboats' majestic progress, enhancing, broadening, and deepening the passengers' feeling of discovery, fluid motion, and renewal. The moving quality of the music that passengers heard set them to dancing, shifting them into a anticipation of adventure, recollection, and imagination. For as long as it might last, they could imagine themselves moving beyond the limits of a short excursion and into the mythic realms of America's River Nile. Americans dreamed of getting somewhere.

Beginning in 1927, the popularization of life on the inland waterways was repeatedly moved to Broadway in New York City, charming millions of Americans long after the paddle wheelers lay scuttled deep in the Mississippi mud. Americans outside the Mississippi and Ohio valleys have come to enjoy commercialized images of that life largely because of the 1926 novel *Show Boat* by Edna Ferber.[11] This popular story appeared just before a terrible Mississippi River flood that, with official guidance, swept away the homes of tens of thousands of poor black Americans.[12] Ferber often bragged that she had no need to actually see or personally experience something in order to write about it: "I have never been on the Mississippi or in the deep South. I wrote *Show Boat*."[13] Her novel therefore extended and popularized minstrel themes found in Mark Twain's *Life on the Mississippi* and *Huckleberry Finn*, giving a leading role to Magnolia, her white heroine and daughter of a show boat captain, who takes over for Julia, a "black" entertainer ejected from the show boat for camouflaging her racially mixed parentage.

The perennially popular musical *Show Boat*, based generally on Ferber's novel, with music by Jerome Kern and lyrics by Oscar Hammerstein, has been regularly revived on Broadway, in touring companies, and in three Hollywood films in the seventy-five years since it first appeared. The jazz excursion boats were technically not "show boats," those floating theaters on barges pushed about the rivers by steamboats, but they definitely were in show business. In contrast, although the musical *Show Boat* did give work to a number of black musical comedy artists, it romanticized, distorted, and minimized black life and music on and along the Mississippi. The show has stirred repeated protests from black communities across North America for thoroughly stereotyping the lives of the blacks who brought their music to the river, thereby creating what Lauren Berland has called a Pax Americana by sacrificing black Americans' long, rich history on the levees, the rivers, and in the Mississippi valley to minstrel show stereotypes.[14] Despite the great Paul Robeson's famous feature number "Ol' Man River," the show's music was never based on that which black Americans had played and sung on the Mississippi. Robeson, in fact, struggled with Kern and Hammerstein over the lyrics to that number.

The musicians who made riverboat jazz, the twentieth-century music of the Mississippi and Ohio rivers, also struggled against insulting and restricting racial oppression. Their migration got under way at the height of interracial tensions in the Mississippi valley. For this reason, control of the aesthetic contours of riverboat jazz by tour promoters limited the amount and kind of freedom with which musical employees were allowed to perform. This careful adjustment of the music's racial elements was designed to express the Streckfus family's idea of what it was like to live on the move within white Middle America. For most excursion boat passengers, carefully rehearsed black jazz musicians offered just the right amount and kind of movement, a level of stimulation calibrated to carry steamboat traditions into the twentieth century.

At the same time, with a telling illogic, riverboat jazz became an important touchstone by which white critics and jazz writers established the "authenticity" of African American jazz. No matter how restricting and "white" riverboat jazz seemed to many of the black musicians who played it, they, more than the white bands, specialized in performing it. Even white riverboat musicians concurred that the best riverboat jazz orchestras were the black ones.[15] Many more major black musicians and all-black orchestras played on the riverboats, and played longer, than did major white ones. The jazz flavor of hot riverboat dance music leapt from Fate Marable's bands in particular. Regardless of *Show Boat*–style conventions, the music of Marable, Charles Creath, Dewey Jackson, and Eddie Johnson, all based in St. Louis, the headquarters of Streckfus Steamers, Inc., was considered "the real thing."

The authenticity of black riverboat jazz in the end stemmed from its popular association with roustabout levee culture as well as its musical excitement. The levees of the Mississippi and the Ohio were intervening areas designed to protect cities from floods and to facilitate the movement of passengers, goods, and services to and from the river. After the Civil War, black American laborers specialized in providing manpower and entertainment in this special zone, moving into and out of the various river cities, onto and off the riverboats. In this transitory world, levee workers developed a roustabout culture, a rowdy, swaggering style of life deeply involved in survival by means of personal strength, group political action, music, and dance. The white riverboat system treated black roustabouts brutally and, at the same time, romanticized them and their lifestyle as indomitable and playful, emphasizing musicality and hiding the physical and emotional cruelty meted out to them.

The capital port of riverboat jazz, St. Louis, epitomized the moving process that carried riverboat roustabouts into and out of black urban neighborhoods. It has rarely received its due as a major center of black music and of popular music in general. Any exploration of jazz on the river immediately reveals this city's rich musical influence and the hidden political and economic significance of riverboat and levee music made from 1865 to 1945 in such St. Louis ghetto districts as Wildcat Chute, Castle Thunder, Clabber Alley, Cross Keys, and Death Valley. The city's famous black folk ballads "Staggolee and Billy," "Frankie and Johnny," and "Bradey and Duncan" and its rip-roaring saloon songs "There'll Be a Hot Time in the Old Town Tonight" and "Ta-Ra-Ra-Boom-De-Ay" provide revealing examples of the process by which black variety and saloon entertainers in the river cities worked to produce popular music. For at least a generation before the invention of riverboat jazz, St. Louis's Death Valley had produced commercialized versions of urban black folk music that were adapted and further exploited by white musical entrepreneurs.[16]

The mixture of musical styles emanating from New Orleans and St. Louis provided the most influential example of a process in which black levee workers created intercity circuits of musical exchange along inland waterways after the Civil War.[17] Waterfront laborers frequently rode the riverboats from city to city in order to unload cargo at various destinations. In the process they labored, drank, and performed music with one another, helping to create what Gerald Early has called "the Black Heartland."[18]

At the time of World War I, riverboat jazz provided a turning point in the history of levee work, a moment when, in the face of radically diminished need for roustabouts, they needed some new form of employment. The Streckfus line hired two ten-to-twelve-piece dance bands that provided a real, if limited, employment opportunity and an opening into the middle-class world of professionalism. Black musical employees remained mindful, however, of the musical traditions of St. Louis's levee culture.

A properly revised *Show Boat*, one more directly responsive to African American history and perspectives, could begin to write back into the story of the riverboats the perspectives of levee workers and black dance band musicians. These musicians, who built professional reputations on the river, had their own agendas and their own opinions of the musical labor they performed. When Fate Marable, their agent, hired them, he created for them a jazz stream in the Great Migration of African Americans through the Mississippi and Ohio valleys. Once embarked, these musicians earnestly pursued the many skills of dance band professionals, using their time on the rivers to mix folk music with show business, earning enough money to move further north and making contacts within a growing network of jazz and hot dance band musicians.

Regardless of restrictions, theirs was what many jazz musicians called "get-off" music, improvisations that departed from the scores. It communicated an aesthetic of release, a taking of leave, a separating from the past, an exploratory aesthetic and an optimistic plunge into the future that ultimately revealed both the confinement and the potential in the Jim Crow music scene in the 1920s, 1930s, and 1940s. In a dangerous time and region, black musicians fashioned their own enigmatic jazz culture, one within which they discovered more about themselves, about music, about fashioning new worlds of their own imagining. Life in the United States created the enduring need for such flights of creative imagination. Happily, however, the inertia of racial segregation could not reach into and crush their inner spiritual mobility.

Riverboats, crews, musicians, and passengers, arranged in a rigidly structured system, played out through changing times an idealized public parade of American national power and identity in the early twentieth century. "Parades, inaugurations, processions, coronations, funerals [and excursion boats] provide ruling groups with the occasion to make a spectacle of themselves in a manner largely of their own choosing."[19] Banners waving, white paint glistening, music gaily playing, the huge paddle wheelers, moving symbols of the Old South, gracefully glided just above the raging currents of our most powerful and destructive rivers. They demonstrated to everyone involved a new commercialized interpretation of American national confidence. In their vessels, on the dance floors, and in their orchestras, Americans thus evoked, and then struggled to maintain control over, forces to which jazz gave such intriguing and enigmatic expression.

Chapter 1

"Masters of the River": Streckfus Steamers, Inc., and the "Swan Complex"

Of course, on a boat, the prima donnas is the band. You got a good band? You got a good boat! If you haven't got a good band, then it don't matter how fine the paddle [wheel] is, you just don't have a boat if it's an excursion.

—David Grant, St. Louis, Missouri

The vaporous exultation not to be confined! Ha, Ha! The animation of delight which wraps me, like an atmosphere of light, and bears me as a cloud is borne by its own Wind.

—Gaston Bachelard

In 1925, Frederick Way, who was to become the leading chronicler of riverboats, bought his first packet boat with help from his father. For him, owning riverboats was like "drilling an expensive well in a field which had been worked over for a generation past—then abandoned—and a sign posted on the premises which would read 'No Oil Here.'" It was "akin to clearing away the wreckage of abandoned derricks, chopping down the weeds and morning glories and drilling a well (at great cost) when every indication in the world pointed to the fact that the net result was going to be a total loss and a dry hole."[1] The *Betsy Ann*, Way's folly, plied the Ohio and the Mississippi rivers for fifteen more years before being dismantled at St. Louis. Way personally experienced the irrational compulsion to take to the river in steamboats whose form, if not function, evoked a slower, less technologically advanced, and supposedly more elegant and graceful time. He was scarcely alone in his fascination with nineteenth-century riverboat aesthetics and technology; many

Americans in the major river valleys shared this desire, one that led to a new riverboat culture and its most notable herald, riverboat jazz.

Way did not exaggerate the odds against making money by transporting goods on the old-style packet boats. Since the last quarter of the nineteenth century, the railroads had possessed mounting advantages in speed and organization. And not only were the old riverboats slow; unlike the railroads, they were not organized into powerful corporations that handled shipments from point of production to final market. No one company, for example, could carry goods all the way from Pittsburgh to New Orleans. Riverboat companies remained small and independent, offering merely to transport their cargoes over relatively limited distances only to unload them, necessitating subsequent reloadings that increased the risks of further damage and thus of increased insurance costs.[2]

The packet companies never managed to promote the systematic construction of steamboat "terminals," similar in function to railroad terminals, where goods might be efficiently transported from packet to warehouse. A few cities such as Davenport and Memphis did construct them, but they were the exceptions to the rule. Riverboat architecture, moreover, featured continuous upper decks that prevented freight-handling machinery from unloading cargo from the lower decks. As if all of that were not enough, steamboats were notoriously flimsy and unreliable. As their official journal put it: "Not only is there an amazing number of ancient, decrepit steamers on the river, tottering about until a snag, a collision, or a boiler explosion sends them to a watery grave, even the new boats show no advance in type. They are still wooden, flat-bottomed sternwheelers, their monumental smokestacks emitting dense clouds of black smoke to obscure the landscape and testify of the coal they waste."[3] Moreover, in general, trade in the United States moved along an east-west axis rather than the north-south trajectory of the riverboats.

Despite the many problems with river transport, cultural compulsion easily overcame impracticality. The cultural history of Mississippi and Ohio excursion boats reveals that these large, antiquated, heavily symbolic vessels stimulated enchanting visions of graceful harmony with the forces of nature, illusions of masterful control over the river's destructive power and over social and political currents that periodically disturbed the nation's public life. Americans liked to dream about their graceful white boats, enjoying reveries in which the vessels resembled wedding cakes, Victorian mansions, southern castles, and even swans paddling majestically through peacefully calm, glassy waters that wedded past with present and North with South. For most white people, riverboats stirred nostalgic longings for gentle voyages into an earlier era, sometime just after the Civil War, when the Mississippi River opened onto a vast national playground in which white Americans might, like happy children, wander, explore, and discover. Stirred by experiences of river water, air, levees, and vessels, the national imagination conjured a compelling anticipation of exploration, expansion, individual liberty, and national power along the watery paths of the American Dream.

The excursion boats of the first half of the twentieth century systematically organized and commercialized these reveries, expressing them with new forms of tourism that had been implied but left undeveloped by the nineteenth-century riverboats. The dominant excursion boat companies defied the dangerous currents of rivers and of race relations that roiled beneath the upper decks of the packets and strategically restaged dramas of mastery over surging waters and interracial tensions, rewriting, directing, and starring in riverine rituals of national power.

Four generations of the Streckfus family, whose German immigrant founders settled along the upper reaches of the Mississippi River in Illinois, dominated the excursion boat era on the entire navigable length of the Mississippi and the Ohio from 1901 to 1950. Like the dangerously powerful river on which the trips took place, the Streckfus family was a natural force and not to be taken lightly. Its enterprising history in the United States began in the spring of 1850 when Balthazar Streckfus (1811–1881) emigrated from Landerbach, Bavaria. He, his pregnant wife Anna Mary (Schaab) Streckfus, and their two daughters Barbara and Catherine set sail on stormy winter seas for New York City. Three months later their battered wooden vessel, far off course, with many of its passengers now suffering from smallpox, dysentery, and diphtheria, finally limped into the port of New Orleans.[4]

Michael Streckfus, the family's first son, was born on that trip. After seeing him baptized in the nearest Catholic church, the family made its way northward on the Mississippi by flatboat, settling on a farm in Edgington, Illinois, about five miles inland from the eastern bank of the river and twenty miles east of Davenport, Iowa. A family photo from that period reveals Balthazar to be a startlingly handsome man with black hair and dark, sharply piercing eyes that challenged the camera. In 1868 he established a successful wagon-building business in Rock Island, Illinois and, when he had accumulated enough capital, built the "Streckfus Block," a large brick building that still stands. It included a boarding house, a dance hall, and a saloon; like the boats that would make the family's fame, it served the needs of Americans on the move.

Balthazar's son John (1856–1925) was the first member of the clan to take to the river as a profession. He founded the family's excursion boat empire. John epitomized the midwestern strain of huckleberry rebellion popularized by Mark Twain. For example, he defied his father's wishes in choosing the boat

John Streckfus surrounded by his four sons. Left to right: Roy Michael, Joseph Leo, John Sr., Verne Walter, and John Nicholas, January 5, 1920. All were licensed riverboat captains. (Photo courtesy of Duncan Schiedt.)

business, setting in motion within his family one of the core psychological dramas of riverboat culture and the jazz life. He is said to have caught what midwesterners called "steamboat fever" as a nine-year-old, stowing away under a sack of corn in order to live out his dreams of independent adventure and discovery. His masterful father, who had determined that his son should become a flour miller, caught him, however. The young John Streckfus dutifully postponed his dreams, working for years in his father's wagon shop at Ninth Street and Third Avenue in Rock Island. When the young man married Davenport's Theresa Bartemeier, he even opened a grocery store with a flour and feed mill attached. As luck would have it, however, flour milling made him ill. A doctor recommended that he pursue a career out-of-doors.[5] He happened to have had one in mind and would later interpret his "tramping" excursion boats and the Mississippi River within the mix of ideas created by Mark Twain about youth and escape from authority on the river.

In 1880, John, then twenty-four, bought his first riverboat, the side-wheeler *Freddie*, and went into the packet business, delivering produce and a few passengers to and from small towns. Bigger boats such as the swifter *Verne Swain* (built in 1886) and the *City of Winona* followed. He started with triweekly trips between Evansville and Rochester but, as early as 1894, grumbling about competition and low profits on the Ohio River, began to talk wistfully about moving to St. Louis, Missouri. He eventually did get there, moving his Acme Packet Company north of St. Louis and developing the Upper Mississippi trade by carrying produce and passengers in the Quad Cities area. He turned out to be a thoroughly capitalistic rebel and earned a reputation for efficiency, punctuality, courtesy and, when he deemed it necessary, a two-fisted toughness. He took inspiration from the rigorous schedules of the trains that ran along both banks of the Mississippi, the same ones that were doing such a good job of running the river packets out of business. No matter how empty, John Streckfus's first packets steamed in and out of port on time.[6]

Large wooden riverboats that had been constructed during the last two decades of the nineteenth century fascinated Streckfus and his customers. They could not help but gaze upon them, imagine the feel of the mighty river flowing under their shallow hulls, and admire the vessels' delicate but stately movements. Writers evoked the various timbres of their throaty steam whistles and the bubbling wakes stirred by their chunking wooden paddle wheels, fleeting trails that seemed to trace and retrace the wakes of the country's national glory. But the business of delivering dry goods and through (one-way) passengers by water was slowly dying, mortally wounded by the powerful railroads that could transport everything much more swiftly and cheaply. River packets were too slow, too nineteenth-century, too inefficient, much too disorganized. Wasn't there some other way to make a life plying the inland waterways?

If he was going to stay on the river, John Streckfus had to find something else to do with his boats. Like all packet captains, he had always carried at least a few passengers. He had been known to deliver a small cluster of avid fishermen to a choice spot along the shore. He decided to try to attract more passengers. At the turn of the century, he had George Kratz make a thirty-seven-whistle calliope to be installed on the *City of Winona*.[7] If its insane whooping didn't get people's attention, nothing else could.

In 1901 he fulfilled a dream shared by many close observers of the river packet business: he placed an order for an excursion boat, a modification of the packet boat idea designed to carry "sightseers and excursionists"[8] rather than produce and overnight passengers. Streckfus designed and paid $25,000 to have built at Jeffersonville, Indiana, an innovative 175-foot "palatial excursion boat" meant to carry from eighteen hundred to two thousand passengers, introducing a number of ideas new to the traditions of marine architecture on the inland rivers. The nineteenth-century packet tradition had dictated relatively long "through" voyages from one port to another. Such trips had required staterooms in which passengers could retire for the night. John Streckfus, however, had no intention of allowing his sightseers to stay aboard that long, and while they were on board he saw to it that they moved through specially designed public spaces. He therefore provided sleeping quarters only for the steamboat's musicians and crew and gave to the public an enormous polished maple dance floor (100 × 27 feet) on which to dance and flirt with water-borne dreams of adventure. The superstructure that surrounded this arena of bodily movement, desire, and negotiation looked much like that of the old packet boats but opened onto long, gingerbread-covered verandas along which passengers could take the air, chat, and wax romantic. Windows shaped like those on a train, a "saloon cabin," easy chairs, cigars, newspapers, a dining room, and a modern electric light plant showed the influence of railroad design on the excursion boats.[9] He began his new excursion boat empire by placing his own initials, J.S., on the bow of his innovative riverboat.

John Streckfus hoped to begin a Mississippi River empire. His new excursion boat would allow him economic protection should his packet business wane. One year after its christening, the *J.S.* was plying the waters between New Orleans and St. Paul,[10] running cruises out of any port that could provide enough customers. His riverboat might winter in New Orleans or in one of the rare Mississippi or Ohio River ports (such as Nahant, Iowa, near Davenport), that provided shelter from the winter's crushing river ice. But the *J.S.* had no home port, and its constant searching for a welcome came to be called "tramping." The term "tramp steamer" soon applied to the growing number of excursion boats in general, and it caught just the right attitude of jaunty and unfettered freedom.

That line between individual liberty and responsibility, an essential trajectory in jazz music as well as riverboat culture, could be as difficult to locate as a snag-free river channel. John's rebellion against Balthazar's plans for a landlocked future seems always to have included a sensible recognition of the need to make a living and earn society's respect, even on its watery margins. From 1901 to 1910, the rebellious son proved determined and well-organized, keeping his excursion cruises on time in a delicate wooden boat that required constant vigilance and upkeep, commercializing as he went Huck, Tom, and Becky's midwestern idyll.

But then, during an evening cruise on June 25, 1910, at Bad Axe Island on the Upper Mississippi near La Crosse, Wisconsin, the *J.S.* caught fire and burned to the waterline. One of the passengers on that cruise had gotten out of line. The accounts do not indicate how, but in those years, before Streckfus introduced the sale of alcoholic beverages on board, passengers could bring

The steamer *J.S.*, built to order in 1901. It burned to the waterline in 1910. Fate Marable led a four-piece band on this vessel beginning in 1907. (Photo courtesy of the Jones Steamboat Collection, Special Collections Division, Howard-Tilton Memorial Library, Tulane University.)

their own. This man probably drank too much and started bothering people. Having had to defend himself, along with his mate, in April 1895 against a charge of having committed assault and battery on one of their deck hands,[11] the captain clearly knew how to use his fists. And he had a responsibility for his passengers' safety, on which depended the success of his entire venture, so he threw the offending passenger into the brig of the *J.S.* The fellow got more than he had bargained for when he flipped a cigarette between the bars of his cell, setting the wooden vessel ablaze and losing his own life in the process.

The burning of the *J.S.* communicated to John Streckfus the terrible power of fire, the element that, when heating water and creating the steam that propelled the old packet boats, often burned them down as well. Fire, the wooden steamboats' ever-present danger, acted, along with water, air, and earth, as a powerful stimulus to riverboat reveries, in which jazz and hot dance music also played major roles.

The tragedy of the *J.S.* brought out the best in John Streckfus. Having gone to the effort and expense of commissioning the construction of a new riverboat only to lose it, he concluded that it would be far easier and cheaper simply to convert outdated wooden packets to excursion boats. The former, after all, could be purchased for a song, and he was one of the very few who had substantial experience in finding something remunerative to do with them.

The Mississippi River entrepreneur seized on the idea of buying out Joseph Reynolds's Diamond Jo Line, which had been running in the red for nearly ten years.[12] That company, like all packet boat enterprises, found it difficult to compete with the railroads in transporting passengers and produce. Moreover, short-term conditions dictated that Streckfus make his move in early 1911. The 1910 season had been a disaster. The water level on the Mississippi had been the lowest since 1865; one of Diamond Jo's leading packets, the thirty-year-old, 221-foot stern-wheeler *Sidney*, had struck rocks, knocking itself out of commission; under the draught conditions, two other Diamond Jo steamers, the 300-foot side-wheeler *St. Paul* and the 264-foot side-wheeler *Quincy*, repeatedly ran aground. Only the 257-foot stern-wheeler *Dubuque* seems to have escaped Diamond Jo's disastrous summer. An epidemic of typhoid fever hit the crews hard, and the company lost an entire season's profits and went deeper into debt.[13]

Moving swiftly to assure himself of a 1911 season, John Streckfus raised money from the sale of common stock in a newly organized Streckfus steamboat line and bought all of Reynolds's wounded packets, a wharf boat in St. Louis, and a string of warehouses that gave him exclusive rights to valuable riverfront landings at all the principal towns between St. Louis and St. Paul.[14] This deal might have created a monumental folly due to draught conditions that regularly left the boats high and dry from 1911 to 1916. Instead, the struggling new company weathered the bad years by means of occasional sales of stock to a carefully limited number of investors, several of whom were family members, and the sale of bonds to the St. Louis Chamber of Commerce.[15] John Streckfus thereby created a family-run riverboat company that soon dominated the excursion trade on the Mississippi River, which the Streckfus family would come to treat as their exclusive domain.

One by one, John and his sons converted their old packet boats to excursion steamers. In order to try to prevent any further disastrous fires, the company banned the smoking of anything but special long stogies that went out when set down. The first of the "new" Streckfus steamers was the *St. Paul*. Transformed in 1917, which World War I turned into a terrible year for the steamboat business, the *St. Paul* started tramping between St. Louis and St. Paul in 1918, when river ice crushed the whole fleet of the Eagle Packet Company. In the boat's third season, an advertisement in the *St. Louis Argus* touted it as follows: "One block long, 75 feet wide, 5000 passengers, three roomy decks open on all sides, 500 rockers, 2,500 comfortable seats, 5000 electric lights, 1000 electric fans. Best dance music in the United States. 1500 couples can dance on the dance floor at one time!"[16] The *St. Paul* hung up on a sand bar at Lone Tree Crossing four miles above Quincy, Illinois, on the twentieth of September, 1918, with two thousand passengers on board, most of them women and children. The long night hours, during which efforts to refloat the huge steamer failed, also produced a bitterly cold wind that thoroughly chilled the waiting passengers. Food at the concession stands quickly ran out. There was no heat, nor were there staterooms to which the unhappy passengers could retire. By 9:00 the next morning, various river craft arrived to take passengers off.[17] Despite this crisis, the new excursion boat had a successful season.

Between 1918 and 1931, a series of locks and dams were finally built on the 729 miles of river between St. Louis and St. Paul. By means of these long-awaited devices, at least nine feet of water could be guaranteed in a channel designated for river craft.[18] By the time they were completed, however, only ten to fifteen years' worth of excursions on the old Diamond Jo boats remained.

Owing to the persistent lack of adequate river water, the *St. Paul* ran its excursions primarily in the area between Cape Girardeau, Missouri, and the Quad Cities. In the 1930s, after many years on the Mississippi, the mammoth craft was moved to the Ohio River. In 1939–40 it was rebuilt and renamed the *Senator* and continued to run excursions from Pittsburgh until World War II forced it out of business.

The huge *St. Paul* was designed to appeal to the youth market, so in 1919 Streckfus converted the packet *Quincy* into the excursion boat *J.S. Deluxe* to serve the "carriage trade" out of St. Louis until replaced in 1934 by the *President*, which catered to this upscale market. The *J.S. Deluxe* carried all-white dance bands led by Jules Buffano, Jan Garber, Louis Panico, and Wayne King. It featured more luxurious appointments than the *St. Paul* in order to attract "the better sort." As another captain put it, the *St. Paul* was designed for "the hoi polloi." As the company explained to its customers: "Mondays and Fridays are special society evenings in the beautiful *J.S.* Steamer Deluxe when invitations are issued to club members and others who appreciate the higher-fare policies that assume a select and limited attendance. Mrs. Julia Laughlin Boehmer has been secured as Social Chaperone on those evenings. Jules Buffano and his famous Montmartre Orchestra of Chicago furnish entrancing music for these delightful occasions."[19]

The *Dubuque* underwent conversion in 1920, reemerging as the *Capitol*, which replaced the old *Sidney* as the winter-season harbor steamer in New Orleans. This was the company's favored boat: its shallow draft allowed it to navigate the treacherous waters of the Upper Mississippi, while its classic stern-wheel design evoked raging cases of riverboat fever.[20] Fate Marable and his orchestra played on the *Capitol*, particularly during the winter months. In 1921 the company rebuilt the steamer *Sidney* as the excursion boat *Washington*.

In 1910 John Streckfus had organized a new company called the Streckfus Steamboat Line, with $150,000.00 in capitalization and offices in Dover, Delaware, and St. Louis. In the 1920s his company was renamed Streckfus Steamers, Inc.[21] The company paid no dividends until 1921, but from that year to 1930, its surplus grew from nearly $18,000.00 to more than $315,000.00. Net profits for the same ten years amounted to $882,720.73.[22]

Financially as well as musically, the 1920s were banner years for Streckfus Steamers. During the depression, too, the company did better than might have been expected. The year 1930 was their worst year as water levels, the lowest in sixty-four years, added drought to depression. Moreover, the company recognized that lines of trade had changed with the unprecedented proliferation of such distractions as movies, radios, and automobiles. (Television would do much to replace river cruises once and for all.) Led by John's eldest son, the indomitable Joseph, the company emphasized the need to compete with the latest trends in popular culture by lowering ticket prices, and, in order to do that in a profitable manner, attracting greater numbers of passengers onto larger boats.

Streckfus Steamers became a family affair. Joseph Streckfus's son-in-law William Carroll enjoyed telling about one of the first jobs to which he was assigned. He was to stand at the head of the gangplank, a small mechanical counter in hand, pressing down on a lever each time a passenger came on board. The small window through which one would normally have been able to see the mounting total had been covered. Carroll was not a Streckfus and therefore was not allowed to know the gross take from ticket sales. Moreover, only members of the family were allowed to touch the money: John and Joe's daughters worked in the ticket booths, and their fathers and husbands counted the cash at the end of the day. Complete and rigid discretion ruled the Streckfus empire: neither junior family member nor mere employee was allowed to talk to the press or anyone else about money or about company affairs.

Streckfus Steamers had the grit and the cash to make the most of the depression years by buying the steamer *Cincinnati*, a luxurious 220-foot packet built in 1924. This boat had covered the Cincinnati-Louisville run, spending considerable time in Pittsburgh, as well. Its parent company fared less well in the depression than did Streckfus Steamers, to which it was sold in 1933. Torn down to the all-steel hull, its superstructure was rebuilt in steel; it reemerged as the *President*, "the first five deck, and all-steel, fire-resistant steamer on the Western Rivers." With twenty-four watertight compartments in its hull, it was said to be unsinkable.[23] The *President*, which replaced the *J.S. Deluxe* in

NEWS AND VIEWS
STRECKFUS STEAMER PRESIDENT

Grand Salon of the S. S. President, largest and finest floating ball-room in the world. Two decks high, with mezzanine all around. Illumination by the unique Rainbow Shadowbox produces more than 80 beautiful effects in colored light. *Below* — The modernistic orchestra stand and corner of the promenade lounge around the dance floor.

Company advertisement for dancing on the S.S. *President*. When launched in 1934, its watertight steel compartments made it the safest of the Streckfus excursion boats. (Photo courtesy of the Jones Steamboat Collection, Special Collections Division, Howard-Tilton Memorial Library, Tulane University.)

the carriage trade in St. Louis, became an instant hit, plying the rivers well into the 1980s. It was, until recently, permanently docked in Davenport, where it served as a casino. In renovating the *Cincinnati*, Streckfus managed to turn the depression into something of an advantage. Because his own ships had fewer and poorer customers, he used his crews to work on the *President*, getting the job done cheaply thanks to low wages and rock-bottom prices for materials.

An exceptionally strong liquidity allowed Streckfus Steamers to strengthen its position during the depression. In addition to the *Cincinnati*, Joseph also bought the stern-wheeler *Greater New Orleans*, thus removing the competition in the Crescent City. It was torn down for parts. The *President* moved into the Pittsburgh trade during the depression, vastly extending the Streckfus empire, which now dominated both ends of the Mississippi-Ohio river system. In the mid-1930s, the system of locks on the Upper Mississippi allowed the large Streckfus craft to work their way up to Minneapolis–St. Paul for the first time since 1918.

The Streckfus men commercialized a new excursion boat culture in which riverboat jazz played a major role, indeed, a far more important role than might have been expected. John Streckfus Sr.'s son Joseph Leo (1887–1960) inherited the company in 1925 on his father's death. A tall, powerfully built, fleshy man, licensed as both a master pilot and a steam engineer, Joe, a pianist, took a deeper interest in music than did his three brothers, Roy Michael (1888–1968), John Nicholas (1891–1948), and Verne Walter (1895–1984). The numerous, energetic, and influential members of the Streckfus family, all of whom worked for the company, together modernized the steamboat experience, marrying the nineteenth-century packet tradition to the popular tourist culture of the twentieth century. Joe, in particular, made jazz a cornerstone of their new interpretation of America's mightiest river system, going so far as to claim that the very term had spun off from the name of their steamer *J.S.*, which they encouraged people to call the "Jess." History, therefore, hereby records that the Streckfus family invented "Jess."

On the simplest level, cruises offered to the public morning and evening round trips from any port along the Mississippi and back between May and September. The boat's first arrival of the season announced the coming of spring, and its departure after Labor Day proclaimed the end of summer, when children went back to school. During the winter, river ice was the greatest danger to the delicate boats. The Streckfus family gathered all but one of their big boats at Davenport, where the topography offered winter-long protection from the crushing power of river ice.

Until the invention and commercialization of air conditioning after World War II, another development that contributed to the demise of the excursion boats, Americans in general and midwesterners in particular suffered from the summer heat and humidity. An outing on the river was supposed to provide cooling breezes, proximity to cool river water, and plenty of refreshing iced drinks. Even when the air over the river actually remained heavy with stifling humidity, just looking at the water brought a measure of relief. Daytime cruises appealed to groups of women with small children, heat-weary housewives, and special women's groups of many kinds. These cruises went from town to town, allowing passengers to get off and see the sites before moving on.

The Streckfus cruises encouraged passengers to think about the association of flowing rivers with history, and their magazine offered reminders of the great white men who had explored the Mississippi all the way from Minnesota to the Gulf of Mexico. Historically inclined ship's officers spoke to passengers about historic sites along the riverbanks, helping them to associate their own excursion with the river's great adventures.[24]

On their daytime excursions southward from St. Louis, for example, passengers could see such sites as the Cahokia Power Plant, the United States Arsenal, Carondelet, the Jefferson Barracks (commanded during the Civil War by Jefferson Davis and Robert E. Lee), Indian Cave (once a home to members of the Osage tribe), and Fort Chartres (from which Chouteau and Laclede came to settle St. Louis).[25] But, try as he might, William Carroll usually found that his history lectures drew tepid responses from the crowds. The public's thirst for historical knowledge seemed all too easily slaked. The Mississippi, moreover, was frequently so wide that everyone had difficulty distinguishing much of anything onshore.

The moonlight cruises, offered from just after sundown to midnight, created the excursion boats' version of romantic excitement on the river. Although music was offered to daytime customers as well, the moonlight cruises always featured the best of the bands that had been hired for the summer. Clark Hawley and Alan Bates describe the customers arriving at dusk to catch their first glimpse of their waiting swan: "White lights outline the graceful lines of her sheer curve, deck above deck, all faithfully mirrored in the placid water . . . there is a particular scent in the balmy air composed of hot popcorn, new floor wax, old, wet wood, and cylinder oil, an odor peculiar to excursion steamers, and . . . it melds subtly with the sharp smell of ragweed, the stink of a too-dead fish, and voluptuous and sulfurous coal smoke."[26]

One-half hour before departure, with all the steamer's lights shining brilliantly, the band played a "calling concert," and young midwesterners dressed in their finest streamed aboard for their mating rituals. After the boat cast off, the dance floor began to pulse with the beat of their feet. The crew obligingly turned out all lights on the uppermost deck of the slowly moving boat so that

The steamer *Island Queen*. (Photo courtesy of the Jones Steamboat Collection, Special Collections Division, Howard-Tilton Memorial Library, Tulane University.)

lovers might neck in relative privacy over the sounds of the hot dance band and under the moon and stars.[27] Riverboat captains liked to joke that the young people "didn't stand a chance," falling eagerly into the sweet melancholy of this pre–World War II dream of moonlight, water, and love, only to awake the next day to find themselves engaged to be married.

The Streckfus family manipulated the major themes of the midwestern cultural interpretation of riverboats. Nineteenth-century society along the Mississippi and the Ohio had created the idea of "the fashionable tour" up the Mississippi from St. Louis, the river and its banks considered graceful playgrounds.[28] The excursion boats shortened and commercialized the fashionable tour. First, using jigsaw carpentry, they carefully preserved and enhanced the wooden gingerbread scrollwork, known as "steamboat gothic," that decorated the edges of most open spaces. In fact, the boats' superstructures had more of this nineteenth-century "wedding cake" filigree because the forward space on the main deck, which had been left open on the sides to accommodate the bulky products carried by packets, was now elegantly sheathed like the rest of the vessel. The Streckfus Line kept the filigree painted as blindingly white as possible. The delicately decorated cupolas under which the river pilots worked, the tall black smokestacks, and the immense and elaborately decorated paddle wheels of the Streckfus steamers created a hyperreal vision of the nineteenth-century packets so lovingly detailed in Mark Twain's *Life on the Mississippi.*[29]

As much as everyone loved the old wooden paddle wheelers, their shortcomings remained all too obvious. Despite the impeccable safety record of Streckfus Steamers, during the mid-1930s the United States Coast Guard insisted that the company install elaborate and expensive sprinkler systems and other safeguards against disastrous fires. Because the old Diamond Jo boats were fast approaching a point at which repairs would cost more than the boats themselves, by 1940 the company decided to scuttle all but the old S.S. *Capitol.* The latter survived its rotting hull only until 1945. To respond to governmental safety concerns and to stay in business, Streckfus Steamers built in 1939 and 1940 a new 374-foot all-steel, inflammable, unsinkable excursion boat named the *Admiral.*

Carefully cleaned, scrubbed, painted, and polished, bedecked with many

The *Admiral,* as it appeared in *Streckfus Steamers Magazine.* When launched in 1940, the all-steel Art Deco vessel was the safest excursion boat to ply the inland waterways. An unknown artist rendered ghostly figures in the sky. (Photo courtesy of the Hogan Jazz Archive, Special Collections Division, Howard-Tilton Memorial Library, Tulane University.)

colorful banners and, of course, American flags, the Streckfus excursion steamers paraded confidently over the Mississippi and Ohio rivers, providing by their marine architecture, the social hierarchies on board, and their carefully arranged hot dance music dramatic public demonstrations of the confidence of a racially segregated nation.[30] The Streckfus family would cling to that vision for more than fifty years.

Having set the stage for a riverboat idyll, Streckfus Steamers did not simply tie up at the dock and wait anxiously for people to come down to the levee. The excursion boats represented a major capital investment that had to be recouped by persuading as many people as possible to buy tickets and get aboard as quickly and as often as possible. This could not be allowed to depend on chance. The company set up an elaborate and clever system to assure that their space produced revenue.

Sometime in early spring, the company sent an "advance man" to the small towns and big city neighborhoods along the rivers to get future customers to share the company's risk that bad weather would ruin the whole enterprise. Advance men sold charter reservations to civic groups, school systems, corporations, and social groups. In this way, the company made money even if the boat never left the dock. Advance men also offered contracts by means of which groups and individuals "sponsored" a future cruise and received a percentage of the gate. This arrangement encouraged the sponsors to sell the cruise for the company in order to ensure a good turnout and a profit on their investment. The company reserved for itself the right to print the tickets in order to prevent the sponsors from overselling the vessel. It also reserved to itself all profits from the concessions sold on board. The margin of profit on food, drinks, games, and souvenirs far exceeded that on the tickets.

The advance men returned to each town a few weeks before the scheduled excursions and plastered walls and telephone poles with posters that usually vastly exaggerated the size and grandeur of the boat. According to Hawley and Bates, one of the best of the advance men was Arch Persons, so persuasive that "he could sell warts." He worked for Streckfus Steamers, always dressed immaculately in the latest style, and admired the company's owners enough to name his son Truman Streckfus Persons. Persons *père* later divorced. When his son moved in with his remarried mother, he took her new married name, becoming Truman Capote.[31]

The system of advance sales of charters and sponsored cruises also lent a veneer of social respectability to the excursion business. In reality, company operatives, who were always ready to pounce on troublemakers and throw them into the brig, carefully policed each trip. But in promoting social dancing to thousands of young midwestern ladies, the company had to reassure parents that their daughters would be treated with the respect they deserved. The system of sponsorship and charters brought more or less cohesive social groups on board, ones that brought with them the mix of people associated with schools, churches, corporations, and small-town civic groups.

Streckfus Steamers also evoked the theatrical matrix popularized in 1927 by Edna Ferber's novel *Show Boat*. The company did prohibit organized gambling on their boats, and the consumption of alcoholic beverages was strictly limited and supervised during Prohibition, but customers were encouraged to think of themselves as casting off from the discipline, routine, and dominance of their landlocked parents and bosses. Passengers undertook a mysterious voyage on a powerful and dangerous river, a voyage that carried them away to a slower, quieter time of carefree youthful high jinks and daring bohemian rebellion before depositing them back on the levee, somehow transformed by their experience.

Excursion boat rides, like the novels of Twain, Ferber, and Frances Parkinson Keyes and the tremendously popular Broadway musical *Show Boat*, romanticized the river. The vessels themselves created the impression of very large but delicate white mansions in the American Gothic style, like floating country houses of St. Louis's "catfish and crystal" elite,[32] gliding smoothly over the waters. Company publicity labeled them "palatial," not unlike the movie palaces of the 1920s and 1930s. One scholar has written of "a palatial boat gliding through the placid waters of the Mississippi . . . the pure white of the freshly painted steamer, the gay costumes of the ladies and the banner waving in the breeze" creating an enduring memory of masterful, stylish grace.[33]

The public spaces opened to customers complemented excursion boat architecture. The steamers' superstructure was opened to the air; railings like white picket fences allowed passengers to lean outward over the water without falling into the river (men tended to dive off when drunk). The decks formed long galleries along which the public might stroll and enjoy the cooling breezes, or if they preferred, to sit in the many rocking chairs placed along their routes.

The slow-moving grace of the riverboats appealed strongly to many Americans, but, inevitably, many others, often boys and young men, found the excursions tedious. According to Bates and Hawley, children nearly always wanted to run throughout the steamer, and many more mature passengers became impatient with the nineteenth-century rhythms of the excursions. These people rushed on board but couldn't wait to disembark. As described by Bates and Hawley: "They are in for a form of torture that is almost oriental in its dilatory pace. They rush aboard and they rush upstairs to get a table and chairs. As soon as they can get a member of their party to table-sit they are off to inspect the boat. This does not take long . . . after a restless eternity the paddle wheel begins to turn but that soon cloys . . . the boat is slow! There is none of the exhilaration of an outboard motor planing across the water . . . time stands still."[34]

A jukebox, arcade games, and the gift shop were soon visited, fed, and abandoned. Young passengers squinted dubiously at the historic sites pointed out to them as being somewhere out there across the water. If the scenery, the boat itself, amusement park games, and the like could not hold people's interest, something else would have to distract them. That something else was a carefully calibrated program of hot dance music for the dancing pleasure of restless tourists who needed to feel themselves in motion, physical as well as imaginative, as the creaking vessel poked along.

As chapter 2 explains in more detail, the association of black dance orchestras with riverboats had roots in the packet era. Black Americans had long played an important role in the white packet boat experience. In the nineteenth century they had worked as roustabouts and stevedores who loaded produce and the passengers' luggage on board. Before departure from a given port, twenty or so of these black laborers would be hired to load the packet and to ride along on its voyage, entertaining passengers from the lower deck. This pattern of activity disappeared in the excursion boat era, when cargo and luggage were no longer involved.

Black roustabouts also had provided musical entertainment for the white passengers, many of whom lined the railings of the second deck in order to watch the hiring and loading process. Officially, in a segregated society, none of the whites really knew much of anything about the roustabouts, but literary and journalistic tradition had it that they were a colorful, comic, happy-go-lucky, dissolute lot. Newspaper reports by Lafcadio Hearn, for example, painted a lurid picture of their carefree lives of dissipation on the levees. According to the American tradition of minstrelsy, all roustabouts were thought to be musical, their rhythmic songs harkening back to the work songs of the slaves.

Streckfus Steamers updated and popularized the roustabout tradition in three ways. First, they kept a few black entertainers on hand to play the roustabouts' role. White passengers looked forward to their evocations of "the days befo' de wah' in the cane and cotton fields of Dixie." Second, the excursion line's magazine published articles filled with what would now be considered blatantly racist stereotypes. For example, in an article in one Streckfus publication passengers were told to look for "ridiculous antics" of "black-skinned, overgrown children" who, in addition to "driving nails with their foreheads," sang and played "plaintive old plantation melodies with the twanging of banjo and guitar."[35] Moreover, the company's yearly magazine published many articles about Mark Twain and identified places along the Mississippi that Twain had interpreted for his readers. Younger customers were encouraged to think of their riverboat excursion in the spirit of Tom, Huck, and Betsy. Twain's Jim reappeared in the guise of the roustabouts, whose lives on and off the river were evoked in such fictional pieces as "Millennium's Luck."[36] *Streckfus Steamers Magazine* explained to the passengers just what the Mississippi, its banks, the excursion boat, and their happy jaunt were all about. Because roustabouts had been an important element in the packet experience but had become redundant with the invention of the excursion boat, Streckfus Steamers published a fictionalized story of a roustabout named Millennium Potts, whom they hoped might be taken as representative of roustabouts in general. The story of this caricatured individual, a lazy but good-natured fellow, moved him through a "typical day" during which he helped feed the boat's voracious furnace, rolled heavy barrels of apples down the levee and up the gangplank, worked a ridiculous scam with a fellow roustabout, fell to rolling dice on his knees with another friend, got thrown into the ship's brig for insubordination and neglect of duty, got hired as a fireman, and finally returned to his wife Mirandy's levee restaurant, where he might be supported by her labors. This version of minstrel stereotypes served to reassure white passengers that innocent, charming, and none-too-bright black men worked somewhere down in the bowels of the boat, far enough away from the whites to be at once exotic and unthreatening and generally there to remind passengers of the packet era.

Third, quite apart from such racist inventions, the actual late nineteenth-century roustabouts' rhythmic vocal music was transformed into a rhythmic instrumental music played by black New Orleans musicians. Like the earlier musical experience, riverboat jazz was supposed to provide, as the Streckfus magazine put it, "Just a Bit o' Color."[37] Impeccably dressed in tuxedoes, seated on a stage behind a thick railing, courteous, discreet, and ultimately mysterious, southern jazzmen injected their racial presence by means of their skin color and the powerful but cryptic hot dance music that carried such inexplicable excitement.

Riverboat jazz was in tune with its time and place in the practical as well as the psychological sense. On the riverboats, jazz stopped blowing smoke. Combined for the first time with the powerful natural elements, hot dance music animated the river experience with racial and musical stimulation. The French philosopher Gaston Bachelard wrote of the imagination as "a kind of spiritual mobility, a kinetic activity of images." He argued that "reverie merely takes us elsewhere, without our really being able to live the images we

Cartoon rendering of typical sights on an excursion cruise, published in *Streckfus Steamers Magazine*. Note the minstrel-show image of a black deck worker and the revealing phrase "just a bit o' color."

encounter along the way." The dreamer "is set adrift. The imagination must be a journey."[38] Bachelard has called the dominant imaginative association of water, air, whiteness, and graceful feminine movement "the swan complex." His analysis of the imaginary symbolism of water helps get to the heart of the excursion boats' expressive cultural meanings, the traditional patterns of imagination and sentiment that explain the phenomenon's continued appeal during the first half of the twentieth century.

For one thing, under sunny skies, rivers such as the great Mississippi and the beautiful Ohio became flowing, transitory, and dreamy, endlessly grouping and dissolving both images and substances in a process of disappearance and rebirth, stimulating naïve, largely unconscious, but still powerful images associated with femininity. These feelings about water, whiteness, and grace dissipated swiftly when skies darkened and winds whipped the water into a fury, its anger seemingly changing its gender. The swanlike excursion boats steamed out onto the rivers only in fair weather. They drew much of their allure from water's feminine associations, but the rivers' underlying destructive powers also confirmed the need for masterful men like the Streckfus captains, whose powerful masculinity might prevail over the elements.

The associations of glassy water and slow, graceful vessels with femininity amounted to culturally specific values, not human universals. Many Americans chafed at the abstracted musings. The riverboat jazz orchestras were intended as further stimuli to the swan complex. First, music's ephemerality beautifully complemented the flowing of the rivers and the transparency of the air. Second, excursion boat dance bands were all-male aggregations. This masculine presence brought to the dance music rhythmic sounds somehow suggestive of the blazing heat down below, where the roustabouts fed wood or coal to the steam engines. The music on the dance floor just above had to be hot as well in order to propel a suggestively intimate rubbing of dancing couples, the latter an apt reminder of the rubbing together of sticks that produced fire in the first place.[39]

Third, the all-black dance bands added to the riverboats' associations of water, air, and fire. Never allowed to dance (or even to speak) with white women on the segregated cruises, black musicians brought to social dance music the diasporic sounds of the levee tonks, juke joints, New Orleans, the Caribbean, and Africa. Given the limited professional opportunities for African Americans in the Midwest before World War II, the black musicians had plenty of reason to play their assigned roles well. In addition, however, the Streckfus family reshaped the powerful evocation of the rivers' sexual and racial associations, replacing staterooms, the moral equivalents of hotel rooms, with huge polished wood dance floors that extended the sexual symbolism of the riverboat with white femininity while at the same time lowering the moral stakes for all.

Because swans can fly, Bachelard emphasized, movement from water to sky "marks a continuity in the dynamic images of water and air."[40] Musical sound waves affect the human imagination, which glides from its water dreams, rising like the notes of a jazz solo and ascending into the air, creating impressions of release, gaiety, and lightness like those of floating effortlessly through the sky. For the passengers on excursion boats, cool breezes in particular were as "gentle breaths" that reanimated those weighed down by the oppressive midwestern heat, especially in St. Louis, where summer heat often becomes extreme. The philosopher stressed that the metaphors of height, elevation, depth, sinking, and the fall are "axiomatic metaphors and the instinct for lightness is one of the most profound instincts in life." The aerial imagination tenders an invitation to travel. As the riverboat's soothing motion cooled passengers' skin, the blessed breezes stirred imaginations with impressions of joy, release, activity, and hope. The boat might be imagined as a floating island suspended in the air or as a bark or, unconsciously, as a cradle rocking on the waves while imperceptibly leaving the water for the sky. Many dreamt of a floating island and then a suspended island and "would ride singing through the shoreless air."[41]

Bachelard taught that "there is no space without music since there is no expansion without space . . . you sing, therefore you fly." Here the excursion boat formula actually provided music to assist struggling imaginations in moving beyond reality toward reverie. Bachelard wrote of the imagined music of water and air: "All profound contemplation is necessarily and naturally a hymn."[42] In the United States after World War I, excursion boat passengers did not usually come on board for "profound contemplation" and wanted something hotter and more secular than hymns. Mixing the popular songs of their day with notably unsentimental African American musical culture associated with New Orleans high life hypnotized Americans with a new, distinctly unsentimental water music played by unknown and therefore exotic musicians. The function of this riverboat jazz was "to go beyond reality and to project a world of sound beyond the silent world."[43] That world could be a religious one or, as on a twentieth-century excursion boat, hot dance music. Music's vibrations, he wrote, created an expanding space into which imaginations, like birds, took flight. The fire in the red hot Streckfus jazz of the 1920s, from slow-burning but radiating coals, cleverly complemented and completed the imaginary takeoff, flight, and ascension of the river experience.

To experience a modern American swan complex, passengers needed music, music made by musicians who were themselves in geographical and spiritual motion. Their diasporic sound waves stirred the air like wind. Slow but stylish dance band music made by black musicians, known only as racist stereotypes, energized the excursion boat reverie of release as vigorous young white men and white women began their intimate swaying.

The color scheme of the swan complex in the United States placed African Americans on the levees, creating an intimate association of skin color with mud. Bachelard labeled the mixture of earth and water "la pate," the doughlike paste from which bread, pasta, and a variety of other essential foods are made. The French word, therefore, is not taken only to mean "mud." The French word for mud is *la boue*. *La pate* also refers to bodily constitution and temperament, as in the French phrase "Il est d'une pate a vivre cent ans" (He's built to live to be a hundred). For Bachelard, therefore, *la pate* also referred to the very stuff of which we all are made, life itself, both physically and psychologically.[44]

Despite the elemental and creative French definition, one that touched on the creative heart of jazz more than did the English word "mud," along the inland waterways mud triumphed over the "pate" of life. Because of unsavory, racist associations of dirt with darker skin color, mud was associated with African American levee workers. This facile stereotype muddied the lyrics and spirit of Harry Barris's 1928 popular song "Mississippi Mud." Barris, a pianist and composer of several other jazz standards of the 1920s, sang with Bing Crosby in a vocal trio called The Rhythm Boys that appeared with the Paul Whiteman Orchestra from 1926 to 1930. When Crosby launched his long career as a solo act, Barris became a character actor in movies, usually playing what Roger Kinkle has called "a small, slick, jive-talking personality [and] fit perfectly Hollywood's idea of [a] typical band musician."[45]

The Whiteman recording of "Mississippi Mud," which also features a solo by cornetist Bix Beiderbecke, emphasizes Barris's lyrical portrait of "darkies" who, when the sun goes down and the tide goes out, gather 'round and "beat their feet" on the Mississippi mud. These fictional roustabout-like characters perform quite a dance; they dance so well that no band is needed; they keep time by clapping their hands; and they're as happy as barnyard animals.[46]

These American ideas about the mixture of water and earth denigrated the viscous stuff of life by treating it as a vicious racial stereotype, the inevitable extension of the color symbolism of the old wooden paddle wheelers. Riverboat jazz on the *Sidney*, the *St. Paul*, and the *Capitol* reflected the immediate context of the excursion boat experience. In 1919, at the end of their first summer season, Joseph Streckfus made it crystal clear that the famous New Orleans jazz pioneers would not be allowed to rely solely on the polyphonic improvisations that they had invented in and around the Crescent City. His subsequent interventions in the orchestra's rehearsals transformed the group's sound.

Out on the river, allowing too much of the hot improvisation that Fate Marable and Joseph Streckfus had heard Louis Armstrong playing in New Orleans, the very music that had so powerfully attracted the steamboat captain, would interfere with the delicate whiteness evocative of the swan complex. Streckfus later spoke specifically of two ingredients of New Orleans music that he felt needed to be changed: tempi and repertoire. First, the musicians tended to play music whose rhythms seemed either too fast or too slow for the dreamy grace of steam-driven swans. Moreover, when the company tested the waters by taking their new jazz show up the Missouri River in 1919, they soon discovered that many patrons sat and stared at the band rather than dancing to its music. Streckfus Steamers had built dance floors into their excursion boats and hired a dance band. Passengers were to dance. If they didn't dance, they would become bored. If they became bored, they wouldn't come back.

Marable, Armstrong, and Dodds would eventually get them up off their feet with the power of their rhythms, but an old wooden vessel such as the *St. Paul* could not long survive the pounding of two thousand perspiring customers simultaneously dancing the Charleston. Streckfus thought of the problem in terms of southern versus northern tempi. He believed that good southern hotel bands such as Dedroit's at the Gruenwald Hotel in New Orleans "had the tempo, syncopation, and rhythm, and played the right pieces for dancers . . . our band's tempo was just 20 counts faster per minute than Dedroit's band."[47] They would have to harness these young Turks and get them to slow down, because rhythmic images of New Orleans and the old South dispatched the passengers' imaginations far downriver to the land of cotton and its capital.

But when playing slower numbers, the captain believed, his musicians tended to play too slowly for the Streckfus Line's version of southern swans. One danced dreamily and, above all, properly at moderately slow tempi; very slow ones often led some dancers to undue sexual arousal. Streckfus was a devoted Catholic whom the church eventually named a Knight of Malta. In St. Louis, he involved himself actively in civic affairs and was a member of the Board of Directors of St. Louis University. He believed that his excursion boat rides provided a major cultural foundation for that city. He was not going to have two thousand customers rubbing their lower abdomens together, doing the "slow grind" to tunes that traditional jazz musicians still call "belly rubbers." Not on his watch! Nor were they going to flay his wooden boat to splinters with the wild stomping of four thousand feet. He therefore dictated moderately slow tempi appropriate for a good New Orleans hotel dance, probably not very different from "the businessman's bounce," a tempo selected for tired businessmen in East Coast clubs. If the excursion boat no longer provided lovers with staterooms, its music might at least suggest the sounds of New Orleans hotels.

Fate Marable, who led the most famous hot dance bands for Streckfus Steamers, had to work within the confining structures of such excursion boat stereotypes. He had his own reasons for accepting such work. He and his musicians had agendas of their own, ones that were to coexist uncomfortably with their assigned roles on America's River Nile.

Chapter 2

Fate Marable, Musical Professionalism, and the Great Migration

These roustabout songs possess more interest for us if we remember their setting—a regal steamboat; passengers traveling in luxury on the upper decks; below, hard labor and toil for 'the white folks' without the aid of modern equipment; and through all of them, the background of the river with its power and its force as part of the fabric of our national life.

—Mary Wheeler, *Steamboatin' Days*

[When we came up river from New Orleans], . . . this was in Louisiana, . . . and we never got up for breakfast, we'd get up around eleven o'clock and lunch would be ready then and we had, of course, a very lovely table, and we would eat and then we'd rehearse usually a couple of hours, and then we'd just loll around the boat watching these white boys work. And I've never been looked at more angrily.

—B. David Grant, St. Louis, Missouri

Like palimpsests, the anecdotes and interviews about riverboat jazz on the Mississippi have always contained a subtext that was never directly discussed. Without this key unacknowledged historical and cultural context, none of these polite and decorous stories fully makes sense. The suppressed element involved all the terrible forms of oppression that white America visited on African Americans: "whitecapping," disenfranchisement, inferior educational facilities, unfair treatment in the courts, peonage, lynching, and other indiscriminate forms of physical brutality carried out in the South and designed to terrorize black Americans. The wave of lynchings peaked after World War I and did much to unleash the Great Migration of African Americans from the

South, notably through the Mississippi valley, toward such northerly industrial cities as St. Louis and Chicago. The captains of the Streckfus steamers never spoke of either systematic racist cruelty or of the Great Migration during their interviews about riverboat jazz. Neither did the black musicians that they hired. But the historic unsettling and reordering of African American life lent increased danger, fear, and liminal power to the river experience, to the boats, and especially to riverboat jazz.

The story of riverboat jazz—acknowledged and unacknowledged— swirls about the controversial pianist and bandleader Fate C. Marable, who came on board in 1907, eleven years before Louis Armstrong arrived. Marable was still playing piano and calliope, recruiting and organizing musicians, and directing the hot riverboat dance bands as the United States prepared to enter World War II. His unmatched career on the excursion boats became a major symbol of new opportunities for blacks in a more highly professionalized music business. Marable's life and position represented important transformations in black riverine culture.

Because of his "uncanny talent for uncovering great musicians"[1] and his dominant influence on the selection of musicians for his orchestras, Marable played the central role in directing a major musical stream in the Great Migration. He used his position as leader of the best black dance bands on the leading excursion boats on the Mississippi and Ohio rivers to personally recruit ambitious musicians who were looking for a way to explore the more northerly reaches of the Mississippi valley as professional dance band musicians. Once Marable had them on board, he insisted that they carefully prepare themselves for success in the modern music business. He demanded that as many of them as possible learn to read music at sight. He then rehearsed his ten-to-twelve piece orchestras until they could play commercial arrangements of popular songs in a way that satisfied him. He taught them the exquisitely precise requirements of Jim Crow performance etiquette on the river. He recruited them for membership in the racially segregated locals of the American Federation of Musicians. When they bungled, he represented their interests to the excursion boat captains. When they excelled, he urged that they be hired as sidemen, solo stars, and bandleaders on and off the river. Most important, he frequently made contacts for the best of them with the country's most famous bandleaders. He played a role in sending Irving Randolph and Al Morgan to Cab Calloway, Earl Carruthers to Jimmie Lunceford, Red Allen to the Mills Blue Rhythm Band, Tab Smith to Count Basie, Nat Storey to Chick Webb, Gene Sedric to Fats Waller, and Jimmy Blanton to Duke Ellington.[2] When any of his migrant musicians failed to live up to his standards, he coldly and abruptly fired them.

Marable's persistent efforts to assimilate improvising urban folk musicians into the world of arranged popular dance music represented one major current of thought within the black community in the United States before, during, and after World War I. At that time, such influential writers as W. E. B. Du Bois, Jean Toomer, and Alan Locke argued that training in the artifice of European written music and composition would help lead the race's music out of the parochial primitivism "of the Mississippi headwaters" and into a more cosmopolitan "international ocean."[3] This set of attitudes underwent considerable revision in the 1930s as Langston Hughes, Zora Neale Hurston, and Sterling Brown insisted on the underlying musical sophistication of aural instrumental improvisation. But when, back in 1917, Marable directed the creation of a new hot dance music called riverboat jazz, his assumptions about the need for musical literacy found resonance in national dialogues about the proper meaning of race music.[4]

Marable searched the major river cities for the men he needed. Sometimes he had little need to look far, because they sought him out. Marable then led them out onto the great river, where, together, they explored musical literacy, hot dance music, jazz, and the Mississippi River valley, looking at and listening carefully to life and music "in the North." Together, they fashioned an exciting black dance band style, a synthesis of commercial arrangements with the timbral and rhythmic freedoms of roustabout music. His musicians gained steady employment and advanced their professional skills and contacts. Their presence and their music politely but firmly announced to the crowds of passengers throughout the Mississippi and Ohio valleys their determination to move out of the South and up the social ladder into a profession.

Within the world of jazz Fate Marable held what is still considered a premier job, one that kept him gainfully employed for an extraordinarily long time, paid him by contract, and allowed him to exert an influence in the world of popular music. Like that made by white bandleaders in the major hotels and ballrooms of America's cities, whatever music Marable fashioned also had to conform to the parameters decreed by those running the venue. Marable's German American employers also believed strongly in musical literacy and decorum as integral parts of good order. The story of riverboat jazz, therefore, reveals that Marable drew deeply from his well of self-discipline in order to meet the expectations of John Streckfus the elder and his son Joseph.

Marable made the best of what could only have been a difficult work situation. Born in Paducah, Kentucky, on December 2, 1890, he secured his position as bandleader in 1907 when he was seventeen years old and held onto it until he was fifty. At that time, World War II largely shut down the excursion boat business. It rallied after the war but never matched its earlier influence.

His became the longest and most influential career in riverboat jazz, a masterful negotiation of the undertow of the jazz life, the hazards of those old boats, and the ever-present dangers of racial segregation on board and in the many river cities from New Orleans to Pittsburgh. In those days, as later, black jazz musicians made very little money. By comparison, Marable felt he was doing very well. He had a salary, good, clean living space, plenty to eat, a job in music, a chance to travel, and the gratitude of many of his musicians.[5]

Fate Marable's mother was Elizabeth Lillian (Wharton) Marable, said to have been part Irish and a piano teacher in Paducah.[6] Fate had two brothers and three sisters: Harold, James, Mabel, Juanita, and Neona.[7] Lizzie Marable taught her young son Fate to read music and play the piano. Lizzie's gift became his life's cornerstone.

As a human being and as a riverboat musician, Marable "lived in an intervening social space between white and black."[8] Born with a light reddish shade of hair, light brown eyes, and a few freckles on skin of a pale hue, Marable was able to pass for white[9] in a time period and region that were painfully sensitive to skin color. He grew to a height of 5 feet, 10.5 inches, sported a mustache, and carried himself like a sailor, wearing hats cocked at a jaunty angle, a special steamboat stogie clamped between his teeth.

For a musician whom jazzmen described as a fast, skilled reader of music, an excellent calliope player, and a strict bandleader, Marable also fashioned his own version of Midwestern riverine hip: "Fate had a magnetic personality. He was a handsome man who sat at the piano with great dignity. He moved the band with his eyes, every section, every soloist, every accent rarely escaped his gaze. He was respected by all his men for his leadership and his really great musicianship."[10]

Marable's stylish endurance of the Streckfus Line's stubborn racial segregation created a musicianly interpretation of riverboat hip. He had an enduring lightness of spirit, one that comes with a sardonic reaction to the struggle for survival.[11] He dressed well and enjoyed music, the nightclub and dance hall scene along the river and in Chicago, female company, cigars, fine sipping whiskey, and betting on the horses. He was a discreetly funny person. Often described as shy, Marable negotiated the challenges of river life in Middle America by keeping a "stone face" firmly in place.[12] No matter what the challenge, and there were many in the white-dominated space where he lived and worked, Marable simply did not visibly react. According to Clarence Elder, for example, Marable said that he was eating a slice of sweet potato pie when opportunity knocked in 1907: Charlie Mills, then the pianist on the *J.S.*, had told Marable that the Streckfus job might be his because Mills was leaving the river to study and perform in New York City.[13] Marable, who was shining shoes in Paducah, sauntered down to the docks, took a bite of pie, and suddenly encountered a Streckfus. He mumbled, as best he could, that he was a pianist who happened to find himself between engagements. He got the job.

John and Joseph Streckfus quickly informed him, however, that he also would be expected to play the boat's calliope. The "steam piano," or the "whooper," as it was known, invented sometime before the Civil War and patented in 1855, became Marable's introduction to the riverboats' zany approach to musical advertising. A steam calliope was installed on a Hudson River steamer named the *Armenia* in the late 1850s. Soon P. T. Barnum had them mounted in the circus wagons that he placed at the end of his parades. They became equally infamous on the showboats that flourished from Reconstruction through World War I, announcing the boats' arrivals so powerfully that workers, secretaries, and executives in office buildings high above the river dropped what they were doing and rushed outside to see if the sky had split open over the levee.[14]

Calliopes were painfully difficult to play and, for the performer, hard on the ears and the fingers. Most "perfessers" of the calliope stuffed their stunned ears with cotton. Steam, under eighty pounds of pressure, shot from the pipes through brass whistles when the player pressed down hard on the brass keys, unleashing an ear-splitting blast meant to be heard as much as ten miles away. The technology allowed only a volume setting of LOUDEST. According to veteran riverboat captain and calliopist Clarke Hawley, the brass whistles changed pitch as they warmed up but did not do so uniformly.[15]

According to Hawley, steam pressure made the brass keys very hot, requiring calliopists to wear gloves. Moreover, in the days before electrical solenoids, the keys were quite difficult to depress. As if all that were not insult enough, there were only two and one-third octaves' worth of keys, some of which invariably refused to function. Excursion boat calliopes were usually located on the top, or "texas," deck so that "a gentle rain of scalding concentrate loaded with boiler compound and cylinder oil" descended on the "perfesser" along with flaming ash from the twin smokestacks.[16]

Marable thought of himself as a pianist, an educated pianist, in short, a Musician. As he put it: "I could read because my mother was a piano teacher and I studied later at Straight University in New Orleans."[17] He balked at playing this mind-numbing contraption. John Streckfus insisted. So, placing plenty of cotton in his ears, Marable entered into combat with this miracle of modern plumbing. The initial results were not at all encouraging and never would be for some of those who loved the piano. Hawley describes the problems faced by the beginner: "Like an organ, the only way to sustain a tone is to hold the key down. Very good pianists can seldom manage this aspect of playing a calliope and they make unrecognizable twittering when they try."[18]

John Streckfus and his musical son Joseph took the *J.S.* downstream to a relatively lightly populated section of the river and went ashore to visit friends, leaving Marable with instructions to continue to grapple with the calliope until their return. From high above the river, they gave him several hours to realize that they meant business. He had to learn to let the melody take care of itself because missing notes forced him to change melodic lines anyway. Valves regularly stuck closed or open. With experience, he learned what key signatures would maximize his chances of actually playing a melody, and he, like the other famous calliope players—Hawley, Leslie Swanson, Homer Denney, and Harry Stocksdale—learned to emphasize short melodic lines of narrow range. In order to marshal the necessary downward pressure on those stinging keys, he reduced his chords to two to three notes.

Marable soon got the whooper in hand, stirring up memories of nineteenth-century good times with simple but lively old-time melodies such as "My Old Kentucky Home," "Turkey in the Straw," "Oh! Them Golden Slippers," "Rings on My Fingers," and "Bye-Bye Blues" that yanked amazed Americans in the river valleys out of their homes and offices. He garnered universal praise from jazz autobiographers, other bandleaders, and excursion boat captains. When, in 1909, President Theodore Roosevelt led his entourage on a political excursion down the Mississippi, the *J.S.* pulled temporarily alongside, and Marable's version of "Turkey in the Straw" set the vigorous chief executive to dancing. Under more prosaic conditions, his calliope's music echoed off the water, surrounding hills, and buildings, its whistling, hooting invitations to jazz dancing and river romance seeming to those on shore to float in from somewhere in outer space.

Working in such a rigidly ordered, racially segregated, and therefore dangerous white world presented more than enough crises, insults, and frustrations to fill a lifetime. The early years of the stoic Marable's career suggest that racial segregation on the riverboats grew rather more than less rigid as the twentieth century progressed. Charlie Mills, who also happened to be black, had performed on the *J.S.* for four to five years (1903–1907)[19] with a variety of white musicians that included the Davenport violinist Charlie Hertzog, the Quad Cities cornetist Tony Catalano, and the trombonist Rex Jessup. Marable played ragtime first in a duo with the white Davenport violinist Emil Flindt, who wrote "The Dance She Saved for Me," and then, adding one musician each season, found himself the leader of a four-piece orchestra in which the other three musicians were white.[20] But from the end of World War I to the end of World War II, the glory days of the excursion boat business, racial integration of onboard orchestras was never to be repeated. All the orchestras on the big Streckfus excursion steamers became strictly segregated, with Marable leading all-black bands from 1917 to the end of his career.

He had been playing with his mixed quartet when the *J.S.*, his ticket to ride, caught fire on June 25, 1910, at 8:00 P.M. He later recalled that, as he and his colleagues played on and more than a thousand passengers "danced and made merry" on the return leg of an excursion from Lansing, Iowa, to La Crosse, Wisconsin, a fire broke out in the hold. Despite their orders to keep playing lest the passengers panic, each of the musicians in turn laconically allowed as how he figured he'd just ease on over and "see what was happening to the boat," in order, of course, to report back. Each one in turn slipped out and disappeared, including Marable, who left his drummer to carry on alone![21]

In reading Fate's version of a major excursion boat tragedy, we again encounter that cool, bemused, ironic, and elusive man who, in this case, survived by hiding his emotions. He was someone who knew the score and would go a long way for his employers but was nonetheless prepared to attend to his own survival. The *J.S.*, after all, burned to the waterline that evening. As a local paper reported: "Wild panic broke lose among the passengers, and . . . a general stampede ensued. Screaming, cursing, praying men, women and children fought, jammed, and trampled over one another in mad chaos and confusion."[22] Two passengers lost their lives, and crew members, who jumped into the water to help floundering passengers, later reported that babies rained down on them from the deck railings. After reuniting with his musicians on Bad Axe Island, Marable found that without the *J.S.* he and his band, and the Streckfus family as a whole, no longer enjoyed gainful employment. Happily, John Streckfus soon went out and bought a whole fleet of boats and went back into the excursion business in a much bigger way.

A marvelous, historically significant photo of Fate Marable survives from 1916, the year before riverboat bands became segregated (see page 44). In it we see him standing on deck in front of his five white musicians, his head cocked thoughtfully at the camera, the trademark stogie clamped between his teeth, a generic naval officer's cap tilted to one side. His fresh white shirt frames a precisely tied cravat; a long sport jacket made of a soft cloth is draped from his shoulders to blend with impeccably pegged trousers. The others, who include the cornetist Tony Catalano, the violinist Emil Flindt, and the trombonist Rex Jessup, look relaxed but a bit rumpled. It's Marable's photo, his band. He looks at ease with his authority.[23]

The year 1916 was a good year for the pianist and bandleader. Despite the misspelling of his name, his first and only published composition appeared

Fate Marable's 1916 orchestra (Marable is in the foreground). (Photo courtesy of Hogan Jazz Archive, Special Collections Division, Howard-Tilton Memorial Library, Tulane University.)

that year. Co-authored with the New Orleans music entrepreneur Clarence Williams and published by the Williams and Piron Music Publishing Company, *Barrel House Rag* neatly expressed the musical sensibilities Marable brought to the river by combining the sounds of levee music with ragtime's more refined sensibilities.

In 1917, the year of the terrible race riot in East St. Louis, Marable, responding to the times, disbanded his racially mixed group and for the first time organized an all-black band. Jim Crow had come to riverboat music. He chose musicians from Paducah, his hometown, and called them the Kentucky Jazz Band. He took them downriver to New Orleans at the end of that season. His new racial policy also responded to unionism, which dictated either all-black or all-white orchestras after World War I. The term "jazz," of course, had been popularized in 1917 when the Victor Talking Machine Company issued its first recording by the Original Dixieland Jazz Band. Until 1917, Marable had been leading a ragtime band whose principal musical style was not indicated by a stage name. After several years of racial integration on the river, musical segregation had arrived. The Paducah group didn't last long, even if they did "play jazz real nice," according to their leader.

Marable had begun his career as a ragtime performer but had steadily become a habitué of the black nightlife of New Orleans, St. Louis, and any other river city that had any to speak of. As Louis Armstrong put it: "Every musician in New Orleans respected him. He had seen the good old days in Storyville, and had played cotch with the pimps and hustlers at the Twenty-Five gambling house. He had had fine jam sessions with the piano greats of those days. . . . He always won the greatest honors with them."[24] The pianist himself reported to Beulah Schacht, "We were playing in and out of New Orleans all the time and I began to notice the type of music they were playing there. It just got under my skin."[25]

Marable inevitably dropped in to listen to the talk of Storyville, Edward "Kid" Ory's Co-Operative Hall band, in which a very young Armstrong played cornet. They had a small repertoire and played by ear, but they played a new hot and free music with a great dance beat. Marable brought John Streckfus in to hear them, and they began performing during the winter of 1917–18 on the *Dixie Belle*, which worked charters and showed tourists the harbor sights in New Orleans. The trombonist Jack Teagarden heard them that winter and declared that Armstrong had just descended from heaven.

Marable and the Streckfus family began guiding the musical and cultural evolution of jazz in new directions when Armstrong, the drummer Warren "Baby" Dodds, the string bassist George "Pops" Foster, the banjoist Johnny St. Cyr, the mellophonist David Jones, the clarinetist Sam Dutrey, the trumpeter Joe Howard, and the trombonist William "Bebe" Ridgley signed on for that first voyage upriver of New Orleans jazz. The powers that were had decided that these exceptionally powerful and creative but relatively untutored musicians would play commercial dance band arrangements of the popular tunes of the day in spite of their uncertain command of written music. It took one year's training and work experience in New Orleans to coordinate the musically literate with the illiterate, making them all ready to play during the 1919 summer season "up North." The Streckfus family hired the director of music at the Saenger Theater to help them smooth out the rough spots in waltzes and romantic ballads.[26]

Why, one might ask, had they been hired at all? If John Streckfus was so determined to have a sightreading commercial dance band, why not go out and hire one? There were plenty of them available. Why bring in a group of relatively untested improvisers who were not in the habit of reading mainstream popular arrangements?

There were several reasons. First, they were African American, and they brought the exotic thrill of southern black music to a venue long associated with minstrelsy. Second, they had to accept less than the union scale paid to whites. As one Ohio riverboat musician put it: "Colored bands never made as

Marable at the piano with his S.S. *Sidney* orchestra in 1918. Left to right: Warren "Baby" Dodds, William "Bebe" Ridgley, Joe Howard, Louis Armstrong, Fate Marable, David Jones, Johnny Dodds, John St. Cyr, and Pops Foster. Standing behind Jones and Dodds is Carl Mangan, a Streckfus Steamers operative. (Photo courtesy of Duncan Schiedt.)

much money as some of the other bands that worked out of here. Like along the Mississippi, they would get them for cheap wages."[27] Third, Marable had found a band with a particularly potent rhythmic drive. The excursion boats of the 1920s had inadequate sound amplification, so they had to emphasize a powerful dance beat.[28] Marable's New Orleans band had that and more, bringing life and movement to their rhythm at all tempi. As many as three thousand people could dance at the same time on the *St. Paul*'s enormous dance floor. Moreover, the dance floor was many times longer than it was wide. The bandstand was placed midway along one of the long walls, and it protruded about eight feet onto the dance floor in order to get as much of the sound as possible out into the room. But the dancers' clothing absorbed sound. Those dancing at either end of the floor could, at best, only feel the rhythm of all those dancing feet.[29]

In order for all of the customers to have an equal chance to enjoy the band, couples were encouraged to dance down one side of the floor, across the end, and then up the other side. Even though, as we shall see, customers often preferred to dance or merely stand in front of the bandstand, bouncers forced them to keep moving in that circular fashion, although a certain number were allowed to congregate on either side of the bandstand.

This, his most famous band, the hottest band Marable ever had, was called, depending on the crowd to be entertained, the "Metropolitan Jaz-E-Saz Orchestra," "Fate Marable and the Cotton Pickers," or "Fate Marable's Society Syncopators." This was the group that included Louis Armstrong, the band Marable and everyone else talked about for the rest of Marable's life. Armstrong, of course, was beginning to play solos of unsurpassed eloquence but also sang, whenever he summoned the courage, and played the penny whistle when ordered to do so by Streckfus. Baby Dodds shimmied his stomach muscles in time to his drumbeat. Pops Foster "slapped" the bass by snapping the strings against the fretboard. Marable, who had developed exceptionally strong fingers from playing the calliope, fashioned a particularly powerful chording rhythm.

But there was much more to that first band and to all of Marable's subsequent groups than his jazz improvisers. He had gathered an orchestra with ten players, sometimes more, not a six-to-seven-piece combo. Referred to in its day as a "hot dance band," we have learned to call such a group a "big band" or a "dance band." It was not a polyphonic jazz band. Polyphony becomes too complex when that many musicians improvise simultaneously. Moreover, in order to meet the acoustic challenges of the *St. Paul*, loud playing was not enough. Marable's band had to generate a coordinated attack that could reach as many dancers as possible.

In the months that preceded the *St. Paul*'s first season in 1919, the Streckfus men, personally and with their black bandleader, directed an adaptation of black New Orleans music to the repertoire, tempi, and sensibilities of stock dance band arrangements. At first the musicians resisted some of these innovations. Joseph Streckfus later recalled his efforts to extract from his musicians the kind of social dance music he wanted:

> My efforts at the first rehearsal didn't fare so well; they just could not get the idea, although they tried hard. Our next stop was Cape Girardeau, and my wife and [my]self started up the main street. . . . As we passed a shop with records and Victrola in the window, the idea came to me—why not inquire if they have the records we have at home, which we can buy and demonstrate to our orchestra what we are driving at[?] Fortunately the shop had the records, played by Art Hickman's band at the Palace Hotel in San Francisco—the first Victor Dance Music Records.[30]

Streckfus obviously felt that, within the traditions of riverboat music and German American culture in St. Louis, he knew better than his musicians that commercially arranged popular songs would please the passengers, who were, six days out of seven, white. As he well might, he admired the sort of musicianship found in the Art Hickman and the Paul Whiteman Orchestras. He therefore selected a complexly arranged recording of "Avalon" in which the studio band played a chorus in one key and then modulated to other keys in a series of interludes. He and his wife ordered the delivery of a Victrola with a repeat device and more records with romantic themes such as "Love Nest" and "Young Man's Fancy"—swan complex jazz. "It wasn't long before we were in a rehearsal of these pieces by ear. Louie Armstrong, with his trumpet in his hand, came down alongside of the Victrola and would pick up on his trumpet the notes in the several chords in the modulations, giving the saxophone section their chords, likewise the brass their changes in chords, and by repeating over and over again, all chords were down pat."[31]

Then Joseph Streckfus turned his attention to the band's tempi, dictating that the wild young musicians abandon both their breakneck tempi and their belly-rubbing slow drags. As they rehearsed, Streckfus timed the beat with a stopwatch and concluded that about seventy beats per minute created the danceable rhythm he wanted. Listening to his orchestra, he would begin to bounce rhythmically by slightly bending his knees to the beat. If he couldn't bounce to it, the beat was wrong. For two weeks, Marable and Armstrong took a chance and disagreed with him. They stubbornly refused to allow him to tame all the wildness out of their music. But, finally, at the end of a long afternoon excursion, Marable decided to give it a try. He set the graceful rhythmic pulse of the swan complex. According to Streckfus:

> At the time, I was on the bridge, Captain Roy was in the Pilot House as Pilot. One headlight alongside of me began to shake, the Pilot House shook. We heard loud hollering coming from the Cabin. Both of us thought something had happened and quickly went down to the Cabin Deck. The dancers were going off [the floor]. I saw Louie Armstrong coming toward me with his trumpet in hand, smiling and Louie said—"We's got it." I said, "What do you mean?" He said, "We played it slow like you wanted it, and I's put in a little swing, and did they like it!"[32]

Streckfus also believed that he would have to greatly enlarge the musicians' repertoire because the improvised tunes that they had played in Louisiana sounded too unfamiliar to more northerly white people. The Metropolitan Jaz-E-Saz Orchestra had enough tunes in its repertoire to perform the four-hour programs required by Streckfus Steamers, Inc. Final musical authority over what might have been a more radically new, politically challenging form of black music created by black people was granted with one hand and taken away with the other.

The transition from aural traditions in the musical cultures of black New Orleans to a more commercial musical style performed mainly for white audiences was not one that could be made overnight or without a lot of second thoughts, some of them tinged with the complexities of racial identity. But the Streckfus excursion boats required of their black orchestras a carefully organized evening of musical varieties designed to appeal to as many tastes as possible.

Some of these varied presentations conveyed more of the latest sounds from New Orleans. The first music that people heard came, of course, from the ships' whistles, followed quickly by Marable's calliope as the boat approached its prospective port. After preparing for the coming excursion, the band presented its first number of the evening. This opener often featured the hottest, brassiest jazz of which the band was capable. As Armstrong recalled, when playing his first concert in St. Louis, Marable selected W. C. Handy's "St. Louis Blues," a famous blues-inflected number bound to please the local audience. He pulled out all the stops, leaving the crowd screaming with enthusiasm.[33] When playing for the younger crowd for whom the steamer *St. Paul* was designed, the band had the green light to "swing like mad," albeit at more moderate tempi.

During a typical midnight cruise, Marable's orchestra was to play fourteen dance numbers at the slow tempi. Passengers were given dance cards with fourteen spaces in which to write the names of those with whom they danced. The dances had been scheduled at regular intervals throughout the evening so that the first one began at about 9:00 P.M., as the boat pulled out into the river. The last dance, often "Home Sweet Home," ended at midnight as the boat pulled back into port.[34] Every fourth dance had to be a waltz. This probably taxed the patience of the young improvisers, but with the passing of the years, the waltzes, so redolent of nineteenth-century riverboat culture, probably waned. The other dance numbers had to be either old-time favorites or riverboat arrangements of the hit songs of the day.

Two things are clear: first, the improvisers had opportunities to play their own way, but they had to learn new tunes, tempi, and time signatures; second, the special combination of the Streckfus swan complex with Marable's black swans was a hit. They delivered tunes and songs familiar to the crowds with a new, densely textured rhythmic swing that Streckfus called "syncopation." Armstrong's hot solos put wings to the dancers' heels, lifting their spirits into the air, where, in seemingly effortless flight, they soared in their imaginations beyond the depressing reality of their poor, struggling, often disappointing lives, becoming the beautiful, graceful, desired people of the American dream. Fate Marable and His Metropolitan Jaz-E-Saz Orchestra became the hit of the riverfronts.

Even though Joseph Streckfus reported that he set definite aesthetic parameters for riverboat jazz, his initial imposition of taste was hardly a grinding dictatorship. After all, he was also president of Streckfus Steamers, Inc., and member of the boards of directors of several major institutions in St. Louis. Surely the demands on his time gave him other priorities than personally leading and rehearsing his most famous dance band. It seems unlikely that someone in charge of the largest steamboat company on the Mississippi and Ohio rivers could have regularly spent much time working personally with the members of his band. He must have delegated such authority to Fate Marable, whose long tenure as riverboat bandleader indicates a generally successful, if not always tension-free, synthesis of black and white musical practices.

Two things emerge from Joseph Streckfus's musical regime. First, in order to feel like dancing, passengers needed easily recognizable popular songs played at moderate tempi, but when such music was performed by a group of black jazz musicians, it did not sound merely danceable to them; rather, it sounded different in some ill-defined but exciting way. The New Orleans musicians brought unmatched instrumental power and an array of sounds associated with individual variations in instrumental training and tone production. These musicians showed a desire to "signify" upon (reinterpret) the music they were playing with "blue notes." They brought to the river unequal levels of musical literacy; some were playing at least partly by ear while others actually read the music. They enjoyed improvisation and tended to mix polyphony and homophony. Put more simply, they approached the charts as road maps that outlined the progression of major turning points in each arrangement. The musicians' unique "black" way with southern dance music provided the "bit o' color" that flew across the riverboats' rigid lines of segregation to be unthinkingly welcomed into the sensibilities of white passengers, creating an emotional and aesthetic experience of the river appropriate for the Jim Crow era.

Second, within the complexity of these musical possibilities, improvising black musicians underwent a further process of professional growth. As they lived through and later recalled the process, it seemed to them important to place these musical experiences within the historical context of black music on the river. Those who spoke directly about this historical dimension insisted that their efforts be linked to the earlier music of the roustabouts. Marable put it this way: "Jazz was the outgrowth of Negro life in New Orleans. It developed from the chants of the roustabouts loading cotton boats, singing with perfect rhythm as they lifted the bales."[35] The New Orleans banjoist and raconteur Danny Barker also emphasized the influence of the roustabouts on early riverboat jazz:

> This is how the riverboats got music on them. Those boats had roustabouts on them, and half of those roustabouts played guitar and nearly all sang. Well, when those boats went up the river, the roustabouts were on the lower deck, and the passengers, the gamblers, et cetera, stayed up on the upper deck. But when the people on the upper deck heard the singing and playing of the roustabouts, they would come downstairs, and that gave Streckfus, the owner of the boats, the idea of putting music on the boats.[36]

Although a few writers have noted that some early New Orleans musicians worked on the levees and docks during the daytime, the influence of Mississippi riverfront roustabouts on the invention of excursion boat culture has never received the close attention it deserves. Marable stipulated their critical importance in the creation of riverboat jazz, however, and since he spent his life on the river, his comments deserve serious consideration.

Throughout the nineteenth century, roustabout laborers worked on the packet boats that transported cotton bales and other goods to and from the river cities. They loaded the boats and then rode along on the voyages, becoming well known for entertaining the passengers. On landing in major ports such as Memphis, Tennessee, roustabouts were replaced by longshoremen who unloaded the cargo.[37] But in the smaller town ports, roustabouts also unloaded the cargo.[38] In New Orleans, black and white longshoremen earned their title after a long struggle to organize themselves as unionized laborers who unloaded both riverboats and oceangoing boats.

Although one can firmly distinguish longshoremen from roustabouts, at least one leading black newspaper used the terms interchangeably. The movement to unionize black levee workers, like that of black riverboat musicians, continued well after World War II. Roustabouts formed the lowest level of the black working class in the river towns and cities. After the Civil War, they lacked formal organization, their labor unprotected by union representation, their persons regularly subjected to physical abuse, their reputations clouded with stereotypes. They, like the jazzmen who came after them, were widely considered to be "happy-go-lucky,"[39] "tough," "dissipated," and much given to gambling, drinking, and carousing. "Roustas," also known as "rousters" or "roosters," like many jazz musicians, were said to live outside of families and established communities, spending considerable time in "gambling and prostitution dens, barrel houses along the riverfront, and 'low dives and back dens.'"[40]

If they lacked union organization, roustabouts nevertheless understood how to negotiate wages with the captain's mates who were sent to hire them. As long as a dollar could be found in his pocket, a roustabout would refuse all labor. But roustas also understood the principles of collective action. A group of recently hired roustas would step off the boat, inaugurating a strike just when no one else remained on the levee to replace them.

But, once hired, roustas could expect abusive, violent treatment from foulmouthed, club-wielding ships' officers. Brutality degraded their lives as they were driven like beasts.[41] They found considerable solace in keeping a psychological distance from society, opening up a space for themselves, a hybrid, translational, cosmopolitan space in the Mississippi River's mud sill cities.[42] The lives of black riverboat jazz musicians remained free of this sort of physical abuse. This, in itself, represented a major step forward toward greater self-respect, but jazz became for them "an oppositional culture" that represented "at least partial rejection of the dominant ideology . . . in the struggle against class and racial domination."[43]

Roustas also made music in the levee jukes and tonks in which they spent so much time, and they sang and labored up and down the gangplanks of the packet boats in exquisitely synchronized rhythms. Judge Nathan B. Young of St. Louis writes of their "coonjining . . . jousting heavy cotton bales and toting fabulous weights by balancing and synchronizing their bodies and muscles in a dancing trot."[44] Another source defines the "coonjine" as "the combination song and dance that [was] associated with handling freight."[45] While coonjining, roustabouts sang a great variety of robust songs drawn from lives of maritime labor.[46] Another scholar described them as one of the "waterfaring clans . . . brawny, ragged, indomitable 'rouster' crews who 'coonjined' up the slanting stage-plank bearing incredible burdens and sang as they labored, singing steadily, loudly, and sometimes beautifully . . . with their nimble feet that cut scallops and pigeon wings to show how tireless they were."[47]

Once they had loaded or unloaded the packet, roustas turned to a variety of jobs on board, but many of them also specialized in entertaining the passengers with song and dance, work songs becoming show business. For many white passengers, the roustabouts provided a window through which to gaze on black riverfront comportment and behavior. Their music served as a bridge between the races and as a theatrical form of southern communication. The packet boats epitomized the disorganized economy of the South, in which lower-middle-class white people learned to accept lives of poverty and toil because the black people they saw seemed so much worse off.

The nineteenth-century roustabout tradition encouraged black folk music as an important ingredient of riverboat culture. The editor of one important collection of roustabout songs says that their songs dealt with "memorable cruises, with lamentable love-affairs, with wrecks, with great bullies and humble heroes, with murder trials and mourners, with hangings and with funerals." Rather than extolling rural southern life, the songs of these "reckless bravos" developed "bolder" themes "shot through with pistol fire and the tally of disaster or . . . some great river race, some splendid achievement of navigation."[48]

Having struggled to establish themselves within riverboat culture, roustabouts partly disappeared from the major river cities in the 1890s as the railroads took over the movement of raw materials in the Mississippi River valley. As Barker noted, the Streckfus family, seeking to commercialize the packet boat tradition, replaced the roustabouts with black dance bands. Their musicians built on the roustas' struggle against oppression, carrying it into new realms of professional instrumental music, opening up new cultural space on the river.

A few packet boats survived into the 1920s, especially those that served the hundreds of small river towns that still lacked railroad lines. The saxophonist and riverboat bandleader Raymond F. "Peg" Meyer, who lived in Cape Girardeau, Missouri, played the polite small-combo dance music preferred on the packets (which carried far more produce than passengers). As he described returning to the *Cape Girardeau*, a packet that carried goods back and forth from St. Louis, after a night on the town, he and a pal finally reached the levee but had to step carefully around and over the many roustas sleeping on the cobblestones there.

According to Meyer, when a steamer with an empty hold tied up at the small-town levees, a mate went ashore with twenty tickets in hand. Met by sixty or more roustas, he, and he alone, selected twenty of them. Those twenty laborers carried the produce on board, the boat left port, and the roustabouts were then fed just before the boat docked again and they unloaded its cargo. In the fall season, they often reloaded the packet with sacks of wheat and were paid a supplement of a penny per sack. The mate sometimes asserted his power and made them suffer by handing out one penny at a time to each man just when he was carrying the heavy sack. Because their hands were full, the roustabouts took delivery of the penny in their mouths.[49] On the return to the port of embarkation, the mate also paid them their day's wages. The passengers and the musicians then enjoyed watching the roustas shoot craps.

Fate Marable's riverboat jazz would contain both musical and psychological elements of the roustabout experience while determinedly "revisioning" the black steamboat experience, seeking to make riverboat music more commercial, professional, and unionized than roustabout work. Like the roustas, his musicians were often wild young men on the move, seeking freedom and opportunity throughout the Mississippi valley by working on riverboats. White people in the river valleys seemed unable to stop staring at them. As Baby Dodds put it: "We played up the Mississippi River and I think people used to come on the boat more for curiosity than anything else. And they sat down and looked at us. That's embarrassing. I figured this: I knew what the object was. They'd look at you startled and for curiosity than anything else. So I just took it that way. All I looked at it was, 'Well, I'm doing something big or else there wouldn't be such astonishment.'"[50]

Marable's men introduced a new era in black riverboat music. Unlike the roustas, the only manual labor the musicians performed involved the manipulation of musical instruments. In their careers music would be treated as a skilled profession practiced by duly unionized musicians in touch with those in the main currents of the music business and in the media that were open to African Americans. Middle Americans, particularly those from small towns along the river, had never seen such a thing. Baby Dodds recalled that their racial label was never omitted when Streckfus Streamers took them to into any port for the first time: "[They'd say,] 'You're Colored,' so people won't be disappointed. You're something that's just crazy. And people would come to see you, they'd look at you, look in on the dance floor. Perhaps they'd say, 'Are they Negroes? We don't want to go in.' Then when you'd go back to that place, why, the boat would be packed." Hannibal, Missouri, was a particularly difficult port. People there stubbornly sat down and stared at the band in silence. Dodds emphasized that the only African Americans that most white passengers had seen before were roustabouts: they "never saw a Negro with a collar and tie on, white shirt, playing music. They just didn't know what to make of it."[51] The sudden appearance of blacks wearing something other than overalls and sitting in a dignified manner while playing instruments signaled a reordering of the social structure.

Shocked passengers were on to something. Moreover, as noted, Marable's musicians were unionized. The first thing Marable did with his first New Orleans band was to take them north by train, not to the St. Louis offices of Streckfus Steamers but to Paducah, Kentucky, where he got them all signed into the local of the black musicians' union. This was Marable's hometown, of course, and perhaps the local musicians were willing to settle for a statement that Fate's recruits could read music. In St. Louis, one had to audition by sight-reading a piece not seen before. Once they were union members, however, they could readily transfer their membership to the St. Louis local.

This was an important step toward professional careers. In 1918, New Orleans had no black musicians' union. Moreover, the Streckfus brothers strongly supported the musicians' unions. They added needed leverage in their yearly negotiations for dance bands. In addition, white musicians owned all the better-paying jobs and had long proved willing to throw the riverboat jobs to members of the black locals of the American Federation of Musicians. Being unionized gave black musicians at least some measure of job security, taking away from the whites any possibility of labeling the black musicians as "scabs." The unions also worked to shorten the hellishly long working hours. As Clarence Elder described the Streckfus music policy, "The hours were terrible with the long all day trips and moonlights. On tramping trips all bands played until unconscious."[52]

As we shall see in detail in chapter 4, the black musicians' locals of the 1920s and 1930s encountered myriad obstacles. Their very existence, never officially recognized within the American Federation of Musicians, expressed the segregationist assumptions of the white locals. Generally, unionized white musicians refused to perform or meet with unionized black musicians. The white locals forcibly reserved all of the most lucrative jobs for themselves and even took a percentage when black bands landed better-paying jobs. Black bands routinely played for lower pay than white musicians. When jobs became scarce for white musicians, they forced black musicians out of long-standing gigs, taking them for themselves. Secretive, under-the-counter negotiations landed black musicians whatever inferior wages they actually received. They routinely played below scale in their own unions, and the local union officials knew it.

But membership in local chapters of the American Federation of Musicians brought a definite long-term moral and ethical advantage, no matter how empty were its short-term promises. Whenever the white locals and the national organization repudiated their black locals, as they did during the depression, when jobs were much scarcer, the blame would have to be placed squarely on those who talked union solidarity while repudiating their laboring brothers.

Despite Marable's important role in recruiting musicians, unionizing them, training them, and promoting their careers, some resented his imperious manner. Most refused to speak plainly about it, but they regularly hinted that their leader frequently treated them badly. He seems to have asserted his authority and his sense of possessing a superior musical literacy by using sharp sarcasm. In public, Armstrong's impenetrable diplomacy allowed him to say only that Marable was "high strung."[53] In a private letter to the drummer Leige Shaw, however, Armstrong referred to Marable as "that little 'Hatchet-Mouth Boy.'"[54] Baby Dodds struggled to find appropriate words when describing Marable to the historian Larry Gara: "I can't exactly explain to you what—he was a pretty stern fellow."[55] Marable did not act like one of the boys. He saw to it that his orchestra members took their places early and stood respectfully until he had seated himself at the piano.[56] All of the famous jazz musicians who worked for Marable noted his authoritarian manner. When they least expected it, he would spring a new piece of music on them and demand that a particular musician, often one with a wild streak, stand up and play it at sight as written. Armstrong recalled that Marable always remembered where individual musicians had stumbled in performance and demanded that they play their parts solo in front of the others, usually on the morning after the night before. The trumpeter Clark Terry recalled that while rehearsing a new piece written in the key of F major, Marable would proceed to modulate to F# major, just to watch his musicians panic.[57] Marable stung fragile egos, and several of his musicians never forgot it. All of them particularly resented his way of firing someone who had faltered persistently: when the poor fellow finally settled down for the night, he found a fire axe in his bunk. Who did Marable think he was, anyway? One analyst of popular culture, Daniel F. Havens, calls Marable "cruel and intimidating" as well as "diabolic."[58]

A portion of the problem seems to have stemmed from alcohol. The trombonist Leon King recalled that Marable "liked to occasionally pour himself a tall one, and then another tall one or two, although he was known to fine his own bandsmen for drinking. Anything, beer, whiskey, anything. I think he was the worst leader I ever had as far as drinking goes. . . . He could be sloppy drunk, but he'd hit that piano."[59] This drinking pattern helps explain the seemingly diabolical edge to Marable's treatment of his musicians. Vertna Saunders recalled that Marable "would ride everybody . . . if you made the least little mistake, you'd hear him laugh above the band. He kept little articles on the piano, such as a metal fountain pen, a tray, a marble. Then when somebody would make a mistake, he would drop it, throw it down on the floor so it would make a sound."[60]

There is general agreement among the riverboat musicians that Marable himself played all the music well. No one praised his ability to improvise; rather, they noted his sightreading skills, his ability to lead the band, and his powerful beat. Recalling the times when they used two pianos, with the great Burroughs Lovingood as second pianist, the drummer Floyd Campbell recalled that "Fate had good execution, we called it all 'school.' He had a way of swinging that band, a 14 piece band. And with two pianos, if Fate would get up the bottom would drop off the band and the minute Fate would come back you would feel it. He was strictly a band piano man. Fate was a foundation man."[61] Marable had the beat. Ironically, the calliope had strengthened his touch on the piano keyboard, just the quality that riverboat dance halls required in those days.

Some musicians tried to dismiss his strict regard for the basic skills of orchestral performance as slightly darker reflections of the attitudes of his German American employers. Marable seemed to some musicians to be a pale reflection of the Streckfus family. But all that is what one expects from jazzmen. They proudly defended their attachment to improvisation, leaving largely unanswered inevitable questions about their own levels of musical literacy. Several mentioned, as if in passing, that at the time they left the river they were beginning to be able to read at sight. Had he cared to, Marable might have written his own memoir revealing how he carried these learners.

He "was especially proud of his musicianship and the fact that he was not self taught."[62] Marable's critics never wrote about the larger context of his determination to make his musicians into full-fledged professionals. He had discovered and recruited them. They had accepted positions in his arrangement-reading dance band. They were now his responsibility. He expected them to learn. One good way to keep the Streckfus brothers out of his domain was to show them that his orchestra could perform the arrangements well without their intervention. How could the leader maintain his authority over his musicians if he allowed them to arrive late, improvise their arranged parts, and get drunk? Marable could improvise acceptably, but he would undermine his own life and authority if he failed to champion sightreading and professional comportment. His infamous trick of playing in F# proved his point: the clever but illiterate improvisers couldn't play along by ear in that key! Armstrong was the only one of the musicians whose written recollections seized the point of Marable's intimidation tactics: "I still think it is good psychology."[63] Armstrong noted that "Fate Marable's band deserves credit for breaking down a few barriers on the Mississippi—barriers set up by Jim Crow. We were the first colored band to ply most of the towns at which we stopped, particularly the smaller ones. The ofays were not used to seeing colored boys blowing horns and making fine music for them to dance by."[64]

Within the context of the Great Migration, the riverboat bandleader's emphasis on musical literacy and versatility made excellent sense. He insisted that his musicians become professionals able to control their instruments, sightread, compose, arrange, comport themselves properly, and allow union officials to represent them. Marable had been chosen to lead what were often untrained musicians into the world of professional music. He valued the jazz skills they brought on board with them, skills that could evoke the spirit of the roustabouts, and regularly featured them during the "calling concert" and on two or three tunes of every dance set. He also insisted that they get themselves together with the nonimprovisers and smartly attack arranged dance numbers.

In 1918, as in 1928, as in 2004, traditional middle-class musical values might cause one to doubt that a significant number of jazz musicians would be able to build lives and careers on improvisation alone. A few exceptionally talented improvisers did manage to become successful full-time jazzmen, of course, but at the time, prudence would have dictated that one become as versatile as possible, just in case. That was exactly the policy pursued on land in and around St. Louis and East St. Louis by highly successful black bandleaders such as Eddie Randle and Chick Finney. By agreeing to work on the riverboats with Marable they had chosen to begin new lives in music. His musical instruction on the Streckfus Line was, as several of them admitted, "our conservatory."

Marable's Cotton Pickers, his Society Syncopators, and his Metropolitan Jazz-E-Saz Orchestra dramatically, even theatrically, announced to all customers, white and black, advance musical notice of the Great Migration, of an elegant, liminal new world emerging for whites and blacks, a world of new possibilities and dangers. Black customers adored them on the special segregated Monday evening cruises of the *St. Paul* and the *Capitol*. They looked and sounded like sharply dressed, well-groomed professionals who could make you want to dance or rock in time in the rocking chairs while taking the cooling breezes, listening to fine music floating over the water. No coveralls, no bandanas, and no work boots! The Mississippi might still be the white man's river, but on Monday night trips out of St. Louis, black customers, surrounded by fellow members of their social clubs and community leaders, could contest the deck spaces and remind themselves, as well as the many whites who came along to watch and the Streckfus brothers, that there was now, because there had always been, a black Mississippi.

And for every musician who resented Marable's haughty emphasis on musical literacy and discipline, there were several who appreciated what he was doing. Armstrong and Terry explicitly praised the bandleader's good pedagogy, though for Armstrong such praise and euphemistic criticism came from later experience and maturity. From 1917 to 1921, Marable insisted that the young Armstrong learn to read music: "'Now, Louis, you are a special trumpeter but you must learn to read. I will teach you every morning at 10:00.' He needed the discipline, needed to learn it. I told him that if he didn't take my lessons, I would fire him. Louis didn't show up for his lessons. He had agreed to them. He said 'Yes,' but didn't show."[65] In 1921 Marable fired Armstrong and added that he could not come back. He always felt bad about it, especially when, subsequently, he watched a large riverboat paddle by his own vessel, one with a huge banner advertising the great jazz improviser. Armstrong was such an exceptionally talented jazz musician and entertainer that he got on without Marable's lessons. Most other musicians, however, saw their importance. Al Morgan joined Marable's band on string bass in 1925, having played that instrument for only one year. Morgan described Marable's contribution in this way: "Fate made many musicians and when the ability was already in a man in full force, he helped form it. The four years I spent with Fate were the most important to me musically, for, during that time, I learned the rudiments—and much more—of the bass."[66]

The drummer, vocalist, and bandleader Floyd Campbell, who also joined Marable's band in 1925, felt that Marable's haughty insistence on musical literacy produced both his greatest achievements and most of his personnel problems: "Fate did himself more harm than anyone. He was a firm musician and he knew how to select men and he would goad you to get the best out of you and compliment you when he saw you doing good."[67]

Marable, as we have seen, recruited fine musicians, tried to make them literate professionals, and tended to treat some of them coldly. He led his bands well in performance. Although he had come up as a ragtime pianist and specialized in numbers such as "Nola" and "Kitten on the Keys," he learned how to make his contribution to hot dance music. Campbell, who was in a position to know, praised Marable's rhythmic contribution.

Jazz fans adore their star improvisers, however, so the small literature on Fate Marable and riverboat jazz usually emphasizes such great soloists as Louis Armstrong, Red Allen, Harold "Shorty" Baker, Tab Smith, Clark Terry, and Jimmy Blanton. Practically nothing has been written about all "the other" musicians whom we see in the band photos: players who were already musically literate when they came to the Mississippi River. We tend to forget altogether members of the first band such as the trumpeter Joe Howard, the trombonist Bebe Ridgley, the violinist Boyd Atkins, and the trumpeter Sidney Desvignes, while recalling David Jones only for the sightreading tutorials he gave to Armstrong. The jazz clarinetist Johnny Dodds, seen in a famous photo of that first riverboat jazz band, never worked regularly with the band and was merely covering for Sam Dutrey, who was unable to make the photo session. For many years, a fine multi-instrumentalist from St. Louis by the name of Norman Mason played first trumpet, saxophone, and clarinet in Marable's bands. Louis Armstrong played second trumpet to him in 1919.

Most of these less famous musicians were some of the music readers of Marable's orchestras and essential to defining the band's sound. They played several important roles: sightreading the commercial arrangements when Marable first rehearsed them, teaching the improvisers how to play specific new arrangements, providing the improvisers with daily tutorials in sightreading, and acting as section leaders who gathered the other musicians into a more powerfully unified attack. Some, perhaps most, of the lesser-known musicians may have been able to improvise, but they had not been hired to play that role.

Marable's riverboat jazz mixed elements of musical literacy and popular music commercialism with elements of African additive rhythms in which each of the ten instruments played with a slightly different rhythmic emphasis.[68] He himself played a key role in reading the arrangements and playing them for the musicians who couldn't read them. What they couldn't grasp visually, they learned aurally. The trombonist Druie Bess, who worked in the Marable band on the *Senator* out of Pittsburgh, in the late 1930s recalled what it was like to "read" dance band music as a young musician: "I was playing everything they was playing. I'll tell you how I was playing a lot of it, though. See, a lot of it . . . I had a very good memory. Memory and good ear. Some of it I was reading. A lot of it I had a very good memory of it. That's the way I learned it. I kind of half-fooled them, to a certain extent."[69]

This is the way that many of the aural improvisers got on, at least for a time. Verne Streckfus confirmed the aural approach when he insisted that "Marable's band didn't have to read, as Marable would play it on the piano and they would learn it that way. The non-readers had music in front of them and they would change it."[70] Regardless of Verne Streckfus's sweeping generalization, some of Marable's musicians were skilled readers when they arrived on board and others became skilled readers under his tutelage. But many, probably most, got by on this mixture of musical memory and literacy. It gave a definite looseness and diversity of attack to the arrangements. This quality of "playing together separately" did much to define the thick rhythmic texture of black riverboat jazz. Their freer, less regimented unity mixed elements of the aural, polyphonic tradition with section work, all of it swinging to a great beat.

Marable's groups did very little recording. Making records was vitally important to the careers of musicians who wanted to make reputations as jazzmen. Many of them came and left Marable's bands on their ways to New York City and the top bands in the country. One can't help but think that had Joseph Streckfus wanted to use records as advertising for his excursion boats, he would have seen to it that his bands recorded more often. But, like many other musical entrepreneurs, he seems to have thought it best that people be forced to pay to come on board his boats if they wanted to hear his bands play.

One way or another, in 1924, Fate Marable and His Society Syncopators made a record for Okeh, a race label. On the two sides of this disc were "Frankie and Johnny" and "Pianoflage." Louis Armstrong had left the river several years earlier, as had all of the other original New Orleanians who had

Marable's New Orleans Harmonists aboard the S.S. *St. Paul.* Left to right: Zutty Singleton, Norman Mason (standing), Bert Bailey, a grinning Fate Marable, Walter Thomas, Willie Foster, Sidney Desvignes, Amos White (trumpet, kneeling), Henry Kimball, Harvey Lankford, Barnet Bradley. (Photo courtesy of Duncan Schiedt.)

played with him. Of those who played on Marable's record, only the pianist himself, Zutty Singleton, and Sidney Desvignes would later turn up in the jazz history books. The musicologist Gunther Schuller notes that the two recordings represent an intermixture of regional styles and the "swing and lilt and relative freedom of a modified New Orleans style" with "an early arranged dance band idiom."[71]

"Frankie and Johnny" (Okeh 40113), of course, was a commercialized folk song about a tough St. Louis woman who shot her man 'cause he done her wrong. As such, it drew on the water-borne orchestra's close associations with nineteenth-century St. Louis and its roustabout nightlife. "Pianoflage," on the flip side, was a novelty piano vehicle written in the ragtime tradition by Roy Bargy, who worked as a pianist and leader in the prominent Benson Orchestra of Chicago. The Benson Orchestra, often under the leadership of the trumpeter Louis Panico, worked on the tonier Streckfus boats. Bargy is remembered primarily for his keyboard feature on the first recording of George Gershwin's *Concerto in F.*

Three aspects of the two sides stand out. First, and most important, both pieces are interpreted nearly identically to feature the ensemble's jumping performance of the arrangements. The trumpeter Sidney Desvignes does take a pleasant two-chorus solo. The expected solo by Marable on Bargy's piano feature fails to materialize. Despite his early hopes, Marable had had to become a leader, calliopist, and band pianist. In 1924, his band lacked any other major soloist. With only one instrumental solo and no vocals or even solo breaks, the recordings tend to sound repetitive. Second, the tempi of the two performances are also much the same, a moderate dance beat with a good rhythmic kick. The sides would have set young listeners to dancing, while alerting popular music professionals that Marable's musicians could read music.

But, third, the band does play with a notably rich rhythmic texture. In addition to the jumping ground beat, the wind instrumentalists play their parts with individualized rhythmic phrasing. Some are playing on top of the beat, others play fractionally behind it, still others anticipate it, all without altering the performance's "steady swinging groove." This rhythmic conversation enriches the recordings.[72]

Fate Marable must therefore go down in history as a talent scout, bandleader, orchestral pianist, and calliopist, in that order. The *St. Louis Argus*, a black newspaper, put it best: Marable was an unsurpassed producer of orchestras. He produced them in the sense that he took the time to visit the bars and dance halls of the river cities up and down the Mississippi. He listened to the way the musicians there sounded, sat in with them, and tried to imagine what this or that musician could bring to his own band or what this or that band could bring to the paddle wheelers' dancers. Marable played a major role in the politics of the black heartland in the Mississippi valley, meeting, greeting, listening, chatting, networking, hiring and firing musicians. He was, after all, the crucial link between local musicians, regular employment on the Streckfus Line, exposure to the regional scene, and introductions to great national bandleaders such as Fletcher Henderson, Duke Ellington, and Joe Oliver. Marable could make and break careers, and everyone along the river knew it. This network was his major historical contribution to black music. Inevitably he frequented some cities more than others. For example, the bandleader took particular care to know the musical circuits in New Orleans, the cradle of jazz, and St. Louis, the home of Streckfus Steamers. When, after three years, Armstrong left, too great to continue to sacrifice his solo talent, Marable went without a major trumpet soloist until he finally replaced him with Red Allen. When Allen, like Armstrong, expressed apprehension about reading the arrangements, Marable got in touch with the St. Louis bandleader Eddie Randle, who agreed to give Allen lessons immediately at an affordable price. Allen made his own professional contacts in Memphis and was soon working in New York City. When Baby Dodds left for Chicago, Marable immediately hired the great St. Louis and New Orleans drummer Zutty Singleton. When he, too, moved on, Marable found the great singing drummer Floyd Campbell, the first black male vocalist to record a blues.

Marable worked in his recruiting to introduce a rugged New Orleans street music sound into the synthesis of aural and literate musical traditions. His star musicians, such as the young Armstrong, favored as much improvisation, polyphony, and polyrhythm as possible. The drummer Warren Dodds thoroughly enjoyed the band's music: "That was a wonderful band. The music would sound so pretty, especially on the water . . . sounded so beautiful on the water."[73] The trumpeter Clarence "Perch" Thornton, who prized his 1997 award from the National Black Music Hall of Fame and Museum, took a more radical position: "To play for Streckfus, you had to go backward musically. The music was like Jeckyll and Hyde. . . . the same tunes that we knew, but they sure sounded different! New Orleans was supposed to be the jazz capital, and with Louis Armstrong playing on the boat, that supposedly made it Jazz, even if it really wasn't."[74] Marable was charged with reconciling the disparate opinions within his orchestra. What with the volatile, flawed personalities that are often found in music, the peremptory attitudes of his employers, and the weight of his obligation to make aural musicians literate, his job could not have been easy. The emerging jazz groove stubbornly went its own way. He pointedly did not encourage his children to follow him into the music business, telling them that it was just "too difficult."[75] Armstrong's relations with Marable certainly demonstrated the point.

Chapter 3

Groovin' on the River:
Louis Armstrong and Riverboat Culture

In April 1919, several years before moving to Chicago, where he cut some of his most important records, Louis Armstrong determined to see where his burgeoning talent as a jazz cornetist, vocalist, and entertainer might take him. In September 1918 he had started playing on a Streckfus Steamers excursion boat that plied New Orleans harbor but, still restless, announced to friends and colleagues that he would be shipping out to perform along the Mississippi River from New Orleans as far north as Minneapolis. Armstrong, who had been born on August 4, 1901, was then seventeen years old. He had decided to accept what looked like an exciting job offer from John Streckfus and his bandleader Fate C. Marable to play in their new hot dance band on board the steamer *Sidney*. He had not then ventured much beyond the neighborhood of his birth and had only quite recently decided to become a professional musician. But having been left to his own resources from an extremely tender age, he was prepared to embark on what turned into a restless life of touring the circuits, playing for junkets for three seasons on the river. He would later permanently leave the river but continue to travel, taking his restless, fugitive music on a train north to Chicago's South Side. He then traveled by jalopy to New York, by transatlantic steamer to Europe, and ultimately on ocean liners and airplanes that carried him to West Africa and around the world. His youthful decision to work out his future on America's greatest river set into motion a lifetime of exile from his southern home, forcing him to translate for new audiences the music he had pioneered back in New Orleans, rethinking and reinventing himself, exploring his musical capacities and creating new meanings while on the move.

Most of the early historians of jazz linked the emigration of its musicians from New Orleans to the official closing in 1917 of Storyville, the city's vice district, in which some jazzmen had found performance opportunities. That narrow interpretation ignored in Armstrong's as in Marable's case the rich context of the black migration out of the South after World War I, a major chapter in the African American diaspora.[1] A closer look at the outpouring of musical creativity that accompanied the Great Migration indicates that New Orleans jazz pioneers, and those with whom they performed on the river, became the heralds of their people's migration northward.[2] Whereas the blues singers became its musical voices, the jazzmen, led by Armstrong, trumpeted the Great Migration primarily to the wider white world of the racially segregated excursion boats. As heralds and modernist troubadours, they experienced this great movement of people in a way that both paralleled and contrasted with that of the majority who were not musicians.

Armstrong, the many musicians who played with him, and those who followed him onto the riverboats did not migrate in the simplest sense of moving from some point in the South to settle down in Chicago. But neither did many male migrants, who tended to move in a generally northerly direction from one job to another before taking on a major industrial center such as Chicago or Pittsburgh.[3] Although the riverboats did paddle northward up the

Three brilliant stars of early riverboat jazz. Left to right: the trumpeter Henry "Red" Allen, the trumpeter Louis Armstrong, and the drummer Zutty Singleton. (Photo courtesy of the Historic New Orleans Collection, accession no. 92-48-L, MSS 520.)

river, they also steamed eastward and westward across it, before paddling southward back to their original point of departure after Labor Day, their musicians usually still aboard.

Armstrong, for example, worked his way from one small town to another up and down the river for three seasons, reconnoitering the major Mississippi valley urban areas, creating a network of professional contacts that helped him find his way in the world. When he first arrived in St. Louis in 1919, he was stunned by its tall buildings:

> There was nothing like that in my home town, and I could not imagine what they were all for. I wanted to ask someone badly, but I was afraid I would be kidded for being so dumb. Finally, when we were going back to our hotel I got up enough courage to question Fate Marable.
> "What are all those tall buildings? Colleges?"
> "Aw boy," Fate answered, "Don't be so damn dumb."[4]

He learned quickly by playing after-hours sessions with St. Louis musicians. His meetings with them epitomized the black musical migration in the Mississippi valley. After demonstrating his unsurpassed improvisational talents, Armstrong listened to them and much admired their literacy and musicianship. Together, they all talked about Chicago.[5] This after-hours networking within a context of further migration and travel would continue for many years, creating what the scholar Gerald Early has called a "Black Heartland."

Armstrong, of course, permanently left the riverboats in 1921 to return temporarily to New Orleans. His further migrations to the North came when he boarded an Illinois Central train to travel to Chicago to join King Oliver's Creole Jazz Band. He could not have gone there by riverboat, there being no waterway deep or wide enough between the Mississippi River and Chicago to convey him there. While working on the river, Armstrong occasionally returned to New Orleans, and he continued to spend much of his time performing on the road around the world, becoming the prototype of the traveling musician who often seemed to live in trains, planes, taxis, hotel rooms, clubs, and recording studios. His career as the single most celebrated jazz star was a most exceptional one, but he, like most of his colleagues, spent long periods moving from one gig to another.

From the point of view of most Americans, Armstrong's restless world was even more elusive and mysterious than that of Marable. Black musicians were strictly segregated from the white passengers on the riverboats, as, later, from the patrons of the clubs and dance halls of the northern cities. "More than white musicians, black ones were usually excluded from the more stable engagements (of a week or longer),"[6] and often lived through careers filled with musical "one-nighters," their more frequent displacements making them harder to locate at any given moment. Armstrong later described what it was like to be on the road in the South: "Lots of times we wouldn't get a place to sleep. So we'd cross the tracks [into the black section of town], pull over to the side of the road and spend the night there. We couldn't get into hotels. Our money wasn't even good. We'd play nightclubs and spots which didn't have a bathroom for Negroes. When we'd get hungry, my Manager, Joe Glaser, who's also my friend, Jewish and white, would buy food along the way in paper bags and bring it to us boys on the bus who couldn't be served."[7]

Employment on the tramping riverboats offered many of them one of their longest-lasting engagements and was, for that reason alone, a milestone in many careers. But however slowly, the paddle wheelers kept moving, too. Elusive black musicians, for whom Armstrong became a figurehead, lived and worked for months at a time in reasonably close proximity to the white crew and passengers. But, thanks to the Jim Crow regulations on board, they still remained essentially enigmatic to whites, their music new and puzzling, their dress and comportment unlike that of the more familiar levee roustabouts, their after-hours destinations and activities a mystery to most white people.

Calling Armstrong and his fellow musicians "mysterious" presumes, in part, a middle-class white perspective that preferred black musicians to remain largely unknown, the better to stamp them all with racist stereotypes. The musicians could be "known" mostly within the traditions of riverboat entertainment. In the 1920s, American audiences still looked for exotic characters when stepping onto riverboats for their musical entertainment. Given the long tradition of minstrelsy, most whites thought that any black roustabout, deck hand, or musician carried an air of mystery, gaiety, and danger. During his years on the river, Armstrong, who, as we shall see, remained largely docile in the face of racial oppression, began to think about the need for an on-stage persona from this artificial racial perspective, one that would reinterpret elements of the minstrel show stereotypes.

His arrival on the excursion boat scene found him near the start of his long career as a crossover musical entertainer, and he was then a timid young man, as yet unsure who he was. But even he could not ignore his amazing talent, so Armstrong gradually discovered the courage to confidently project an image, one at which American audiences marveled in the 1930s and 1940s. By then, he had conjured an "in-between" restless persona in which he mixed his unsurpassed instrumental improvisations with an unusual jazz patois, hoarse yells, scat singing, an eyeball-rolling, handkerchief-waving, leering humor mixed with pathos, and a mysterious musical sensibility that keened in its joy.

Smiling and bowing reassuringly, Armstrong nevertheless seemed a subversive enigma, his music and gruffly masculine presence slyly creating ironic reversals of beloved lyrics and melodies, his fevered imagination an unpredictable, surging force.[8]

The new riverboat musician's early experiences had engendered a tough resilience and a determination to succeed as a musical entertainer. According to Laurence Bergreen, his had been a "wretched" childhood. His memories of its pain and promise had led Armstrong, like the true artist, to signify on it (reinterpret it) onstage, in his music, and in his patter. On the typewriter that he brought on board with him, he initiated a long life of banging out jazzy letters that rarely failed to mention some detail from his "gruesome" days and nights as a timid child in a dangerous world on the grimy sidewalks and in the squalid brothels and cabarets of Storyville. Yet, as Bergreen insists, Armstrong was full of surprises: thanks in large part to music, he later came to insist that his childhood had been an ideal one for a jazz musician. In so doing, he usually reached for the laugh but still revealed an "edge of anger" and hurt stemming from the fact that his father had not only abandoned him and the family but had then paraded proudly through the streets of black New Orleans. His stories about Mardi Gras high jinks included stark recollections of the routine beatings and "head-whippings" the New Orleans whites meted out to inoffensive black workers. His soaring music expressed the mingling of joy and sorrow in his heart. Some of his colleagues "thought they detected a voodoo ethos about" Armstrong, and, indeed, he was familiar with voodoo and included some of its seemingly nonsensical chanting in his vocals.[9]

Armstrong's painful recollections of his errant father, his own forced incarceration in an orphanage, his betrayals by powerful figures of the New Orleans demimonde such as "Black Benny" Williams, and the terrible racial oppression that forced him into a life of exile all brought sounds of sorrow and melancholy to his carnivalesque jazz. The poet Nathaniel Mackey has explained that for those who, like Armstrong, have been subjected to the "social death" of racism and abandonment by a parent, "song is both a complaint and a consolation dialectically tied to that ordeal, where in back of 'orphan' one hears echoes of 'orphic,' a music that turns on abandonment, absence, loss. Think of the black spiritual 'Motherless Child.' Music is wounded kinship's last resort."[10] When discussing Armstrong's scat vocals, Mackey argues that "scat's blithe mangling of articulate speech testified to an 'unspeakable' history"[11] of racial oppression that only worsened during Armstrong's years on the river.

In his published statements, Armstrong maintained an impenetrable diplomatic silence about the many difficulties of his decision to leave New Orleans. He admitted to feeling homesick, missing his mother and sister, friends and cronies, but he clearly signaled that he had exchanged his hometown for an excursion steamer in hopes of finding a better life. Most of the leading New Orleans musicians who had made a deep impression on him were leaving. The cornetist and bandleader Joseph "King" Oliver had decided to move to Chicago. The trombonist and bandleader Edward "Kid" Ory had determined to give Los Angeles a try.[12] A surprising number of jazz musicians traveled the Gulf Coast network of waterways, railroads, and highways in search of greater employment opportunities in music.[13] Among them were John Handy, Sam Morgan, Edmund Hall, Cootie Williams, Lee Collins, Buddy Petit, Oscar Celestin, Clarence Desdunes, Billie Pierce, Sadie Goodson Peterson, and Ida and Edna Goodson. The trumpeter Don Albert joined the migration of African Americans who lived west of New Orleans, on the western side of the Mississippi River, to Texas.[14] The reedman Sidney Bechet had headed for Europe. All of them would live their lives in transit, a bag packed, a telegram announcing the next gig sliding under the door. Many of them ranged as far west as Texas, well up into the northern Midwest, and south to Mexico and Cuba. Many others joined Armstrong on board the vessels of Streckfus Steamers.

Armstrong became the most celebrated representative of a broader and more diverse movement. Looking back after becoming jazz's first superstar, he left no doubt that working from 1916 to 1918 as a musician in and around New Orleans in Kid Ory's band had offered him his start toward professional advancement. The cornetist's wonderful ebullience gave a can-do, Horatio Alger tone to his memoirs of black Louisiana. But working with Ory never would have paid enough to free Armstrong or any of Ory's other musicians from long hours of manual labor during the week. Several other musicians worked as longshoremen and stevedores. In Louisiana, they could only hope to be part-time musicians who played for local black audiences, their wages modest at best.

The "moldy figs" of the post–World War II years—people who clung desperately to early jazz in the face of the bebop revolution of the 1940s—spied purity and authenticity in black New Orleans music before it responded to white riverboat audiences and the big city media, but it would be easy to romanticize the musicians' struggles. Kid Ory had had so much trouble getting gigs that he had started promoting fish fries on a plantation in rural Laplace, Louisiana, one whose grounds reached down to the Mississippi. Ory and his friends caught fish straight out of the Big Muddy. His uncle, who ran a grocery store in Laplace, gave Ory whiskey and beer to sell, as well—five cents for a drink, five cents for a fish sandwich.[15]

Refusing to sit about waiting for gigs to come to him, Ory organized parties, becoming bandleader, promoter, bookkeeper, treasurer, and fish fryer.

He sought out houses left empty by people who had migrated elsewhere in search of work. Such structures worked well for dance parties because they contained no furniture to get in the way. He also worked his party and picnic scheme at local baseball games and eventually earned enough to go into the musical instrument business as well.

As a seven-year-old Ory had begun by making his own banjo, guitar, string bass, and violin in order to organize a band of young musicians. As his "spasm band" began to make some meager profits at baseball games, he gradually bought several real musical instruments: a trombone, of course, a violin, a twelve-string guitar, a string bass, a trumpet, and drums. When poor youngsters such as Armstrong accepted an invitation to play in Ory's band, the leader would rent them instruments on which to perform, reducing their wages accordingly. Despite the fact that Peter Davis had given Armstrong a cornet when Louis left the waif's home, the Streckfus family insisted that he arrived on board without an instument.

The modest, localized, and rural setting of these initial musical endeavors, in which young part-time musicians played by ear on homemade instruments, defined what came to be seen, from a later vantage point, as "authentic" black jazz. But, in fact, the musical world of Kid Ory's band had also led naturally to the margins of more professional musical activities. The leading black bands from New Orleans ventured out to the Louisiana plantations every payday during the winter season when the sugar cane was ground. Buddy Bolden, for example, played on the Yazoo and Mississippi Valley line's excursion trains, which ran between New Orleans and Baton Rouge. Such trains stopped at Laplace, where Bolden would play a number or two from the baggage car as advertising for an afternoon picnic and dance from 11:00 A.M. to 4:30 P.M.

As soon as Ory secured his real instruments, he went into competition with these big-city professionals, dressing up his musicians in jackets and bow ties and leading them at picnics on weekends between performances in Laplace and Baton Rouge. His band's repertoire showed a debt to Buddy Bolden's by playing such tunes as "When the Saints Go Marching In" that he had taken from evangelical and Baptist churches. Those denominations used drums and piano accompaniment with their singing. Ory later admitted to Neshui Ertegun of Atlantic Records that his group's repertoire was more than two generations behind that of the churches.

But Ory had been moving inexorably into more urban settings in which his rural roots intertwined with more commercial venues. He performed at Pete Lala's New Orleans bar as early as 1907 and landed his first job as leader of his own band in Gretna. Soon thereafter, he secured his historic gigs at

Economy Hall in New Orleans and at Cooperators Hall in Treme by renting the halls himself and promoting dances. In 1917, the thirty-eight-block area called Storyville, in which prostitution had been made legal in 1897, was officially closed, leaving the musicians and the prostitutes who had worked there scrambling for jobs. Not long thereafter, the riverboat bandleader Fate Marable began talking to Armstrong about playing in his hot riverboat dance band.

As he thought about Marable's offer, Armstrong imagined it within the context of a search for freedom. He metaphorically recalled the time that he had entertained with a group from the waifs' home at a picnic under a broiling sun. Dizzy and exhausted, he had taken refuge in a nearby cypress swamp, where his thoughts had turned to the generations of slaves who had fled into the swamps from the plantations. Thinking of his own predicament, he had imagined his fugitive ancestors sitting on the knee-shaped tree trunks just above the snake-infested waters. Exhausted, he had perched on a knee and fallen asleep.

Armstrong had awakened, blinded by an impenetrable blackness. Terrified, he had stumbled out of the cypress swamp, grateful to find the sun setting, his young fellow inmates packing their instruments, the interminable job finally played. According to his published autobiographies, Armstrong never went back to the swamp, opting instead to attempt a career as a professional jazz musician outside the South. Starting on the Mississippi River, he demonstrated to those that could hear new spaces between the beats, new notes with which to fill them, and a correspondingly dynamic, elusive, and original lifestyle.[16]

In a second metaphor, Armstrong speaks of the Mississippi as taking the contours of many poorly formed letters M and W when viewed on a map, likening his travels up and down the river to a young person's lessons in literacy. He notes his relief when, sitting on deck, he saw the cypress swamp slide past his northbound steamer.[17]

Much of Armstrong's unusual persona came from his childhood of extreme poverty and limited education, but his unusual and ultimately entertaining translations of his past also found encouragement in the process of his migration to the North and his subsequent chasing after the gigs. He and his jazz, even the partially tamed jazz that he played on the excursion boats, took some of its optimistic spirit from an important link between music and movement. Like the blues, jazz is a form of culture that readily travels. In the first half of the twentieth century, all sorts of Americans lived in motion, migrating from abroad to new homes, from the country to the cities, from east to west, and, most important for jazz and for African Americans, from the South northward. They inevitably left behind them much of their earlier thought and behavior but readily learned to redefine themselves by the contrasts between what they recalled of what they had been and what and whom they saw and heard around them on their journeys. Moreover, the riverboat musicians, proud of their craft, possessed an unparalleled ability to carry their musical identities with them. The elements of their New Orleans musical lives swiftly became what W. T. Lhamon Jr. calls a "lore cycle," an open-ended loop of musical gestures[18] that brought an exotic excitement to riverboat dance music. Jazz may have been invented in New Orleans, but its new context on the Mississippi and the Ohio and in the major river cities changed it.

Forward motion animates dynamically played notes into movement toward "the next expected tone," unfurling melodies moving toward completion, while developing harmonic progressions and stepping rhythmic patterns create an impression of "unfinished being."[19] So the music that was commercialized as "jazz" throve on many varieties of exciting, adventurous travel. Its slang, like the music itself, came to incorporate metaphors of movement. Practiced players said they had "traveled miles and miles" through the paths of song; a musically rich performance was "a trip"; fans wanted to be "moved" by the music and pleaded with the musicians, "Go, go, go!" or "Send me!" Jazz's close relation to dance brought it joy in physical movement as dancers "hoofed it," "legged it," "beat the leather," "hopped," "trotted," "shimmied," and "toddled" to the music. Perspiring scholars tried to pin jazz down, but, of course, it was "in process," always becoming something new depending in part on where it was played, its freshness carrying a powerful message of solace and hope to those able to hear it. As we shall see, riverboat jazz even moved to the rhythmic chanteys of nineteenth- and early twentieth-century riverine laborers.

The riverboats and lives of incessant travel also encouraged what have often been described as the "joyful," "joy-making," "festive," "happy," and "fun" sounds of Armstrong's music. Well-established patterns of minstrelsy and the tourist trade indicated that bar and nightclub music by New Orleans blacks had to be upbeat and exuberant. Thus Armstrong's impossibly large stage smile.

But the music that Armstrong recorded and that he wrote about is too easily dismissed as merely "happy music." It was not "unhappy music," but neither was Armstrong's jazz a cartoon music like that of the Original Dixieland Jazz Band's "Livery Stable Blues," which was conceived and performed with caricatured low-comic intent. So, too, Jelly Roll Morton's "Hyena Stomp" drew in a similar manner on broad-brush vaudeville slapstick. During the 1950s, Armstrong and, in particular, his vocalist Velma Middleton entertained their audiences with plenty of pratfalls.

Nevertheless, most of the recorded music that Armstrong performed in his Hot Five and Hot Seven recordings and his Mississippi River numbers of the 1930s and 1940s could more accurately be described as sharply glinting, in flight, agitated, and excited, not simply happy or joyful, a rough, tough-spirited music that resisted easy labels. Polyphony and polyrhythm gave it substantial complexity. Armstrong himself contributed a nearly operatic virtuosity. As Nathaniel Mackey insists, sadness lurks in his tone and expressiveness and, when blended with the Roaring Twenties spirit of nervous excitement, lent emotional depth to his music. Thus his music flew well beyond the comic minstrel mugging with which it was delivered.

Much of this complexity expressed the hazards of the Great Migration, a mixture of eager anticipation and danger. For Armstrong, as for the musicians who played with him on the riverboats, jazz was, in addition to musical entertainment, what James Clifford has called a habitus, a space in time between past and future where one lived while on the move, a set of musical and social practices and associations that could be remembered and through which one could simultaneously remember one's hometown while far from it.[20] Jazz skills, jazz ideals, and jazz's alienation from mainstream middle-class culture functioned as a body of knowledge with which and within which one could live and work while on the move, particularly on the water. Armstrong owed much to his musical experiences in New Orleans. But from 1919 to the end of the summer of 1921, he tramped the Mississippi, Missouri, and Ohio rivers. He had no fixed home. He worked in order to change his place and position in American society. He never made Chicago his permanent home, either, and when he bought a home outside of New York City, he spent as much time away from it as in it. His music expressed the special kinds of movement characterized by migration, diaspora, and steamship voyages. It had great energy, ambition, daring, courage, undercurrents of the voyagers' nostalgia for home, and a tough alienation from sentimentalism and from mainstream culture.

As he had in that frightening swamp, Armstrong found strength in the long history of African Americans who had plied the Mississippi River before him. As W. Jeffrey Bolster has written, for many West Africans who had been transported to Louisiana during slavery times, water was thought to purify and transport the soul.[21] For Ibos, Kongo peoples, and West Africans in general, water was a potent metaphor for life beyond this world. The scholar Melville Herskovits notes that wherever West African religious beliefs were found within the United States, there also could be found the river cult or, more broadly, the cult of water spirits.[22] Armstrong, after all, visited with and took guidance from his fugitive ancestors in a Louisiana swamp.

According to Sterling Stuckey, during slavery times, immersion in and reemergence from water carried people into interstitial spiritual spaces linked to memories of Africa. A cycle of ceremonial death and resurrection began with the sacred ring shout, in which the people shuffle-danced in a counter-clockwise direction, often around a barrel of water, as if the dancers were moving eastward and upward through the North American air in order to fly away from slavery, descend into the Atlantic Ocean, and reemerge back on the shores of West Africa, their roots remembered and replanted in North American soil.[23]

The ritual spiritual power in black Christianity of baptism by full immersion in rivers also flowed through the black levee culture through which Armstrong traveled. Even in the more secular circles within which jazz musicians felt most at home, the spiritual power of rivers moved. Such African American hymns as "Deep River," "Down by the Riverside," "I've Got Peace Like a River," "Joys Are Flowing Like a River," "Lord, My Soul Is Thirsting," "On Jordan's Stormy Banks," "Shall We Gather at the River?," and "Wade in the Water" blow gently soothing breaths over lonesome, weary travelers.[24]

The music scholar and theorist Samuel A. Floyd Jr. argues that the spirit and function of the West African ring shout extended to the "second line" (people who followed the musicians at funeral parades in black New Orleans), one of Armstrong's major influences.[25] Here the worship of the ancestors mixed with the wildly secular celebration of life when the parade headed back from the burial ground. Here the bands improvised on such themes as "Oh, Didn't He Ramble!" The musicians learned to signify on the spirit and themes of the music. Louis Armstrong became the greatest stylist of this tradition.

In the experiences of the black Mississippi lived a "poetics of relocation and re-inscription" in which the young Armstrong excelled. The Mississippi and Ohio rivers had long offered greater freedom of movement to African Americans, movement that launched the music in new directions.[26] Riverboat musicians were heirs to this tradition, as well, and assimilated into their music the rhythms of the old black sailors' chanteys. Boats paid relatively well, and slaves had been allowed to hire their labor out to the boats' owners. Such mobility had given a higher social status to black laborers in slavery times. Enslaved individuals had sometimes been leased to steamers; they and free blacks worked as musicians, roustabouts, deck hands, firemen, cooks, porters, waiters, and watchmen. Though subject to rigid, often cruel discipline onboard, these laborers still associated water, rivers, boats, oceans, and ships with the freedom of black sailors. Despite the fact that officers routinely whipped, cursed, kicked, pushed, and hit their deck hands, cabin workers and musicians were not usually so abused. The combination of rigid racial segregation, cruel discipline, and the sense of enjoying the possibility of greater liberty encouraged a black riverboat culture that included a sense of rootlessness, horrendous working conditions, a distrust of authority, and a proud masculinity.[27]

Boat workers enjoyed obvious liberties, particularly when in port. According to the historian Tom Buchanan, riverboat slaves and free workers connected widely separated slave and free black communities from New Orleans to Cairo, Illinois, into a black intercity network along the Mississippi that allowed them to make contacts, create networks, and form opinions about the state of the wider white and black worlds in the United States.

In ways that have not been understood heretofore, Armstrong played a particularly influential and controversial role in the riverboat experience. In 1919, 1920, and 1921, the young musician was deepening his initial discovery of the wellspring of improvisation that he had gradually revealed to himself in the aural world of black New Orleans, a powerful groove that he could not but bring on board with him. However, his unusually rapid improvisational progress accelerated on the Streckfus Line excursion boats, just where the orchestra leader Fate Marable and his employers so vigorously pursued their policy of musical literacy. For three summers, Armstrong therefore became the focus of a highly symbolic cultural struggle between oral and literate approaches to musical performance. His spectacular journey through this conflict made him the figurehead of a new musical interstice called jazz.

When he first crossed the gangplank in his tattered shoes, Armstrong performed only in the aural world of Kid Ory's band. But the young cornetist subsequently assured the reading public in his 1936 autobiography that he had, under the tutelage of mellophonist David Jones and pianist Fate Marable, learned to read music.

Subsequent events would prove that Armstrong exaggerated and oversimplified his progress in musical literacy. When in 1924, three years after leaving the river, Armstrong joined Fletcher Henderson's hot dance band, one for which Fate Marable's band had provided excellent training, he still felt uncomfortable reading arrangements. His rhythmic swing helped transform that orchestra, but he still had to listen to someone else play the notes arranged for him so that he could then play them from memory.

> Where I had come from I wasn't used to playing in bands where there were lots of parts for everybody to read. Shucks, all one in the band had to do is to go to some show and hear a good number. He keeps it in his head until he reaches us. He hums it a couple of times, and from then on we had a new number to throw on the bands that advertised in the wagons on the corner

A handsome and dynamic young Armstrong (third from right) looks ready to fly off his chair. The other players, left to right: Henry Kimball, Boyd Atkins, Fate Marable, John St. Cyr, David Jones, Norman Mason, Norman Brashear, and Baby Dodds, aboard the S.S. *Capitol,* c. 1919. (Photo courtesy of Duncan Schiedt.)

> on the following Sunday. . . . I had left Chicago, where the way we used to do it was just take the wind in and take what's left and blow out and now I got to watch this part.[28]

While rehearsing with the Henderson band, Armstrong, for example, missed the dynamic markings and blasted out his part while the rest of the musicians brought theirs down to *pianissimo* (abbreviated as *pp*), as instructed in the arrangement. In response to Henderson's criticisms, he tried to cover up with a joke—"Oh, I thought that meant '*pound plenty*'"—when explaining his failure to follow the chart.[29]

Beyond the initial step of learning to recognize the basic musical notation symbols, "reading music" becomes a relative matter. Some musicians come to specialize in it, becoming precise musical technicians. Others learn to read about as much as they need to play the gigs they manage to find. Armstrong came on board a musical illiterate who lived in the aural musical world he had shared with people in his neighborhood. He then learned to read music, perhaps not swiftly or at first sight, nor perfectly thereafter, but, with sufficient rehearsal, he did learn enough to play his parts well in performance. In the process, he discovered that in some important ways he didn't really want to read music. As he described it, the sheets of music distracted him, got between him and his audience, diverting his inner aural concentration on the sound of swiftly passing chords and rhythms with the external imperative of visual concentration.

He became, after all, the most impressive "get-off man," or improviser, since Sidney Bechet. Early big bands such as those of Marable, Henderson, and Ellington clearly recognized a division of labor between the musicians who had been hired to read the charts and those who had been hired to "get off" into the surprising world of musical improvisation. Armstrong, therefore, moved beyond his initial illiteracy. Like many of the other New Orleans musicians, he dutifully learned to name the notes and to mathematically divide and subdivide their rhythmic values. He was, moreover, linguistically literate. He would use his typewriter to write letters to his old friends for hours at a time. When, in 1936, he wrote his first autobiography, he described the Mississippi as one might when looking at it on a map. The river looked to him like a winding series of poorly formed but recognizable signs whose form and meaning would emerge with greater clarity only with more direct riverboat experience. Armstrong was one of those who preferred to apply literacy to language while keeping music aural.

He had excellent reasons. The oral world from which he sprang treated music and language in similar ways. Both partook of what Walter Ong has called an "oral, mobile, warm, personally interactive life world." Writing, whether linguistic or musical, reduced "dynamic sound to quiescent space." Written words and musical notation "isolate sound from the fuller context in which [they] came into being": "The word in its natural, oral habitat is a part of a real existential present. Spoken utterance is addressed to a real, living person or real, living persons, at a specific time in a real setting which includes always much more than mere words."[30] Written notes were only that. Those played by ear, like pronounced words, naturally relied heavily on individual manipulations of intonation, pitch, and a grand variety of colorings and shadings. The black musical tradition had developed minute rhythmic variations in the way notes were articulated. The written score, on the other hand, seemed to musicians such as Armstrong a cold, unresponsive, unchangeable final statement imposed on the musical imagination, a Dead Sea scroll that remained outside any give and take of real persons, beyond discussion.[31] In his written recollections of his hometown, in many of his letters, and in interviews, Armstrong emphasized the rich social context in which he had come to music.

And here was the crux of his continuing attachment to playing music by ear, just as he was learning to read it at sight. He found in the world of sound, far more than in that of sight, emotional fulfillment. This is, according to Ong, part of the essential psychological meaning of music. It, like human consciousness and human communication, gives the impression of emanating from somewhere profoundly deep within oneself. Like river water, music seemed always in flux, moving toward the next discovery. A gifted musician such as Armstrong gathered and then immersed himself in sounds coming from all directions and sources, making himself the center of his own personal and original synthesis. Whereas sight dissects and isolates elements of experience, sound brings experience inside us and harmonizes our perceptions of the world. As Ong puts it, "The centering action of sound . . . affects man's sense of the cosmos, unifying, centralizing, and interiorizing." Improvised music, "like the spoken word . . . proceeds from the human interior and manifests human beings to one another as conscious interiors, as persons; the spoken word [and music] form[] human beings into close-knit groups."[32] Music, and, more particularly, improvised music (and even hot, agitated varieties) can generate, more than can a written arrangement, a sense of a sacred circle. These styles of music seem to emanate from an unknown source very deep within the musician, one that he or she experiences as a unifying harmony that is being shared with others.

This aural worldview emphasizes a participatory give and take between audience and musician, plenty of leeway in exactly how one recalls a favorite tune, and a nonabstract, situational manner of understanding the communication process. Armstrong and the other black migrant musicians developed their own vocabulary to describe the major techniques, strategies, and culture of playing jazz. They spoke of "heads," "turnarounds," "the sock chorus," "licks," "getting off," and much more.[33] The externalized authority of the tradition of musical literacy must have felt like the imposition of an oppressive new authority, little connected to Armstrong's musical background.

That strong aural tradition formed the core of an interstitial musical life that included many other ingredients, as well. A poor, uneducated black man from the lowest social level of wicked Storyville, someone who nonetheless clung to certain old-fashioned American values, an African American much influenced by the Karnofskys, his adoptive Jewish family, a man traveling into a life of exile from his southern home, an individual moving through a time of crackling racial hostility calling for the strictest discretion and diplomacy—here was a man living between social and cultural categories. Striking out in search of a better life, he began to reinvent himself as a black musical entertainer, becoming a mysterious mixture of gifted solo improviser, comedian, and original vocalist with a guttural, rasping sound capable of suggesting pathos in humor.

Even at that early stage in his career, Armstrong was in the full bloom of an unprecedented journey into a life of solo instrumental improvisation. As jazz musicians used to say, he was beginning to "own that thing." Instrumental control engenders a sense of personal stature and power within the world of music and in life generally. A life of improvisational development is a rare privilege. More often than not, literate musicians simply cannot improvise. His special gift intimately linked him through musical memory to his people and his ancestors.

He had to know, far better than did Streckfus, what his gift might do for him in the world of musical entertainment. He liked and respected Fate Marable and made an on-going, two-and-one-half-year pass at learning to read his charts but stubbornly acted as if he knew that he would never live out his life and career as a section player. Marable might be right. He might live to regret his stubbornness. But, in fact, he did not. He was Louis Armstrong, and there never was another musician like him.

Armstrong may also have had his own reasons for avoiding Marable's lessons. His exceptional talent raised complex questions about career planning. True, reading the riverboat charts offered poor musicians such as Armstrong a special Streckfus kind of economic opportunity—real enough, but strictly limited. They paid the average sideman $35.00 plus room and board or $65.00 per week without room or board, as when, for example, the boat worked for several weeks at one city and the musicians found rooms in the black sections of town. Given the Herculean labor of playing both a daytime and an evening cruise, this was downright parsimonious, but the Streckfus brothers probably were aware that Kid Ory paid his musicians only $17.50 per week (albeit for much less labor).[34] In 1919 John Streckfus had paid only $37.50 per week without room and board, but he gradually increased the benefits and shortened the work hours. Much earnest, respectful negotiation convinced the Streckfus brothers to divide the orchestra into smaller units during the daytime cruises. That way, at least, players got some time off. They subsequently decided to hire a different band for the daylight cruises, saving their best band for the moonlight excursions.

By 1926, when Henry "Red" Allen, following Armstrong's career trajectory and improvisational ideas, came aboard, the starting salary had increased to $45.00 per week, but room and board were not included. In order to keep exhausted musicians from jumping ship, they also offered a bonus of $5.00 per week, paid at the end of the summer season. If a musician could refrain from splurging in town after his night's work, if he would dutifully spoon in the

The S.S. *Sidney* (on the right) seen from the bow in this early photo. Louis Armstrong played on the *Sidney,* and Walter Pichon, James Blanton, and Erroll Garner performed in its dance hall when it was recommissioned as the *Washington*. (Photo courtesy of the Jones Steamboat Collection, Special Collections Division, Howard-Tilton Memorial Library, Tulane University.)

starchy steamboat cuisine, sleep in the tiny, crowded bunk room, and save his pennies, he could welcome Labor Day with more cash in his pocket than he had ever had before. If such restraint faltered, he was still a young man with a bankroll in what looked and sounded like a glamorous job. In levee-front bars, that earned considerable respect. Armstrong wrote glowingly about rolling back into his old Storyville haunts, a wad of riverboat dollars in his jeans.

The Streckfus brothers preferred to pay one flat rate negotiated between the black musicians' union and the company, and their experience with Armstrong led them, slowly and reluctantly, to modestly increase the salaries of their star players. He and other gifted improvisers such as Red Allen, Nathaniel Story, Earl Bostic, Clark Terry, Harold "Shorty" Baker, and Jimmy Blanton managed to eke out another $10.00 or $15.00 per week. The Streckfus brothers never fully accepted the star system because it led directly to higher wages for the star and less work from the sidemen. Nor would they allow them to accept gigs in the river cities after the midnight cruises. They insisted that if midwesterners wanted to hear their red hot band, they would have to pay to come on board. The same logic may have led them to discourage their musicians from recording, at least under the Streckfus banner.

Armstrong wanted to become the featured soloist and vocalist in Fate Marable's dance band. Both Streckfus and Marable resisted the innovation. In 1921, therefore, Armstrong left the riverboats for good. He had found much to admire in the experience, but his employers' intransigence would leave a permanent wound. In his first autobiography, Armstrong characterized his last months on board as stormy weather and, many years later, took particular satisfaction in seeing that a Streckfus entourage had made the effort to come to a club in New York where he had star billing to hear and see him perform. Armstrong returned the gesture by going over to their table between sets.

Although he has exaggerated his case, the musical theorist Jacques Attali has offered an important interpretation of radically new popular music styles such as the jazz Armstrong played on the river between 1918 and 1921. Attali insists that such musical breakthroughs act as heralds of emerging new social orders.[35] Two of his many provocative points about the social functions of music offer potential insights into the social significance of Armstrong, the Great Migration, and riverboat jazz. First, Attali likens radically new musical styles to "noise" that has the potential to disrupt and silence the usual ritualized harmony of musical styles that have been designed to help people forget violent disruptions to the social order. Second, the manipulation of music by the powerful usually serves to ritually domesticate and therefore to "sacrifice" music's radical potential in an effort to restore listeners' belief in the political and social order. Riverboat jazz, a partially tamed adaptation of New Orleans jazz, eliminated violence, affirmed the possibility of social order, and offered a promise of racial reconciliation.

Armstrong and his famous New Orleans jazz brothers had "brought the noise," black noise, through the Mississippi valley at the height of the region's racial tensions.[36] Their astounding music might easily have reached hundreds of thousands of white Americans from New Orleans to Minneapolis. But many were deeply troubled by the social changes set in motion by the Great Migration. Within the "confidence game" played by the excursion steamers, power moved to make the nation's past live on into very unsettled modern times. In order to make twentieth-century midwesterners believe in the continued dominance of Mark Twain's world, the musicians had to sacrifice the blues, the radical challenges of their free polyphonic improvisations, fleetingly fast and grindingly slow tempi, and sexually frank lyrics. This suppression of what would have been to many white passengers the more threatening (because unfamiliar) qualities of New Orleans jazz also sacrificed Armstrong and Dodds, the two most spontaneous, innovative, and entertaining musicians in Marable's Metropolitan Jaz-E-Saz Orchestra. The riverboats had provided but a limited venue for Armstrong's solos. In the fall of 1921, he performed a solo titled "La Veda" accompanied only by piano. It received such applause that it became a featured act.[37] But Armstrong had signed on to act as a section man in an arrangement-reading orchestra. In 1921 he would finally jettison his regimented role in the riverboat dance band. He postponed the daily quest for mastery of Euro-American musical literacy and moved on to the nightclubs of Chicago, a musical world where, on one hand, his individuality and expressive freedom found greater encouragement, while, on the other, the number of his professional choices was correspondingly limited.

Because of the Streckfus policy against recording their bands, Armstrong never recorded with the celebrated Metropolitan Jaz-E-Saz Orchestra. As if that were not unfortunate enough, he had to wait twelve years before recording any tunes that evoked rivers in general or the Mississippi River in particular. But during the depression and World War II, he did express his new, remarkably unsentimental spirit in several recordings with river themes. Indeed, were one to include all the recordings that tapped into the general themes of parting and returning, leaving someone (and being left), and finding that person again, the number of his recorded movement tunes would rise dramatically.

Armstrong created a new jazz interpretation of the black Mississippi, one that combined his musical roots with the lessons of his riverboat years if not their often melancholy spirit. His river recordings began on April 5, 1930, well after his famous Hot Five and Hot Seven sessions of the 1920s. They crop up in daring, wonderfully successful sessions held during the worst of the Great Depression. The first of them was "Dear Old Southland," created in 1921 by the African American songwriting team of Henry Creamer and Turner Layton when they had "borrowed" two spirituals, "Deep River" and "Sometimes I Feel Like a Motherless Child," and stitched them together to make their commercial hybrid.[38] Armstrong recorded it as a solo in 1930 with accompaniment by the vaudeville dancer and pianist Buck Washington. The trumpeter launches into this musical voyage with a slow, haunting, dignified statement of the two sacred themes that is worthy of a New Orleans brass band marching to the cemetery. But then, following the musical tradition of the funeral parades, he leaps into double time, his joyous shouts sending sorrow flying into the glinting rough and tumble of hot jazz.[39]

He was a hip, secular, itinerant musician deeply influenced by the music of Storyville. Indeed, according to Marable, he was a "wild young man." Although such black intellectuals as W. E. B. Du Bois and Alain Locke felt a strong attachment to the spirituals, or "sorrow songs," interpreting them as sacred expressions of a lost time of greater folk purity,[40] Armstrong had grown up far from the halls of academe. Music critics for the Harlem paper *New York*

Age joined forces with the National Association of Negro Musicians and the Hampton Institute's journal *The Southern Workman* to condemn the jazzing of the spirituals.[41] But Armstrong created a hot commercialized river spirit by both respecting and jazzing the spirituals, working into his wild trumpet improvisations direct and heartfelt statements of the sacred old melodies.

"Deep River" first attained great popularity in this country's publishing houses and concert halls in 1917, the year that Ell Persons was lynched in Memphis and a murderous race riot tore apart East St. Louis, Illinois. Nearly blasphemy in relation to Du Bois's sorrow songs and certainly "a moment when the subject-matter or the content of a cultural tradition [was] being overwhelmed, or alienated, in the act of translation," Armstrong's musical announcement of a new era[42] was a transgressive act.

In 1933–35 the trumpeter recorded with a twelve-piece band, similar in number and instrumentation to Marable's bands. Indeed, some of the musicians on these dates—Zilner Randolph, Harry Dial, Red Allen, Leonard Davis, Lawrence "Snub" Mosely, and Pops Foster—had played their ways through the Mississippi valley, too. A remarkable Victor session in 1933 produced "Mississippi Basin," "Dusky Stevedore," "St. Louis Blues," "There's a Cabin in the Pines," "Mighty River," and "He's a Son of the South." Sessions for Decca in 1939 and 1940 waxed the culturally rich "Shanty Boat on the Mississippi" and "Lazy 'Sippi Steamer."[43]

Armstrong's river recordings seem to me to be among the more successful records he made. They can be seen as his creative response to Joseph Streckfus and Fate Marable, the records that he would have liked to make with Marable's Metropolitan Jaz-E-Saz Orchestra ten or eleven years earlier, had he been allowed. On several of these sides we hear Armstrong leading orchestral arrangements, indicating how much he had learned from Marable's tuition despite their falling-out. At the same time, Armstrong is the star instrumentalist and vocalist who leads the band, asserting an individual authority in the recording studio denied to him on the river.

Armstrong's river recordings create an "in-between space" in black music history. He interprets major themes of the black Mississippi, an important experience in the Great Migration, in his own hot, stomping, swinging manner, often at much faster tempi than the riverboat captains had allowed. His lyrics often allude to the sadness of the black South, but Armstrong frames all such moments with his sunny optimism. With Andy Razaf's lyrics for "He's a Son of the South" (Vic 24257), Armstrong, riding high over a fleet rhythm section that included the pianist Teddy Wilson and the banjoist Mike McKendrick, turns the Great Migration into a seemingly effortless but stylish strut. He's a son of the south very much on the move, dressed even better than Fate Marable, and, moreover, stepping to some really hot jazz, much too searing for old wooden paddle wheelers. He pulls out all the stops, his trumpet blistering his joyful, shouting notes, his slick journey through the lyrics slipping, gliding, and veering through the syllables.

He slows the tempo a bit, switching into a minor key, to play and sing "Mississippi Basin" (Vic 24335). In singing these lyrics, Armstrong becomes a levee worker: "Even though the weight was heavy, I was happy on the levee. Want to take my rightful place in the Mississippi Basin back home. Everybody was for me there, all the folks will be there, used to like to wash my face in the Mississippi Basin back home." He wonders aloud why he left but recalls that he's going to make a beeline back home.

He flips on full afterburner when blazing through Andy Razaf and J. C. Johnson's "Dusky Stevedore" (Vic 24320), his second recording about maritime labor. At a tempo that would have reduced the *St. Paul* to splinters, Armstrong doffs his hat to the roustabouts down on the levees of the Mississippi, singing that though the loads they carried were heavy, they still had a song to sing and "a ragtime shufflin' gate" to their steps. These tough, strong, stylish men demonstrated how to come through slaughter, offering an artistic rendering of the roustabout experience to counterbalance the meanness of the Streckfus Steamers' magazine story about Millennium Potts.

Profiting enormously from his back-up band, one that also included Albert "Budd" Johnson and Scoville Brown on tenor and clarinet and St. Louis's own Zilner Randolph on trumpet, Armstrong slowed down just enough to hit a swanlike note of dignity for Billy Baskette's "Mighty River" (Vic 24351). The lyrics actually celebrate the sound of a departing steamer's whistle and bell, announcing a slow voyage back home to a girl (like Daisy Parker) whom migration had left behind. He even slips into these lyrics a statement that the best part of the trip will be getting to its end.

Decca and Victor, labels that plied the nation's more commercialized musical markets, were many steps removed from the Okeh race record label, on which Armstrong's most famous Hot Five and Hot Seven sessions appeared. Armstrong's last two river recordings followed the standard ballad form with vocal. Terry Shand and Jimmy Eaton's "Shanty Boat on the Mississippi" (Decca 2729) and Armstrong's own "Lazy 'Sippi Steamer Going Home" (Decca 3283) provide a counterpoint to the advanced thinking of the other recordings. On the latter, according to Charles Garrett, Armstrong celebrated the social and economic potential of life in Chicago for a talented immigrant. On the former, however, he plays and sings hot interpretations of what he had left behind on his migration. "Shanty Boat" evokes the jerry-rigged house-boats of poor black people along the Mississippi, singing the feelings of an ex-hausted laboring man who looks forward to kicking back on his own shanty riverboat. He's gonna take him a wife, eat fish from the river, and "ain't gonna work no more."

Chanteys were labor songs sung by sailors on boats. Although the lyrics of some of these songs refer back to British tars, many of them reveal black origins, so many, in fact, that one expert argues that the old sea chanteys derived from the West Indies. There, black islanders, defending themselves against severe weather, for example, moved their simple dwellings by mounting them on rolling platforms. The owner acted as both a shantyman and a chanteyman, singing out the call of a laboring song, while those pulling him and his house furnished a rhythmic response.[44] "Shanty Boat on the Mississippi" commercializes and modernizes the shanty tradition, rearranging the old themes of labor, recreation, and music. Armstrong's river recordings are chanteys in jazz time, full of the music and images of riverboats and their traditions. The identity of the group mentioned in the lyrics depends on the listener's point of view, but black jazz lovers would have had no problems creating their own memories of the South and their migration in the performances. Armstrong's original manner of performance might have given his river recordings a little of the rebellious spirit of the black maritime tradition that extended from the eighteenth-century Atlantic trade to the nineteenth-century sail and steam vessels to the early twentieth-century packets and excursion boats.[45]

"Lazy 'Sippi Steamer," like "Mississippi Basin," celebrates the anticipation of a black laboring man like the composer or one of the black seamen or roustas returning home down the Mississippi. Armstrong evokes the powerful, mixed emotions of one returning to the South, the familiar sights and sounds along the banks of the Lower Mississippi evoking home and the lives of one's friends and family, all the beautiful but terrifying experiences that migrants like him had fled.

Armstrong sings these songs straight, without scatting or adding comic interjections such as those he injected into his recording of Hoagy Carmichael's famous song "Lazy River" (OK 41541) and of "Lonesome Road" (OK 41538). The first might have seemed too romantic, the latter too full of self-pitying lyrics. He transforms the former by doubling the tempo and scat singing, the latter by erecting all around the melody and lyrics a scaffolding of vaudeville-style satire. His recording of "When It's Sleepy Time Down South" (OK 41504) compensates for the many little implied racial stereotypes in the lyrics by opening with a conversation between Armstrong and Charlie Alexander, the pianist in the session. They contextualize the song with signals of their solidarity in the Great Migration, discussing how long they've been "up here" and their plans to touch base back down South, the lovely old melody becoming a memory of the beauties of a less intense, slower-moving past.

In the big band river records that Armstrong made during the thirties and very early forties, the great musician and entertainer turned all the hope and labor of his migration into his own interstitial interpretation of the Mississippi. He and his all-black recording orchestras recalled via their own experiences the black laboring men who had come before them. In the recordings of Louis Armstrong and His Orchestra, excited emigrants fairly flew through the air, with style and grace, their travels animated by the adventure, energy, and mystery of gifted young artists on the move.

After World War II, a time of somewhat less violent race relations in the Mississippi valley, a time when more militant attitudes about how to deal with the white majority swept through black communities, Armstrong appeared to some to have accommodated himself too fully to racism and segregation on the river and elsewhere. The trumpeter Miles Davis, raised in East St. Louis, Illinois, lamented "all that grinning" by Louis Armstrong and placed Armstrong's photo alongside those of Beulah, Buckwheat, and Rochester in his autobiography.[46] Davis had never lived through the post–World War I riots and had never been so poor, and was therefore unable fully to appreciate how dangerous those times had been to a musician such as Armstrong. Whatever his practical spirit of accommodation, the older man had never granted whites in general nor the Streckfus family in particular dominion over him. Despite his reluctance to help free the drummer Baby Dodds from the clutches of John Streckfus Jr., Armstrong did not fully accept the riverboat captains' vision of white dominion on the Mississippi.

In his second autobiography, he recounted it thus: one night, a mate roused him from his sleep with word that the captain had demanded his presence in the pilot house. Worried that he might have done something wrong, Armstrong rushed to the captain's side only to discover that the white-bearded gentleman wanted to point out to him Jackson Island, where Mark Twain's Tom Sawyer had cavorted with his friends. "I looked up at the old gentleman, not knowing what was to come. Then I saw he was smiling. He said, 'Louie, come in here. We're working up to Jackson Island in a few minutes and I thought you would like to see it.' He had remembered my telling him about my reading 'Tom Sawyer' and asking him if he had known Mr. Mark Twain." Streckfus placed a heavy, kindly hand on Armstrong's shoulder. After a lengthy silence, he finally said:

"This is Mark Twain's country. He was a very great man. I never pass this part of the river without feeling that his spirit rests over it." I began to see a dark patch of woods standing out ahead of us on the left. Then I heard his voice again. "That is Jackson Island," the old gentleman said. I knew the time had come when I should feel something he wanted me to feel. I remembered from the book about how Tom Sawyer and Huckleberry Finn and their friend Little Joe Harper had gone to that island to be "pirates," and had cooked their food over a wood fire and had had a good time, but that seemed a long way back to me, and the island, as far as I could see it in the dark, looked just the same as a hundred other islands we had passed in the river in the long time we had been going since we left New Orleans.[47]

Although he has been accused of being a weak person whose spirit was broken by racial oppression,[48] Armstrong, beneath his ever-present diplomacy, remained quietly resilient and independent in the face of pressure from such white authority figures as John Streckfus Sr., the president of Streckfus Steamers and captain of the boat on which he was working. In fact, this is a major lesson that can be learned from the history of his years on the river.[49] Armstrong and Marable's other musicians took what the excursion boats could offer them and then got on with the greater goals of their migration. Their experiences in major cities along the Mississippi ultimately led them away from the South—and the riverboats.

Chapter 4

From Beale Street to Market Street: Music and Movement Through Memphis and St. Louis

At the foot of Beale Street in Memphis, where the river lapped lazily at the dock, bales of cotton covered the levee like huge flakes of snow. Clustered about the waterfront were half a dozen packets, their tall smoke stacks standing black against the sky, all hungry for cotton.

—George Lee, *River George*

In St. Louis, the Mississippi River laps onto a cobblestone levee laid by enslaved workers in the nineteenth century. Steamboats tied up to steel rings anchored in stone. At night, on those cobblestones, the roustabouts slept as best they could. Musicians coming back on board after a late night in town had to step carefully around their sleeping bodies.

—Jazz musician Eric Sager

One Ohio roustabout song commented:
"Steamboat done put me out of do's, oh Baby.
Out on the cold frozen groun'."

—Mary Wheeler, *Steamboatin' Days*

Between New Orleans and St. Louis, the two leading urban centers of riverboat jazz, the largest port city with a long-standing reputation for vernacular music was Memphis, Tennessee, the "Bluff City," perched on Chickasaw Bluff, from which Hernando de Soto first saw the Mississippi River in 1541.[1] Located at the crossroads of eastern Arkansas, northern Mississippi, and southwestern Tennessee, Memphis became the largest inland cotton market in the world, the "capital city of the Mississippi Delta."[2] Thanks to the convergence there of three different railroad lines with several riverboat lines, Memphis became a crossroads of country and vaudeville blues, blues-influenced jug band music, dance bands, brass bands, and restless jazz musicians worried about a persistent lack of gigs.

Over the long run, Memphis earned a reputation as the blues capital of the United States. Beale Street, the city's black commercial center, the "Main Street of Black Memphis," ran up from the Mississippi for a bit more than a mile through the center of town before disappearing in the mud flats of East Street. As McKee and Chisenhall have written, although black people also shopped for food and clothes and saw doctors, dentists, and lawyers on Beale Street,[3] that part of town was permanently labeled the Saturday night sin district of Memphis.

Diverse blues styles from adjacent communities mixed in Memphis with ragtime piano, with a number of instrumental wind ensembles led by W. C. Handy and Jimmie Lunceford, with the vaudeville blues of Memphis Ma Rainey and Alberta Hunter, with gospel singing, and with music delivered to the foot of Beale Street by the packet boats from New Orleans and St. Louis.[4] A number of African American folk music traditions blended on Beale Street, the "Saturday night heaven of country Negroes who wrote the expressions from the tall, white cotton fields of the sloping river bottoms."[5] Up on Beale near Second Street, country sharecroppers gathered at a place called the Wagon Tongue. Mixing their Prohibition gin and smoky barbecue with the music of their own banjos, guitars, and Jew's harps, "they would ease their souls with ready-made songs." George W. Lee, the poetic novelist of Beale Street's blues, wrote of "a song flowing in quick tears and laughter straight from the unhappy heart of man," the song of "a lazy, tall, county rube prying down a dusty, country road in the moonlight."[6]

Blues traditions were further enriched in this "hell-roaring river town"[7] by roustabouts who, with glinting cotton hooks hanging from their jeans, swaggered up Beale Street, eager to drink, gamble, and charm "winsome, pocoduloas brown figures,"[8] the better to escape punishing riverboat discipline in the company of their own people. To the diverse mix of rural blues traditions roustabouts added their bluesy songs of powerful steamboat captains, wild and alienated deck workers, and loves lost and found on a riverboat in the moonlight.

Beale Street's blues contributed in major ways to jazz on the river before World War II. The folk blues sound would permeate jazz. Jazz musicians often backed the vaudeville blues vocalists on stage and in the recording studios. But musically ambitious Memphis instrumentalists, who would come to work under the "jazz" label, tended either to emigrate from or work outside of that city. The Bluff City was a deep southern cotton town. Jazz instrumentalists, like many other emigrants, sought better wages further north.

Like everyone else, early jazz musicians made their compromises with Jim Crow, but, by means of their music, sought greater freedom and ways to mix inventive and accomplished sounds with show business. The reasons for their tendency to leave Memphis are not hard to find. The city had for many years attracted large numbers of black immigrants from Mississippi and Arkansas. After 1900, thousands of these relatively recent migrants, who had fled flood damage, the boll weevil, the peonage system, low wages, lynching, segregation, poor housing, and poorer schools, emigrated from Memphis further north. According to Gloria Brown Melton, by 1930, almost a third of Tennessee-born blacks had left the state. But, as Michael J. Honey reports, "many more came to Memphis, fleeing from even worse conditions in rural areas."[9] As James H. Robinson relates, that city was a rural as well as an urban center. Because of this, according to William S. Worley, "from the 1890s to 1940, Beale Street music was mostly blues [that] . . . resounded of poor rural backgrounds."[10]

The elite of the city, the ruling families whose patriarchs dominated the Memphis Cotton Exchange and who owned offices on Front Street (popularly known as "Cotton Row"), indirectly encouraged their city's dedication to blues. Disturbed by the alarming departure of black workers during World War I, they dedicated their economic leadership to keeping exceptionally cheap labor readily available by recruiting more and more workers from Arkansas and Mississippi. Doing so, they believed, would attract industries from around the nation. The results, however, were not strong, and Memphis generally failed to diversify its economy, remaining basically "Deep South" in its reliance on cotton and on extractive industries such as hardwood lumbering. The depression of the 1930s weakened Memphis industry for twenty years. Despite the continued immigration of blacks from the countryside, a social pattern that played an important role in the popularity of a rural music such as the blues, the city's black population declined from 70 percent in 1879 to 40 percent in the 1930s. Some of those emigrants headed up the river, up Route 61, and up the tracks.

Owing to the exceptional need for the transportation of cotton by river, the packet boats also injected their musical influence into Beale Street's rich mix of blues styles. Because cotton remained the major business of Memphis, packet boats with their roustabouts continued to be a major feature of the city's port life long after their numbers had diminished in more northerly industrial ports. As a result, although excursion boats managed by the Streckfus Line and by other companies did stop at Memphis, that port did not become a major home for jazzy excursion boat dance music in the way that St. Louis did.

Any outside company that might have introduced modern excursion boat service in Memphis quickly encountered an "understanding" among a "clan" of packet operators that included Peters Lee, Ed Nowland, James Rees, and Matt Downs. These men managed to protect themselves from competition. "Each respected his neighbor's fences."[11] Their packet boats dominated the trade southward to cotton-exporting ports such as Pine Bluff, Vicksburg, and Greenberg. The Lee Line dominated upriver trade to St. Louis and beyond.

Beginning in 1915, Peters Lee and D. W. Wisherd ran the *Majestic* as an excursion boat out of Memphis. Lee owned a hotel there of the same name. The S.S. *Majestic* tramped as far away as New Orleans, Kansas City, Peoria, and most towns in between until it burned in May 1922. The West Memphis Packet Company sold excursion cruises out of Memphis on the *Idlewild* from 1915 to 1928.[12] The St. Louis dance band musician Eddie Johnson, with and without his Crackerjacks orchestra, played excursion cruises on the *Idlewild* from Cairo, Illinois, to Cincinnati.

Despite the heavily rural musical tastes of many Memphians, musicians skilled at playing wind instruments using written arrangements migrated to Memphis in order to play in the brass bands of W. C. Handy, George Bynum, and others. Such versatile bands vied with each other for popularity, playing for the rallies of white political candidates, particularly the authoritarian Edward Hull Crump, whom Handy helped elect mayor in 1909 with a campaign tune then titled "Mr. Crump" and later renamed "Memphis Blues." Handy's band played the number aboard the 150-foot excursion boat *Pattona*, named in 1909 when President William Howard Taft steamed into the city to plug the creation of a deep channel waterway from Chicago to the Gulf of Mexico.[13] The *Pattona* was the resident excursion boat of Memphis until she sank in 1914.

Like Handy, most of the Memphis musicians who went on to make migratory careers in jazz had been born into a literate black musical culture that emphasized familiarity with European concert music, as well as more ethnic musical traditions. The distinguished clarinetist Buster Bailey, born and raised in Memphis, "played from the sheets" in circus and dance bands before visiting New Orleans. He also heard what he called "embellished" music on the records of the Original Dixieland Jazz Band and of Wilbur Sweatman in 1917.[14] So, too, the Memphis-born pianist Lil Hardin grew up taking formal piano lessons and rarely improvised before migrating to Chicago in 1918. Like Bailey, she moved in order to find greater musical and economic opportunities. The trombonist George Williams, a native of New Orleans, worked in Handy's reading bands but also improvised.[15] All of these trained musicians moved on from Memphis, each discovering his or her own personal experiences of frustrated professional ambition.

For all of them, as for black Memphis as a whole, the experience of the composer, arranger, and bandleader William Christopher Handy in Mississippi and on Beale Street took on symbolic importance. Handy did not improvise. He was no jazzman, but he, like the Memphians who adopted the label, tried to create a synthesis of the blues with the emerging patterns of the popular music business. Unlike the others, he thought to translate the blues into through-composed popular song forms. His "Memphis Blues," "St. Louis Blues," "Beale Street Blues," and "Loveless Love" played an important role in the early jazz repertoire on the river and in the success of riverboat jazz thereafter.

According to Adam Gussow, Handy's increasing empathy for the blues, a folk music far from his own middle-class world of formal composition and written music, related to his terrifying and frustrating experiences performing amid the "vicious Negrophobia" of the Mississippi gubernatorial campaign of James Kimble Vardeman in 1903 and 1904.[16] Handy's orchestra played music for political rallies during which Vardeman promised to withdraw all state funding for Negro education. These campaign promises unleashed a wave of lynchings around Tutwiler and Cleveland, Mississippi, where Handy first began to notice the blues. Once elected, Governor Vardeman signed a vagrancy law that bore heavily on poor rural black males such as blues singers.

Handy's awakening to the blues as a musical vehicle for reactions to Jim Crow—humiliation, despair, cold chills, violent revolt, and the release of laughter—reactions that he, too, had felt but repressed—came from a riverboat musician just back from months on the river.

> His eyes were deep-set with weird shadows. His name was William Malone, and he had been earning his salt by playing up and down the old Streckfus line between St. Paul and St. Louis. A kindly, self-educated boy, I prevailed on him to join our show, and he and I became berthmates. Then it was that I discovered his unearthly affliction. Periodically during the night a strange, tortured sound would escape his lips. I cannot describe the sound. It was as if the woe of the entire world was suddenly rolled upon the lonely young man. Over and over again, as long as he slept, this moan was repeated.[17]

The Father of the Blues, moved by the plight of people subject to the violence of lynch law and deeply concerned about his own complicity in that oppression, began to hear catharsis in the repetitions of a folk blues guitarist whom he later encountered in the Tutwiler railroad station. Gussow argues convincingly that far from merely commercializing what Handy described as "the nightmare of those minstrel days," the bandleader's increasing urge to translate the blues stemmed from his deepening empathy with black suffering.

Although Memphis's racial politics proved somewhat less demeaning to Handy than did Mississippi's, playing music for Boss Crump from 1909 to 1914 offered a difference in degree only. Happy to use black music as a vote-getter, Crump quickly trimmed his sails under pressure from moral reformers. As George Lee put it: "In order to please the religious folk, the Bible people, every time the town had a revival, they would send out the order, 'screw the lid down.'. . . Crump didn't want to get tied too closely to what he thought were Negro songs."[18] Crump never admitted that he owed a large measure of his success to Handy's music. In response to pressure from reformers, he closed Beale Street down. He still lost power in 1915. He was followed by no fewer than seven mayors and acting mayors from 1915 to 1919. In the 1923 mayoral elections, the Ku Klux Klan greatly increased its influence in Memphis.[19] When Handy left the city, therefore, it had lost much of its attractiveness to ambitious black musicians.

Many traveled the 350 miles north to St. Louis. North of New Orleans, Saint Louis, Missouri, and East St. Louis, Illinois, just across from it on the eastern bank of the Mississippi, played the most prominent roles in the development of riverboat jazz. Far more than Memphis, St. Louis had a long history of mixing its folk music with many varieties of popular theater, concert music traditions, and German American musical education. The city lacked the recording enterprises so necessary to careers in jazz, but, in most other regards, its rich nightlife scene skillfully prepared its musicians for careers in Chicago and New York.

Musicianly innovations accompanied the city's industrial growth and diversification. Because St. Louis's industrial activities—steel, iron, meat-packing, glass, brick, railroads, and tobacco—outstripped those of any of the other cities that opened onto the Mississippi, African Americans migrated to the Mound City in the hope of finding jobs. Its industrial base included St. Clair and Madison Counties in Illinois, so that growth of the combined areas outpaced the national average during the 1920s. Blacks came to outnumber foreign-born immigrants 11.5 percent to 9.8 percent.[20] As a result, black migrant musicians, who necessarily performed for those with money to spend on leisure activities such as music and dance, often spent considerable time in there before moving on to Chicago and New York. Many settled in St. Louis as well.

On the border between the South and the North, St. Louis could not claim to be a haven of freedom. The city's older black population believed that the immigration of whites from Arkansas, Mississippi, Texas, and Louisiana lent a distinct southern pattern to its life.[21] Homeowners associations and restrictive covenants hedged a growing black population into strictly limited sections of the city.[22] So, too, "the great mass of Negroes were in unskilled or semi-skilled work, much of it irregular and poorly paid."[23] But by compari-

On the levee in St. Louis, Missouri, c. 1915. (Photo courtesy of the Historic New Orleans Collection, accession no. 92-48-L, MSS 520.)

son to Memphis, the black population in St. Louis enjoyed certain important though limited freedoms. In addition to promising steady jobs, St. Louis did not racially segregate streetcars, waiting rooms, or public restrooms, although the city's restaurants, theaters, playgrounds, and riverboats were segregated. Blacks in St. Louis, as in Memphis, could vote and also serve, with full powers of arrest, on the police force.[24]

From 1910 to 1920, St. Louis's black population grew rapidly, more than doubling to 9.1 percent of the city's population.[25] Between 1900 and 1940, the city's black population grew from thirty-five thousand to more than one hundred thousand,[26] another doubling to 18 percent of the total,[27] but remained significantly smaller than the black population of Memphis. A large proportion of St. Louis's black residents did come from Arkansas, Mississippi, and Louisiana, so the more northerly river city also enjoyed their country ways. Miles Davis would label St. Louis and East St. Louis "country towns" that were "full of country people," adding, significantly, that they were "kind of hip in their countryness."[28]

Davis's father, a prosperous dentist in East St. Louis, a major landowner in Illinois, and an active Republican politician, would best be characterized as

middle- or upper-middle-class. It was from that vantage point that his son admired the immigrant country people and their blues. Moreover, he and his
family were the leading edge of a significant social segment of middle-class
professionals in St. Louis. In 1935, the *St. Louis Argus*, relying on a report by
the Department of Race Relations of the St. Louis Community Council and
on the United States Census, reported that 636 business and professional enterprises were owned and operated by blacks in the city. Moreover, a considerable group of 1,701 black professionals included 36 lawyers, 105 physicians,
41 dentists, 144 social workers, 210 ministers, about 110 graduate nurses, 487
employed teachers, and 108 substitutes.[29]

From this stratum of black St. Louis came a notable strain of political ac-
tivism intertwined with ragtime and jazz. In 1918, city Republicans nomi-
nated Charles Udell Turpin, the wealthy owner of the Booker T. Washington
Theater, for constable. He became the first black elected justice of the peace.[30]
Turpin and three others organized the Citizens' Liberty League within the
Republican Party to mobilize black voters.

Such black leaders of the 1920s as Charles U. Turpin, George Vaughan,
Homer G. Phillips, and Joseph Mitchell enjoyed notable success in securing
for their followers greater educational opportunities and improved medical
care. In 1875 blacks pressured the city to build Sumner High School, the first
comprehensive black high school west of the Mississippi. Sumner faculty and
graduates exerted the political pressure necessary to create Homer G. Phillips
Hospital, the first full-service teaching hospital for black people west of the
Mississippi during the twentieth century.[31] From 1928 to 1932, the death rate
for blacks in the city was 21.5 deaths per thousand compared to 11.9 per thousand for whites. Blacks were more than four times more likely to die from tuberculosis and other respiratory diseases.[32]

Thus, during the first half of the twentieth century, St. Louis mixed the
grim reality of Memphis-style low wages, unemployment, and racial oppression with isolated but significant instances of greater economic, social, and
cultural opportunity. The hope for good jobs in St. Louis's more diversified
economy often proved illusory as black workers faced unrelenting opposition
from unionized white laborers. In the midst of an ongoing migration and daily
struggle for freedom, the African American minority created a remarkably active, creative cultural life in which music played a major role.

In addition to its strategic geographical location and its historic role as the
leading packet boat port in the nation, by 1918 St. Louis had established an
impressive forty-year history of commercializing and popularizing African
American music. In a town that had done so much to invent ragtime and
Gilded Age popular music, the musical development of riverboat jazz came

naturally. Most important, however, St. Louis's exceptionally robust roust-about tradition had been hit hard by the decline of the packet boats. Were African Americans to have any role in the excursion boat era, they would have to place musicians in a position to extend packet boat music into the twenti-eth century. The city had the black musical traditions at a time when the rem-nants of the riverboat industry needed them.

Black roustabouts had long provided the vital link between St. Louis's riverboats and African American variety saloons, often referred to as "dens of iniquity," "dives," and "free and easies," bars that also featured onstage musi-cal entertainment. The infamous Bloody Third district of St. Louis included an area close to the river bounded by the levee, Franklin and Washington Av-enues, and Eighteenth Street. According to contemporaries, this area "was infested by low-bred Negroes, river roustabouts and drifters."[33] Two of the most notorious neighborhoods were called Wildcat Chute and Clabber Alley. Racially integrated street gangs with such names as the Limehouse Gang, the Collins Street Gang, the Round Top Gang, and the Jim Blue Gang enlivened these neighborhoods. The particularly tough, all-black Red River Hall Gang established its headquarters on the second floor of Tom Morgan's saloon on Wash Street between Sixth and Seventh.[34]

The city's black variety saloons maintained close ties to riverboat roust-abouts, providing them with room and board, liquor, and entertainment and acting as their loan brokers, employment agents, and Republican political or-ganizers. Economic relations between roustas and their concert saloons fol-lowed a seasonal pattern. During the winter months, when shipping declined, saloonkeepers provided roustas with credit but pressed for repayment when work on the river resumed in the spring. The decline of the packet boat busi-ness caused by the rising power of the railroads, however, seriously limited the roustas' ability to uphold their end of the agreement. As roustabout jobs dis-appeared, some new form of riverboat employment would become vital.

Many of St. Louis' "variety theaters," which combined popular music with "leg shows," were large second-floor saloons with staged entertainment. They sprang up six to seven blocks west of the levee. Male customers, primarily clerks, salesmen, and young boys, outnumbered the prostitutes, who dressed in short skirts and sat on the men's laps to encourage them to buy drinks. This sort of procedure led to powerful reform movements in St. Louis, as elsewhere in the United States. The moral reformation of variety theaters created vaude-ville, a proper "family" entertainment that featured the songs and dances mi-nus the liquor and prostitutes. Jazz's move onto the excursion boats repeated this process.

Variety theaters nevertheless provided fertile ground for the roots of jazz. The Theatre Comique, the Canterbury Theater on South Sixth Street between Spruce and Poplar, the Globe Theater between Sixth and Seventh Streets on the south side of Morgan, the Crystal Palace on Seventh and Elm, and the Alhambra at Seventh and St. Charles all created a mixture of circus, minstrelsy, sporting life, and improvised music: "Variety musicians had to be able to fake a song in any key. Vocalists and dancers rarely read music. As the performer sang, the musician felt his way along to the end."[35]

From 1880 to 1900, many variety saloons mixed southern black folk music with urban show business. The ragtime music publisher John Stark and many other St. Louis music merchants believed that ragtime had been invented in St. Louis during these years. Along Market and Chestnut Streets west of Twelfth Street was the notorious Death Valley, a neighborhood of saloons, bordellos, and gambling dens. The high priestess of commercialized black popular music in Death Valley was Sarah B. "Babe" Conners, a six-foot-tall redhead from Nashville with diamonds and gold embedded in her teeth. Babe Conners ran a famous bordello and variety theater called the Castle Club at 212 South Sixth Street. In her stage shows, Babe featured "Mama Lou," a St. Louis street singer and "voodoo priestess" whose real name was Letitia Lula Agatha Fontaine.[36] While Babe sported big-city opulence, Mama Lou dressed down as a poor country woman, the two ladies representing the urban and folk roots of African American life.[37]

Mama Lou introduced many original popular songs onstage at the Castle Club, songs that became national hits when appropriated by East Coast music entrepreneurs. Among these songs were "Ta-ra-ra Boom-de-ay," "I'm a Natural-Born Gambler," "There'll Be a Hot Time in the Old Town Tonight," "That Ain't No Lie," "Mr. Johnson, Turn Me Loose," "Mamie, Come Kiss Yo Honey Boy," and May Irwin's "Bully Song."

From 1880 to World War II, St. Louis, more than Memphis, tended therefore to create hybrid musical styles such as ragtime and hot dance music that combined folk music roots with a variety of more formal musical influences. The powerful cultural influence of nineteenth-century immigrants from Germany combined with the aspirations of early twentieth-century African American immigrants to create in St. Louis a strong interest in classical music and legitimate musical education. This musical current found institutional encouragement at Sumner High School, to which students came from surrounding states and other towns in Missouri. Music teachers at Sumner held degrees from Oberlin College, Northwestern University, and the New England Conservatory of Music. Jesse Gerald Tyler, who taught at Sumner High from 1911 to 1922, for example, had graduated from Oberlin and went on to become the music supervisor of the black schools in St. Louis.[38] The noted musical educator Nathaniel Clark Smith taught at Sumner from 1930 to 1933.

Such institutional music education led to the creation of several orchestras, four bands, and several choirs and glee clubs at Sumner High. But the strong interest in classical music in St. Louis's black community also influenced the city's creators of vernacular music. During the closing years of the nineteenth century, the city became a major center for composers, publishers, and performers of ragtime, a form of notated piano music.

Thomas Million Turpin became the patriarch of ragtime at his Rosebud Café at 2220 Market Street, a variety saloon in Death Valley to which the itinerant pianist Scott Joplin was attracted. Joplin wrote some of his most famous works—"The Entertainer," "Gladiolas Rag," and "The Cascades"—while playing piano at the Rosebud. (Joplin lived at 2658 Delmar, just a short streetcar ride away.)[39] Tom Turpin (1873–1922) was a composer himself, as well as a creative inspiration for a generation of ragtime musicians as notable as Joe Jordan, Sam Patterson, Louis Chauvin, and Charlie Warfield. His "Harlem Rag," which appeared in 1897, was one of the first rags published for piano.

According to the St. Louis Municipal Court judge Nathan B. Young,[40] Turpin's father owned, among other things, a saloon on Sixth Street. Tom's parents had sent him for piano lessons to one of the best German American piano teachers in St. Louis. The six-feet, one-inch-tall young man, described as a "mulatto with dark auburn hair," had to travel to his lessons at night in a closed horse-drawn shay in order to hide his social transgression of neighborhood racial frontiers.

John Stark moved from Sedalia to 3848 Washington Boulevard in St. Louis, fusing "folk music and learned music," "prairie and town,"[41] setting important precedents for the city's subsequent influence on New Orleans jazz. The city attracted a number of pianists, including included Louis Chauvin, who attended Sumner High School. Chauvin and his pal Sam Patterson organized a vocal quartet that they called the Mozart Comedy Four, in which they alternated straight light opera with comedy routines. When Tom Turpin, Louis Chauvin, Sam Patterson, and Joe Jordan formed a four-piano quartet, they performed, in addition to ragtime syncopation, light classical overtures and concert waltzes "straight with precise spacing and beautiful counterpoint."[42] The ragtime movement in St. Louis culminated at the 1904 Louisiana Purchase Exposition. Thereafter, newer styles of musicianly popular music began to emerge in black neighborhoods.

Tom Turpin and his brother Charles promoted their nightlife enterprises as self-consciously black cultural institutions. In January 1916, for example,

Charles staged a gala entertainment titled "For His People," its advertisements stating, "Race Pride and Race Patronage Go Hand-in-Hand."[43] He spoke to the Negro Business League that same year, describing "the power of the Negro in business." He estimated that $50,000 a day in business was then going into the coffers of white entrepreneurs in St. Louis. Turpin urged his audience to "harness that power."[44]

Black jazz in St. Louis emerged within this black community of musical and entertainment enterprises that provided cultural and political continuity over time. The decline of ragtime and the rise of jazz in the Mound City took place in the same stretch of Market Street that had seen the birth of ragtime. Josephine Baker, the great international dancer and entertainer, got her start in the Market Street clubs. The offices of the *St. Louis Argus* at 2341 Market Street promoted ragtime concerts in cooperation with the Booker T. Washington Theater. The newspaper, of course, enjoyed selling advertising space to black theaters, restaurants, and night clubs. In 1919, Tom Turpin opened a dance hall called Jazzland at 2216 Market Street, right next to the old Rosebud Café. The pioneering hot dance bands got their starts there, playing well into the early hours of the morning so that people on the night shift could enjoy the music and dance.[45] During the late spring of 1920, the trumpeter and bandleader Charles Creath opened an office at 2234 Market Street from which to promote his "Sensational Jazz-O-Maniacs dance band."[46]

The black nightlife scene on and around Twentieth Street along Market and Pine Streets was the most centrally located but not the only black enclave in St. Louis. By the time of World War I, blacks also lived in five other areas of the city: (1) north of the central business district; (2) south of Market Street, along Mill Creek Valley from Union Station to King's Highway; (3) the largest neighborhood, called Elleardsville, beginning at Vanderventer Avenue on the east and spreading west to Taylor Avenue, south to Easton Avenue, and north to Fairgrounds Park; (4) four blocks south of Elleardsville beginning at Vanderventer and extending west along Finey Avenue; and (5), Carondelet, in the southern part of the city.[47]

The piano had anchored black music in the city during the ragtime era; the trumpet would play a similar role in the jazz age. A school of trumpet players arose among young black male musicians who had been born around the turn of the century. It included Robert Shoffner, Leonard "Ham" Davis, Irving "Mouse" Randolph, Eddie Randle, Harold "Shorty" Baker, Charles Creath, Dewey Jackson, Ed Allen, and Clark Terry, to mention only those who gained a degree of national fame in jazz. Many others remained known only within the region. Pittsburgh's great trumpet star Roy Eldridge, stranded in St. Louis in 1927, found work at the Grand Central Hotel on Pine Street.

Few, if any, trumpet players ever bested the fiery Eldridge, but in St. Louis he was challenged by "a whole posse of really good trumpeters." At Sunday jam sessions, no fewer than five of them—Jackson, Creath, Andrew "Big Baby" Webb, Baby James, and a man called Cookie—"came down and tore me apart." All of them sounded more or less like Louis Armstrong, according to Eldridge, but they had added a guttural rasp that influenced Eldridge.[48]

The trumpet played an important role in European concert hall music, of course, but that is not where young black musicians encountered it. Early in the twentieth century, grassroots musical training for boys in black St. Louis emphasized the cornet and trumpet at the Pythian Temple at 3137 Pine Street. The Mound City Company C of the Knights of Pythias and the Fourteenth Regiment Odd Fellows Band both championed military-influenced wind ensembles heavy on brass instruments—cornets, trumpets, trombones, French horns, and alto horns. The pioneer jazz musician Dewey Jackson, who became president of the black musicians' union Local 44, for example, started playing trumpet at age thirteen in the Odd Fellows Band under the instruction of P. B. Langford.[49] The saxophonist Sammy Long took lessons for fifty cents a week in the Pythian Lodge Children's Band, learning "the fundamentals of music."[50] The *St. Louis Argus* underscored the importance it attached to the involvement of young men in musical education. The paper reminded its readers that young boys in these bands learned "discipline," "deportment," and "self confidence" in addition to music. Such qualities, the paper editorialized, were particularly important to young black males, who, "unlike whites, had little prestige and race development behind them."[51] Robert Lee Shoffner and Edward C. Allen, two St. Louis trumpeters who performed in a number of different jazz groups during the 1920s, appear in newspaper photos as proud young Odd Fellows musicians.[52] The two organizations' music programs for youth disappeared from the newspaper's pages after 1916, so those grass roots of the St. Louis school of trumpet may have disappeared, as well. Pythian Hall, however, remained the black community's major dance hall throughout the jazz age.

The East St. Louis trumpeter Charles Creath, who was born in Ironton, Missouri, in 1890, pioneered jazz on both sides of the river. Just after World War I, Creath, who became the most famous jazz trumpeter in the region during the 1920s, started leading his own bands in dates at the most widely publicized black St. Louis venues, such as the Keystone Club at Compton and Lawton and Tom Turpin's Jazzland. In late 1919, he sallied forth to the St. Louis Country Club, where his Keystone Jazzers bested Chicago's all-white Gene Rodemich Orchestra in a battle of the bands. As early as 1920, he was sending out a variety of bands from his Market Street office.[53] His newspaper advertisements read: "Give a Thought to Music. For Real Time, Rhythm, Jazz Dance Music call C. Creath, 4257 Kennerly Ave." and "The Water's On! There'll be a Hot Time in the Old Town."[54]

During the winter months, Creath's Jazz-O-Maniacs performed in all of the city's major dance halls—the Paradise Dance Palace at 930 Sarah Street, Pythian Hall at 3137 Pine Street, Bohemia Dance Hall at 2246 Market Street, and Argus Hall at 2312–2316 Market Street, owned and rented by the *St. Louis Argus*. His bands varied in size from three to as many as twelve musicians and usually included the drummer and vocalist Floyd Campbell and the string bassist Pops Foster.

Creath, the founding father of St. Louis jazz trumpet playing and of the city's jazz in general, recorded with his Jazz-O-Maniacs for the Okeh label in 1924, 1925, and 1927.[55] The leader excelled in the hot, cup-muted style related to that of Joe Oliver, but the St. Louisan played with his own ringing purity of tone. His range seems narrow, especially on the earliest of his recordings, but that tone is burnished, centered, and sure. He urgently punches out his leads, his lines paraphrasing the melody. His nine-piece band of two trumpets, a trombone, three saxes, piano, banjo, and drums blends jazz band polyphony with the harmonized saxophone choir, defining the early hot dance band style. The trombone, clarinet, and cornet improvise polyphonically, while the saxophones chant the melody with heavy vibrato. Creath lost his first band to Floyd Campbell. He built another one and recorded his slickest sides in 1927, his solos as hot as before but more adventuresome, his sax choir tighter, the arrangements showing the influence of Fletcher Henderson.[56]

Miles Davis later remarked that musicians from St. Louis knew how to play the blues, and Creath's Jazz-O-Maniacs prove the point. The band recorded popular songs and novelty songs but mostly stayed with blues. Their recordings of "Market Street Blues" (a reference, of course, to the black entertainment blocks in downtown St. Louis) and "Every Man That Wears Bell Bottom Britches Ain't No Monkey Man" feature the full, rich vocals of Floyd Campbell, who must have either inspired Jimmy Rushing or learned from him. Campbell insisted that he was the first male vocalist to record the blues.

Creath's enterprising jazz activities extended well into the late 1930s, when he was still to be heard playing on the Streckfus Line. When, from time to time, work disappeared in St. Louis, he moved to New Orleans and played on the *Capitol* with Fate Marable. He was a hard-working bandleader for nearly twenty years and set an example followed by Dewey Jackson, Eddie Jefferson, Chick Finney, and Eddie Randle.

All of them also received the invaluable support of Jesse Johnson, the "kingpin"[57] of jazz bookers in the region. Johnson began his influential career promoting riverboat cruises for St. Louis's African American community. His first efforts predated jazz; starting in 1916, he organized riverboat excursions every spring on the *Grey Eagle* so that civic-minded citizens could enjoy an outing to the orphanage at Montesano Springs. He sometimes combined this trip with one honoring the year's high school and trade school graduates. Johnson negotiated with the steamboat captain, hired a St. Louis band, usually invented a new dance step to introduce along the way, and acted as master of ceremonies. In June 1916, while most of the adults went ashore to picnic with the orphans, the younger set remained on board to make some music of their own.[58] Not long thereafter, jazz became Johnson's music of choice for river cruises.

In 1919, when the first of his promotions of Creath was announced in the *St. Louis Argus*, Streckfus Steamers, despite a long-standing tradition of racially segregated Monday night river cruises in the St. Louis area, had yet to advertise any cruises for blacks. Their first efforts there to attract customers to segregated cruises did not appear in print until September 10, 1920. Johnson had gotten the white company's attention by negotiating with the *Liberty*, the *Grey Eagle*, the *Pilgrim*, and the *Majestic*, all rivals of the Streckfus excursion boats that tramped the Upper Mississippi.[59] Following a tradition of dance music on the river, Creath's band played "sweet strains of music" on the *Majestic*. He and Johnson broke all attendance records, goading the Streckfus Line into belatedly offering a few racially segregated cruises.[60]

Johnson promoted cruises for black people on the *Grey Eagle* from 1916 to 1918, at which time that steamer was crushed by river ice. He then teamed up with Creath aboard the *Majestic* during the summer of 1921, when Creath went one-on-one against the Streckfus Line's biggest and most famous boat, the *St. Paul*, and the acclaimed Metropolitan Jazz-E-Saz Orchestra (whom, the *Argus* said, "other bands are trying to imitate"). The Streckfus Line subsequently beat its St. Louis competition by default when, in May 1922, the *Majestic* unexpectedly burned in its winter quarters on the Illinois River.

The following summer found Johnson and Creath in charge of the music on all but one of the *St. Paul* Monday evening "colored boats." They refused, however, to give in completely to the segregated Streckfus Line and promoted cruises for African Americans on the smaller steamer *Pilgrim* four nights a week. They advertised this boat as "The Only Steamer on the Mississippi Operated by Colored People. Concessions are also Operated By Our People. Steam Calliope, Four Spacious Decks, 1500 Chairs, 500 Rockers, 3000 Jazz Lights!"[61] Johnson even promoted Marable's bands, known to history as the house bands on the Streckfus Line's "colored boats," in order to compete with that dominant company. He did so, moreover, explicitly to fight the estab-

lished pattern of segregation on the river. On May 14, 1926, Johnson promoted an inaugural cruise on the *City of Cairo*. Taking out a full-page advertisement in the *Argus*, Johnson, always involved in dance as well as music
promotions, featured "Prof. Jesse Johnson and his Paradise Boys and Girls"
demonstrating to the music of Fate Marable and His Jazz Syncopators in a
"Big Saturday Nite Midnight Ramble" for "the Exclusive Use of Our People."
The "officers on our steamer are members of our group":

> Churches, Social Clubs, Fraternal Organizations and Labor Organizations
> will not have to group together to secure a date on the "City of Cairo," due
> to the fact that our steamer is not confined to Monday Night only but EVERY
> NIGHT.
>
> We feel sure that each and every one will appreciate this step forward
> and will cooperate individually and collectively to make this mammoth un-
> dertaking a grand success.[62]

Somehow these efforts to unite music and dance in the name of greater racial
freedom on the river repeatedly foundered in tragic accidents: just as the *Grey
Eagle* sank in 1918 and the *Majestic* burned in 1922, the *City of Cairo* suddenly
sank during the winter of 1923. The *Pilgrim*'s draft proved too deep for the
river, and it was towed to Tampa, Florida, where it rotted away.[63]

Despite these maddening reversals, the St. Louis riverboat pianist Chick
Finney insisted that Jesse Johnson be remembered as a great benefactor. "He
was a great contribution to St. Louis and to our race, I have to say that. He
worked in civic, religious, and he had a dream like Mr. Randle said, to give
St. Louis something to put them on the map for entertainment." The bandleader Eddie Johnson added: "Jesse Johnson was the black Streckfus. If you
wanted to play the boat then, you came to Jesse Johnson. He made a lot of contributions to the black community."[64] Jesse Johnson epitomized the spirit in
which Miles Davis learned the roots of jazz.

Johnson also promoted the jazz careers of orchestra leaders who followed
Creath: Dewey Jackson, Floyd Campbell, Eddie Johnson, and Chick Finney.
Born in St. Louis in 1900, one of eleven children of Augustus and Nettie
Jackson, Dewey Jackson took his first lessons with the Odd Fellows Band in
1912 and 1913.[65] He organized his first band in 1920 with Harry Dial on
drums, Boyd Atkins on violin and sax, Sammy Long on tenor sax, Andrew Luper on trombone, and Jane Hemingway at the piano. He led his St. Louis Peacock Charleston Orchestra on a Vocalion recording date in 1926, performing
both on the riverboats and at Jesse Johnson's Regal Nite Club and Paradise
Dance Hall.

Advertisement in the *St. Louis Argus* for a series of excursions out of St. Louis organized by and for blacks in 1936. The *City of Cairo* cruises demonstrated that African Americans were not dependent on the Streckfus Line's segregated cruises for black people. (Advertisement courtesy of the Missouri Historical Society.)

Jackson led his own bands right through the worst of the depression, appearing with them in a variety of black clubs and dance halls, on radio stations, and, of course, on the Streckfus Line's *St. Paul*. He broke race barriers by playing at St. Louis's Castle Ballroom and Sauter's Park. On February 24, 1933, Jackson's orchestra starred in an unusual integrated dance sponsored by the Catholic magazine *Interracial Review* in the St. Louis University gymnasium. This Catholic thrust for greater racial understanding also produced the program "Interracial Hour," broadcast over station WEW. On June 10, 1933, the Dewey Jackson Orchestra performed for a "Depression Dance" at the People's Finance Building, 11 North Jefferson, the proceeds going to the Scottsboro Boys Defense Fund. Whenever times got too tough, he landed back in the Fate Marable Cotton Pickers Orchestra, playing for long periods on the *Capitol* in New Orleans. World War II drove Dewey Jackson, like most of the other jazz musicians of his generation, out of the business.

Eddie Johnson's career in Monday night cruises on the *St. Paul* began in 1929 and was as deeply intertwined with Jesse Johnson's promotions as Creath's earlier work had been. Born in East St. Louis in 1912, Eddie Johnson had played piano in the Oliver Cobb band and took over that group on Cobb's death, renaming them Eddie Johnson and His Crackerjacks. Under his direction, this band played in such St. Louis clubs as the Dance Box, the Chauffers' Club in the Finance Building, the Palladium at Delmar and Franklin, the Paradise Ballroom at Sarah and Hodiamont, the Casa Loma Ballroom, the Riviera, the Carioca Ballroom at Sarah and Finney, and the Showboat at Delmar and Taylor. Johnson, moreover, secured a regular broadcast on station KMOX. Youngsters used to gather in a candy store near Vachon High School to listen to Johnson's programs.

Jesse Johnson promoted Eddie Johnson's Crackerjacks on several successful tours to various sections of the country. The trombonist Winfield Baker reorganized some of the band's members as the St. Louis Crackerjacks with his brother Harold "Shorty" Baker on trumpet. In 1935, Chick Finney joined them on piano; he and William "Bede" Baskerville wrote arrangements for the band. It remained popular until 1938. Under Finney's leadership, they tramped on the steamer *Idlewild*, owned by Henry Meyers, from Alton, Illinois, up and down the Ohio River to and from Louisville and Cincinnati before the Streckfus family invaded that territory in the early 1940s.[66] The Crackerjacks played on the *Idlewild* for five months each year, earning an enviably solid economic foundation.

Chick Finney led the band in a productive Decca recording session in 1936.[67] The group plays with cohesion, crisp attack, and excellent intonation and uses more sophisticated arrangements, moving well beyond the 1920s world of Creath and Jackson. A strong inclination toward the blues and gospel gives the Crackerjacks continuity with the past, but this St. Louis aggregation has jettisoned hot polyphony for the seduction of silkily smooth section work and a big league rhythm section. The original St. Louis Crackerjacks reached for and seized the major concepts, if not the glamour and ballyhoo, of the big band era.

The band may have taken its inspiration from records by the Duke Ellington, Fletcher Henderson, and Cab Calloway bands, but they also had the opportunity to hear these bands in person. During Miles Davis's early years, Jesse Johnson promoted important, musically educational concerts by the best jazz musicians in the country, bringing to St. Louis such national stars as Armstrong, Ellington, Henderson, Thomas "Fats" Waller, Claude Hopkins, Jimmie Lunceford, Calloway, and the International Sweethearts of Rhythm, presenting them on the *St. Paul*, at the Coliseum, and in various ballrooms. Jesse Johnson showed younger musicians of Miles Davis's generation the possibilities for careers in jazz. He first brought Henderson's orchestra to the Coliseum in 1926. In two marathon appearances that would have tested the strongest embouchure, Armstrong performed on Sunday afternoon, February 5, 1928, from 2:00 to 7:00 P.M. at the Paradise Dance Palace and again from 9:00 P.M. "'til Late" at the Capitol Palace.[68] Alphonso Trent's orchestra backed Armstrong.[69] Many eager fans had to be turned away from this concert. Listeners were struck not only by Armstrong's playing but also by that of the saxophonist Lee Hilliard and the violinist Stuff Smith. Hayes Pillars played in Trent's band for that concert and made some contacts that eventually led to a triumphal ten-year gig in St. Louis. Johnson also promoted the Calloway and Ellington bands in 1933, in both cases hiring an airplane to drop thousands of advertising flyers over East St. Louis and St. Louis.

Jesse Johnson always found ways to simultaneously promote the best local bands and the national stars by staging "battles of the bands" pitting locals against the visiting groups or simply promoting a musical bill with at least two bands, one of which came from the St. Louis area. For example, he put the Creath, Jackson, and Marable bands on the bill with Fletcher Henderson, while the Crackerjacks went on tour with Fats Waller from Cincinnati throughout the East Coast. Johnson used national stars to promote concerts in venues such as St. Louis's Forest Park Highland that normally contracted exclusively with the white American Federation of Musicians Local 2. The whites controlled music in the best hotels and in operas and other theatrical productions, but as Eddie Randle put it: "The Negroes had just a better dance band in those days. This is the way that came about. Because this was the only thing that we could play and it was a matter of making it. We applied ourselves. We practiced. We had arrangers that would sit up all night writing to put us in this position where if our kind of work came along, we could do it . . . and we did a good job of it."[70]

The history of A.F.M. Local 44 in St. Louis reveals the drive for progress by means of musical professionalism. According to the drummer Elijah Shaw, who had been born in Jackson, Tennessee, on September 9, 1900, and who arrived in East St. Louis just after the infamous race riot of 1917, African American musicians in St. Louis organized before there was a national musicians' union. In 1896, when the A.F.M. was born, black St. Louis musicians sent the pianist John L. Fields to the first national convention. The A.F.M. formed forty-four unions at that meeting. Because Fields was the only black representative, his local got the last number. After thirty-five years of uninterrupted activity in St. Louis, a combination of racism and economic hardship stemming from the depression combined to kill what was then referred to as "the colored union."[71]

African American hot dance bands, known for their jazz, had sought jobs in dance halls, nightclubs, and riverboats because organized white musicians dominated the vaudeville and silent movie theaters, the legitimate theaters, the opera houses, and concert halls. When sound came to the movies in 1927, white musicians lost those jobs, and, in 1929, the crash drove most of them out of many of the remaining jobs controlled by Local 2.

In 1931, black musicians in St. Louis learned that their union charter had been revoked one year earlier. According to Shaw, the Streckfus Line had requested a low "concession price" from the black and the white local, one that would have reflected the hard times. Local 2 refused. Joseph Streckfus therefore decided that "instead of using three white groups on the two boats they ran out of here at that time, they were going to use four colored bands" from Local 44. Local 2 formed a special committee headed by Harry Lang, bandleader at the Castle Ballroom and the Forest Park Highlands, "to wait on Capt. Joe about this crisis."[72] Inevitably, the whites decided that without a union charter, black musicians could not possibly negotiate with the Streckfus Line. Therefore, the river captains installed three white bands and one all-star black band that included Marable, Jackson, Campbell, and Creath. None of the white bands that now found themselves on board had any prior experience in riverboat work.

For two years, the *St. Louis Argus* made practically no comment on this terrible blow to the economic, political, and racial foundations of black music performance. In 1932 the paper reported "much confusion in local 44," as "hostile forces" worked to get the local "out of all white jobs."[73] Several months later the organization was referred to as the Musicians' Protective As-

sociation.[74] Finally, in September of that year, the *Argus* revealed that the
A.F.M. also had revoked the charters of the black locals in Kansas City and
Denver and reported that the Kansas City musicians had refused to accept the
decree. Similarly, the paper reported that the black San Francisco Local 648
had gone to court to prevent the white local from barring black musicians
from all venues.[75] The *Argus* darkly suggested that the compliance of Local 44
in St. Louis had led to its becoming "a subsidiary local, paying dues to the
white local but not receiving equal benefits in return."[76]

Why did Local 44 acquiesce? Certainly the importance of Streckfus
Steamers to black union membership and the payment of membership dues
had something to do with it. Once a series of reverses had sunk Jesse Johnson's
efforts to establish independent black riverboats, black musicians relied exclusively on the white company that, to its credit, had consistently hired at
least some black bands. Campbell, Creath, and Jackson abandoned their bands
and joined an all-star black unit under Creath and Marable's direction. Had
Local 44 fought the A.F.M., the Local #2, and the complicity of "Captain Joe,"
those precious jobs would have been lost.

During the 1930s, non-union dance bands dominated the black St. Louis
and East St. Louis halls, regularly playing for wages that were under scale.
Racism within the A.F.M. had seriously undermined the union movement
among black musicians in St. Louis. Elijah Shaw remained a steadfast champion of unionism in St. Louis, going so far as to compose a song titled "Close
the Halls to Non-Union Bands." His bands sang it wherever they performed!
For the most part, however, black dance band musicians had to work where
they could.[77]

Black bands did not disappear entirely from the riverboats. Musicians from
St. Louis played for smaller excursion boats such as Meyers's *Idlewild* on the
Ohio River. The Streckfus Line hired bands such as the Jeter-Pillars Orchestra, which had recently arrived in St. Louis after touring extensively across the
nation. New Orleans musicians also worked for them. The pianist Walter
"Fats" Pichon ("Fats Waller's Double") and, of course, Fate Marable made
water music throughout the 1930s. In the meantime, Elijah Shaw took time
off each year to attend the A.F.M.'s national conventions, where he "harassed
the officers" about getting back the charter for the once-robust St. Louis
Local 44. Finally, in 1944, the national organization chartered St. Louis
Local 197. That remained the black musicians' union in the Mound City until 1971, when the white and the black locals were finally integrated for the
first time.

As the economic depression wore on through the 1930s, an increasing
number of black musicians adjusted to the decline in the number of jobs on

the river by taking jobs outside the city for at least part of the year. Creath, Jackson, and Marable were based in New Orleans. Many of the other St. Louis musicians worked with a variety of bands that toured the country, returning to St. Louis when a lucrative job beckoned from the dance halls. Floyd Campbell moved first to Cincinnati and then to Chicago; Ed Allen, Leonard Davis, and Irving Randolph went to New York City. Many of these musicians brought the St. Louis tradition of hot dance music to the orchestras of Fletcher Henderson, Benny Carter, Cab Calloway, Andy Kirk, and Teddy Wilson.

At the same time, St. Louis musicians tried to merge their local bands with national trends by recruiting a number of recognized musicians from around the country into their orchestras, using the connections these men brought to promoters in other cities. During the early 1930s, Eddie Johnson replaced many of the local musicians who had played in his Crackerjacks orchestra with out-of-town musicians such as saxophonist Tab Smith. Excellent local groups always faced this temptation to "go national," sacrificing their river city identity for inclusion in national media circuits.

This blending of St. Louis–based jazz styles with influences from around the United States became more pronounced with the arrival of the Jeter-Pillars Orchestra in 1934. Led by the saxophonists James Jeter and Hayes Pillars, this band settled in for a ten-year run at the Plantation Club, a segregated club catering only to whites. After many years of arduous touring from Arkansas to Maine to Oklahoma, Jeter and Pillars were content to bring rising young instrumental stars to St. Louis. Among these were the guitarist Charlie Christian, the trumpeters Harry "Sweets" Edison and George Hudson, the trombonist Lawrence "Snub" Mosley, the string bassists Walter Page and Jimmy Blanton, and the drummers Joe Jones and Sidney Catlett. Like the city's other hot dance bands, the Jeter-Pillars Orchestra prided itself on musical versatility, playing floor shows with such visiting stars as the Mills Brothers, the Ink Spots, and the Nicholas Brothers. In 1944, the band moved to Club Riviera, a racially integrated establishment run by Jordan Chambers, a prominent African American undertaker.[78]

For many black musicians, St. Louis remained a significant way station on their long musical journeys. But an important core of hot dance band musicians also made their homes there from the 1920s to the 1950s. None of them better represented the quiet, literate side of hot dance bands than Norman Mason, a multi-instrumentalist who started on trumpet before moving to tenor saxophone, and, finally, to clarinet. Mason replaced the trumpeter Joe Howard in Marable's Metropolitan Jaz-E-Saz Orchestra, with which Armstrong had first played. Mason had the second longest riverboat career of any of the immigrant black musicians after (of course) Marable. In some ways, in his ten years on the river he was more deeply involved with life in the Mississippi River valley than was Armstrong, who had been there and gone. Mason's musical contributions also were more representative of the aesthetics of the Marable-Streckfus regime. But like Armstrong, Mason traveled long and hard in order to find his niche in this country's musical life.

Norman Mason was born on the island of Nassau in the Bahamas on November 25, 1895,[79] one of ten children of a strong-willed watchmaker who played the trumpet in the Episcopal church and sold roses to tourists. At eight years of age the younger Mason began trumpet lessons, with his father and with a Scotsman who played in a local hotel band. Under their tutelage Norman learned to think of himself as a concert musician. He showed great promise as a teenager, eliciting stern lectures from his father, who feared that his son would stray from the path of his dreams. To further discourage his son from life's low road, the father took him to a prison and, while leading him around it, suddenly pushed his son into a cell, locking the door after him. That was as close as Norman Mason would ever get to a jail.

But money was always a problem. Mason therefore also learned the trade of shoemaking and saved his wages, officially for law school, his second choice should symphonic music remain a dream withheld. But he frequently heard of lucrative opportunities in the United States, so, in 1914, without telling his father, Mason began his own Great Migration as he sailed from Nassau to Florida, where he set to work as a shoemaker by day and a musician by night. His dreams of the concert stage and law school slowly dimmed under the pressures of earning money the hard way. No matter how overworked, Mason insisted that music remain a cornerstone of his life. In 1915, therefore, he began touring with the Rabbit Foot Minstrels and in that group accompanied such great blues singers as Ida Cox, Lizzie Miles, Mamie Smith, and Gertrude "Ma" Rainey as they entertained under tents in unnumbered dusty southern towns. The terrible flu epidemic of 1918 forced this famous group to break up, and Mason headed for St. Louis, headquarters of Streckfus Steamers.

When he secured employment as first trumpet in the Jaz-E-Saz Orchestra aboard the enormous steamer *St. Paul*, he immediately exerted an important musical influence on Louis Armstrong by teaching him to read music.[80] According to one particularly knowledgeable source, Mason would play the lead for a chorus, and Armstrong would just listen. Then the great improviser would play his own version of the lead part.[81] Armstrong did not publicly acknowledge Mason's influence and instead credited Davey Jones with his tuition. Because Armstrong and Mason played in the same two-trumpet section, Mason also would have helped the younger man play what was written.

Mason's versatility and excellent sightreading also helped him contribute to a major musical innovation in riverboat jazz. While playing saxophone with the trumpeter Ed Allen's Whispering Band of Gold aboard the steamer *Capitol*, which provided tours of New Orleans harbor, Mason, Eugene "Honey Bear" Sedric, and Walter Thomas formed the first known saxophone section in black jazz. This choir of saxes was then an important innovation in New Orleans music, a departure from the famed polyphonic approach, and the band became known for it. The orchestra toured the city's schools exhibiting their new concept, and the Buescher Musical Instrument Company gave them new saxophones with which they introduced the idea of sax sections in St. Louis.[82] Because of the professional demand and his dental problems, Mason switched permanently to the saxophone and clarinet during the 1920s.

Mason and his friend Bert Bailey got the call to play their saxophones when on March 16, 1924, in New Orleans, Fate Marable's Society Syncopators recorded "Frankie and Johnny" and "Pianoflage" for one of the Okeh label's field recording units. Moreover, Mason always insisted, despite the lack of supporting evidence, that he had recorded "Grandpa's Spells" and "The Pearls" with Jelly Roll Morton.

The 1920s and 1930s passed in a flurry of movement as the expatriate migrant continued to play on and off the river during the summers, in the clubs of New Orleans and St. Louis during the winter months, and on regional tours with a variety of bands. In 1926 Mason organized his own group and named them the Carolina Melodists. His band was heard on the radio stations WIL and KMOX in St. Louis during the winters, and this advance publicity created regional tours for the group, as well. He even landed a year-long gig in Chicago. Like many other musicians of that time, Mason and his men, as a matter of course, traveled very widely throughout the Midwest and from New Orleans to St. Paul, Chicago, Cincinnati, Pittsburgh, and many communities in between.

But the time did come in 1939 when Mason settled down, his travels to be of a more local nature. He chose St. Louis, which offered him a variety of club jobs, steady labor at the Scullin Steel Company, and the pleasure of becoming the groom of his longtime girlfriend Bernice Bailey. Although the war years were difficult, the late 1940s brought the Dixieland revival to St. Louis. Mason sagely took up the clarinet in earnest, playing at such clubs as the Peanut Grove, the Windermere, the Barrel Club, the Peppermint Club, and the Top Hat. In the 1950s, the heyday of the Gaslight Club on Gaslight Square, Mason played regularly with Singleton Palmer and His Riverboat Jazzmen, the leading Dixieland jazz band in the city after World War II.

Floyd Campbell, who played fewer gigs with Louis Armstrong than did Mason, also braved a hard road to play with the trumpet great on the river, and the story of his travels catches more of the flamboyant side of the Great Jazz Migration. Campbell, a drummer, vocalist, and leader of jazz combos, was born on September 17, 1901, in Helena, Arkansas, fifty-four miles south of Memphis, on the Mississippi River.[83] During his youth, considerable river traffic moved in and out of Helena—packet boats, excursion boats, and show boats. Some of these carried bands, and Campbell later remembered in particular the *Kate Adams*, on which W. C. Handy led his own band. Campbell went to Peabody Elementary School and High School in Little Rock, Arkansas, and entered Philander Smith College there in the fall of 1918.

In 1919, Campbell began spending his summers in St. Louis, 350 miles north of Helena, working for the Pennsylvania Railroad as a dining car waiter. In this way he earned enough to buy clothes for school in the fall. His father owned a barbershop and pool hall on Walnut Street in the black section of Helena. He kept a piano there and even played ragtime numbers on it. When the boats were in town, musicians gravitated to this barbershop, which was very close to the levee, sometimes jamming on a few numbers there.

On his mother's death during the summer of 1921, Campbell returned home from St. Louis to find that a white man by the name of Jack Greenfield had opened a drugstore on the corner of Walnut and Missouri, just a few doors from the Campbell barbershop. Greenfield covertly defied Prohibition by selling potions called "Jamaica Ginger" and "Orange Peel," both said to be 90 percent alcohol. On Saturday nights, Greenfield hired a pianist and a drummer, the latter of whom usually succumbed to his own self-ministrations by 10:00 in the evening. Greenfield asked Campbell to replace the fallen drummer, sweetening the offer by offering to buy him a drum set, paying him $5.00 per night as he learned how to play, and hustling up gigs for him at white country club parties and dances.

Before long, Campbell "decided to [go] to Memphis in hope of becoming more efficient."[84] He discovered that people enjoyed his singing as much as his drumming, and he quickly became one of a small number of singing drummers in jazz. Working days as a waiter at the Peabody Hotel in Memphis, Campbell worked nights with his own band, which included the trumpeter Zilner Randolph and the banjoist Pete Patterson. Back in Helena, a very young Louis Jordan, later a major innovator in rhythm and blues, replaced Campbell at the barbershop. In 1924, the pianist Gus Perryman, leading the minstrel life after leaving his home town Hattiesburg, Mississippi, led a six-piece band at Sayle's drugstore and later emphasized that it was big enough to accommodate an interior bandstand.[85]

Far more gigs were to be had in St. Louis however, than in Helena or Memphis. Jobs were more readily available there, too. As a result, the black population there had more money to spend on leisure activities, so in 1923, Campbell made St. Louis his base of musical operations. He caught on immediately with Charles Creath, the city's top black bandleader, and with Creath's band Campbell sang one chorus of "Market Street Blues." This was the first recording of a male voice singing the blues. Campbell made no bones about his own reasons for recording the blues: "Frankly, I didn't care for the Blues but back in those days that's the only thing they let colored bands record. . . . In my home in Helena, they had a lot of what you'd call Honky Tonks and we played sometimes in those gambling places and people would come up and sing. And it would just go from one to another and that's how we got those different verses. I guess I know 75 different verses to some Blues. And Arnold Wiley came around Helena and I got a lot from him."[86]

Campbell's voice strongly resembled that of the Kansas City blues vocalist Jimmy Rushing, later a great star with the Count Basie Band. Campbell reported that Rushing credited him with being his original stylistic inspiration but also noted that Rushing had the "much bigger, better voice." Campbell was such a hit in St. Louis that he replaced Zutty Singleton as the drummer in Fate Marable's riverboat band. After Labor Day, the company would sometimes "fire" Marable and reorganize a band of St. Louis and New Orleans musicians under the direction of Dewey Jackson on the *Capitol* during the winter months in New Orleans. In the spring of 1926, Campbell recorded with Jackson's band for Vocalion Records, singing "Capitol Blues," "Goin' to Town," and "What You Want Poor Me to Do?"

After the summer season of 1927, Campbell organized his own band, calling it the "Singing Synco Seven." Together they played on the *J.S. Deluxe* and in a great variety of clubs and dance halls as far north as Davenport, as far east as Cincinnati, and as far south as Memphis.[87] In May 1928, his band, which included Irving "Mouse" Randolph on trumpet, Nat Storey on trombone, Cliff Cochran on alto sax, Sammy Long on tenor sax, Red Brown on banjo, Janie Hemenway on piano, Cliff Birdlong on alto sax, and Cecil White on bass, backed Louis Armstrong in a special concert on board the *St. Paul*. Jesse Johnson brought in Alphonso Trent's Orchestra to do battle with the Campbell-Armstrong combo, and although Satch was at his best, Trent's group seemed to be winning the hearts of the crowd of five thousand: "They were getting the best of us—we were local. So Louis told me, go back up there and play 'St. Louis Blues' and when you get to the break fill it up with drums and I'll take it from there, let the boys rip. And you never heard so many high notes. And that was back in '28 and nobody was used to hearing all those high notes. He must have hit 30 high notes and the band is riffing under him and from then on we had it."[88]

Later that same year, temporarily out of club work in Chicago, Armstrong wrote Campbell that he liked his band and offered to front them on a tour of the South. The Streckfus captains got wind of the fact that Armstrong was available and sent Campbell to Chicago to offer him $75.00 a week to play on their boats. Armstrong refused. They raised the offer to $100.00 a week, and then to $125.00. Armstrong refused all offers, noting that even though he had no club jobs in Chicago, he was in the midst of recording (and, indeed, was about to record his great hit "Heebie Jeebies") and preferred to finish what he had begun there.

After the crash of the stock market, Campbell found that audiences shrank drastically in small midwestern cities such as Indianapolis, Lexington, Louisville, Memphis, and Little Rock, all places where his bands had done well over the years. On May 9, 1930, owing to the influence of the depression on the music business, Campbell moved to Chicago, where the black economy would remain stronger than in the smaller cities. He worked with Armstrong again and then took over a back-up band for Jabbo Smith. In 1931 they played opposite McKinney's Cotton Pickers at the Milwaukee Fairgrounds, presenting a torrid battle of the trumpets between Smith and Rex Stewart. Campbell prospered musically in Chicago from 1931 to 1945, at the Rhumboogie Club, in theaters with Sarah Vaughan, and with the Ink Spots, and he even introduced the tune "Sweet Georgia Brown" to the Harlem Globe Trotters basketball team.

Black St. Louis and East St. Louis played a major role in midwestern jazz and in riverboat jazz, sending solo stars and section men on to Chicago and New York City. These cities also produced the most prominent black musical interpretation of the Mississippi River, one that placed skillfully arranged and performed hot dance music within a drive for black enterprise on the inland waterways. The city of St. Louis brought to jazz on the river the sounds that the leading white jazz musicians considered the best, most exciting, most creative, and, inevitably, most "authentic." The great jazz cornetist and pianist Bix Beiderbecke lived 270 land miles upriver from St. Louis, and the pianist Jess Stacy lived 117 miles downriver in Cape Girardeau. Both would credit black riverboat jazz as a major inspiration in their musical careers. Chapter 5 explores their lives, careers, and relationships to the Mississippi River.

Chapter 5

"Blue River": Bix Beiderbecke and Jess Stacy on the Mississippi

Tell me why your song is sad, never glad?
Blue River, Blue River;
Do you hold a memory of a vanished dream?
Sing to me of lips I pressed and caressed,
Blue River, Blue River,
'Til I saw my hopes go drifting down the stream.
When I hear this lonesome song, I know something's wrong,
Blue River, Blue River,
Maybe it's because I'm just as blue as you.

—"Blue River" (Bryan-Meyer, 1927)

The era of riverboat jazz saw many young white musicians who took to the waterways in pursuit of music and adventure. The better known among them worked in all-white bands such as those of Louis Panico, Elmer Schwartzbach, Jules Buffano, and Wayne King. Most of the best known performed for Streckfus Steamers, particularly on the *President* and the *J.S. Deluxe*. In 1958, Joseph Streckfus recalled that his company had hired fifteen bands that did not primarily identify themselves as jazz bands.[1] According to the jazz and dance band discographies, most of them did not record. Although their names can now seem obscure, they still may have played extensively on the river.

Of the jazz-oriented groups mentioned by Streckfus, Iowan Tony Catalano's band lasted an impressive eight seasons, becoming the leading white riverboat dance band that regularly played jazz. Chicagoan Ralph Williams's hot jazz–inflected dance band lasted three seasons, and St. Louisan Gene Rodemich's organization lasted for only one. The Davenport bands of Carlisle

Evans and Doc Wrixon each lasted two seasons. On competing steamboat lines, Clyde Trask's Orchestra played for twenty years on the Ohio River, most prominently on the last two *Island Queen* steamers when they tramped early and late in the season.[2]

The most accomplished, creative, and ultimately famous of the white musicians to live the jazz life on and beside the river were both pianists: Bix Beiderbecke, who, of course, also played cornet with great originality, and Jess Stacy, a famous sideman and soloist with Benny Goodman. Both grew up in the upper Mississippi valley, experimented musically with the flashy popular sounds heard on radio, on records, on riverboats, and in vaudeville and the movies, and played their ways to jazz fame. Stacy worked his way upriver from Cape Girardeau, Missouri, and Beiderbecke, of Davenport, who became one of jazz's first iconoclastic and gifted amateurs, moved downriver to St. Louis. Their paths briefly crossed in Davenport. Stacy praised Beiderbecke's piano playing. Bix did not go on record with comments about the young Stacy's keyboard prowess.

After years of struggle with traditional music lessons, high-school-age instrumentalists such as Beiderbecke and Stacy were drawn to the latest popular bands and their solo stars. Largely unaware of the historical forces that created the jazz age, only superficially acquainted at best with black American life and history, such young musicians were caught up in the flowering of popular culture that followed World War I. The horror of that war, the obvious failure of wartime idealism, and the scandalous inability of the United States government to provide jobs for the returning doughboys set in motion a churning, youthful spirit of searching and rebellion. Beiderbecke and Stacy were budding creative artists who invented from popular music original solo instrumental styles that filled the interstice between white middle-class (and middle-aged) social dance music and black blues and jazz.

Their movement toward jazz benefited from the social and professional advantages enjoyed by all white persons relative to all black ones. Beiderbecke, for example, heedlessly rebelled against dance band professionalism and the excursion boat formula early in his playing career at a time when he was, in all honesty, still unable to meet the profession's demands. Beiderbecke anecdotes interpret him as the victim of conservative musical authorities in Davenport, but there was something stubborn in his rejection of musical literacy. The ability to get away with such rebellion stopped at the economic, racial, and professional divide. He thereafter moved swiftly into the jazz band format pioneered by the all-white Original Dixieland Jazz Band and recorded early and often in this manner. Moreover, as he played his way through their repertoire and increasingly mixed its raucous jocularity with his poised, declarative, and harmonically advanced improvisations, Beiderbecke brought a new, more contemplative artistic sensibility to an older, more slapstick musical style. In spirit, his contributions to jazz cornet and piano moved away from musical entertainment and toward a blend of avant-garde European art music and American popular tunes.

Because of various factors that included his drinking, inability to read music, and desire to treat music as art rather than a profession, Beiderbecke showed himself, for a substantial portion of his life, to be an amateur. The idea of the gifted amateur musician has not played a role in the analysis of early jazz. Antoine Hennion has extensively explored this concept, arguing that, in music scholarship, the "amateur" has nearly always received a negative interpretation as someone who misjudges his or her ability to play music. The amateur, moreover, must not be seen as a mere product of social and cultural conditioning but as an active force in the chosen art. The gifted amateur emerges from a collective history and shapes and reshapes the taste first discovered.[3] Beiderbecke may have absorbed this orientation from his socioeconomic background, from his German American heritage, and from the ambiguous professional position of many early jazz musicians.

By comparison, Jess Stacy showed a far more consistent desire to become a consummate jazz professional who hewed more closely to the path followed by Fate Marable's musicians. He started out in a small combo but moved swiftly and permanently into bigger, chart-reading dance bands. Although Eddie Condon would work him into his small combos in the 1930s and 1940s, Stacy would remain the shy, laconic, hard-working musician who emphasized playing the charts as well as comping for the good of the orchestra. Stacy had never had the social and economic parachute necessary to ignore the basic skills as Beiderbecke did. Rebellion against the job required a certain sense of social and economic entitlement.

In their different ways, Beiderbecke and Stacy still made undeniable contributions to the performance and recording of music that their peers, the music business, the popular music press, and generations of jazz fans and writers considered to be jazz. In a deeply segregated society, neither man went out of his way to familiarize himself with African American life. Beiderbecke did, however, listen to black bands in performance and seek out after-hours opportunities to sit in at black clubs.

Much of Beiderbecke's and Stacy's desire to be involved in jazz stemmed from the personal consequences of their formative years in cities along the Mississippi River. Being young, handsome, gifted, and white made the Mississippi valley their oyster. Just as they reached their teens, society erupted into a controversial youth culture in which new musical styles played a key role. Beiderbecke stayed late at the party while Stacy got home in time to get in some more practice.

While they were teenagers, their discovery of girls and improvisation, their rebellion against academic discipline, their enjoyment of pursuing something that upset their parents, and the growing admiration of their classmates largely brought intense satisfaction. But as they immersed themselves deeper into musical improvisation, they mixed elements of sadness and regret into their musical celebrations of youth, achieving thereby a degree of emotional complexity. The two leading white jazz musicians of the Mississippi valley, like Louis Armstrong, had had tenuous and conflicted relations with their fathers. A sense of sadness as well as Roaring Twenties abandon drew them into jazz. In addition to helping them create for themselves a rich world of sound, their music, like that of African Americans, became a shield of optimism and an emotional solace that made reference to something missing in their lives.[4]

At the same time, however, neither musician's life in music can be explained by historical influences alone. Each man was, of course, a product of his place and time, but Beiderbecke demonstrated a strikingly original jazz sensibility, a persistent drive to live a musical life, and a complex aural background that combined popular music and avant-garde harmonics. Drunk or sober, at the piano or on the cornet, Beiderbecke had latched onto a creative life in music. In his, the most artistic approach to jazz in the Mississippi valley, he returned frequently to river themes as a source of creative inspiration, recording a haunting "Blue River" and several more commercial river tunes. "Blue River" aptly expressed the personal and artistic struggles of an original, greatly gifted, but erratic musician who worked his way downstream to St. Louis and then eastward by land to Chicago and New York City.

Jess Stacy, on the other hand, grew up in poverty. That experience tempered his youthful rebellion. He was easily as withdrawn as Beiderbecke, and snapshots of him reveal a handsome but melancholy-looking young man. By comparison, Beiderbecke looked persistently boyish and certainly much more expensively dressed. Stacy became the more practical, quietly determined, and sharply focused musician. As a youth, he so persistently sought out and found musical education that he managed to study under the leading music educator in southeastern Missouri. He studied and practiced his way out of small-town poverty. As a result, at a young age, he caught on as a riverboat pianist who could not only improvise but also set a rock-steady dance beat, as well as sightread new charts and help the band learn them. Stacy quickly played his way up the river. A touring dance band snapped him up, and he rarely looked back at his Mississippi River roots while steadily climbing to the top of the big band business of the 1930s and 1940s. Unlike Beiderbecke, Stacy found established musical procedures no impediment to his progress in jazz, smoothly integrating his career as a big band pianist with his development as a significant solo improviser. Until his last recording sessions in 1977 and 1981, Stacy showed little interest in recording nostalgic tunes that evoked river themes. Near the end, however, he did return musically to the Mississippi by recording "St. Louis Calliope Blues," "St. Louis Blues," and "Barrelhouse."

The center of riverboat jazz on the Upper Mississippi was neither Minnesota nor the river's headwaters. Between Minneapolis and what was then called the Tri Cities area (now known as the Quad Cities), the river often became too shallow or too turbulent to allow the excursion boats to pass through. A long and complex series of locks had to be constructed by the Army Corps of Engineers in the 1930s in order to allow regular passage up to Minneapolis–St. Paul. During the 1920s, therefore, the more southerly Davenport became the center of northern activities for Streckfus Steamers during the winter months. This attractive, medium-sized, Victorian river city played a major role in the yearly rhythms of the excursion boat business and therefore in the history of riverboat jazz.

The Streckfus family had long cultivated personal and business ties in Davenport. In 1850, Balthazar Streckfus had settled his family in Edgington, Illinois, south of Rock Island, Illinois, just across the Mississippi from Davenport. His first son, John, who started the family in the excursion boat business, married Theresa Bartemeier of Davenport. The young German Americans were, of course, the parents of the four second-generation Streckfus river captains, most notably Joseph Streckfus, who did so much to shape riverboat jazz.

Even after they moved their excursion business to St. Louis, the Streckfus family retained ties to Davenport.[5] The physical configuration of the Mississippi at Nahant, hard by Davenport, provided the fragile fleet of old excursion boats with a natural winter port and, most important, protection from river ice. Many a Mississippi and Ohio steamer's hull was ripped open by floating river ice during winter thaws and in springtime. Of the Streckfus boats, the *Capitol*, the *President*, and the *St. Paul* sometimes found protection during the winter months by giving harbor cruises in New Orleans. The other vessels spent the dangerous winter months in Nahant, where the family and its retainers could keep track of them while preparing them for the coming season.

The Streckfus men tended to marry Davenport women. Compared to tiny Edgington, Davenport had long prized its aura of gracious, substantial Victorian respectability. Beiderbecke's German American grandparents had, for example, arrived in Davenport in the 1850s, as the Streckfuses were settling across the river. German immigrant culture made music an essential part of family, church, and society. More important, despite Davenport's lack of conservatories and major concert halls, the city's leading families proudly espoused a Germanic faith in the uplifting spiritual powers of the music of Wagner, Brahms, Beethoven, and Mozart.

Pride in this musical culture at the turn of the century found expression in the Lutheran and German Reformed churches, in private *soirées musicales*, and in home lessons in piano and voice. Young people of the right sort of middle-class families were taught to read music, not merely to ignorantly improvise on an instrument in a musically vulgar manner. Charles Burnett Beiderbecke, who raised a legendary jazz musician, and John Streckfus Sr., who promoted riverboat jazz, shared this remnant of Euro-American faith and hired private music teachers for their children accordingly. Young musicians who could not read music were thought to be "illiterate," fit only for the shadowy margins of American musical life located in bars and along the river.

Despite this determined strain of European traditionalism, the public musical life of Davenport welcomed the latest in popular music. The city's cultural history is somewhat hidden because the two Davenport newspapers—the *Democrat and Leader* and the *Daily Times*—often chose to report on news from Chicago, the nation, and the world, giving shorter shrift to their own community's activities. Nevertheless, Eunice Schlichting, chief curator at Davenport's Putnam Museum of History and Natural Sciences, surveyed daily news items in 1911, 1922, and 1933 in the two papers and turned up some important data.[6] Moline, across the river, was the home of the Augustana Conservatory of music, which maintained branch studios in Davenport. Despite the occasional concert by a national or regional instrumentalist, the newspapers mainly reported on concerts by schoolchildren, touring pop stars, and celebrated dance bands.

According to the newspaper advertisements, by the early 1920s Davenport supported several of the major institutions of popular music. Six theaters—the Grand, the Columbia, the Family, the Orpheum, the Terrace Gardens, and the Capitol—featured vaudeville and movies, the last two mounting a "jazz jubilee" in February 1922. The Baxter Piano Company, the L. A. Murray Company, and the A. P. Griggs Piano Company sold phonographs and records in addition to pianos. Davenport had its own radio station, WOC, and several semipublic spaces for social dancing, most notably Turner Hall, the Coliseum Ballroom, Terrace Gardens, and Linwood Dance Pavilion, ten miles out of town.

Despite its burgeoning popular musical culture, the trombonist Esten Spurrier, who played often with Beiderbecke in Davenport in the early 1920s, still described the town as a "very predominantly German town, whose music was over legitimate."[7] The daring new improvised sounds of the years 1910–1930 such as the Original Dixieland Jazz Band's "Livery Stable Blues" and "Original Dixieland One-Step" on the Victor Talking Machine label, the dancer "Bee" Palmer's steamy vaudeville shimmy act, and the Chicagoan Frank Westphal's hot hotel dance band mixed with a powerful art music tradition. Jazz and popular music created a much-discussed cultural challenge to the idea of the community's more traditional musical and cultural values.

And then there was the Mississippi River, Davenport's major scenic attraction, its greatest economic disappointment, and its most controversial cultural influence. Just before America's entry into World War I, the city undertook major improvements to its riverfront, transforming it from "an unsightly dump" to "a beautiful riverfront park site."[8] That and subsequent community efforts produced one of the most attractive riverfronts on the Mississippi and a major headache during the inevitable spring floods. Davenport, unlike, for example, Rock Island, built no levee, and thereby sacrificed the safety of the downtown business district, park, and baseball stadium to the scenic beauty of an uninterrupted view of the river from the Victorian homes up on the bluff. Levees provide safety from the rampaging river but block most people's view of it. After mopping up from its regular spring floods, Davenport epitomizes the Huckleberry dream of the good life on the river.

But boosters of business in Davenport deeply regretted that the Mississippi did not run from west to east.[9] According to them, it "pointed in the wrong direction."[10] The great river actually does flow in a south-southwesterly direction as it passes the Quad Cities, but Davenport businessmen of the early twentieth century would have preferred, in order to stimulate trade, an east-by-northeasterly flow directly to Chicago. Davenport also shared the midwestern longing for greater cultural and economic ties to the eastern seaboard. The river city's bankers, commercial leaders, and industrialists, like those in other Upper Mississippi towns, hoped to make their town a "Lowell [Massachusetts] on the Mississippi." The Iowa city, with a population of around thirty-five thousand, claimed major strength in banking, retailing, and the manufacture of cigars and washing machines.[11] Town fathers looked longingly at Chicago's huge markets and immense productive capacity, and citizens with musical interests, like the young Beiderbecke, admired the musical might of Chicago and New York City.

Davenport's longing for a water route to Chicago went well beyond idle fancy. The first of the many east-west canal ventures that attempted to tie the Upper Mississippi River to Chicago had been the Illinois and Michigan Canal, built by the State of Illinois between 1836 and 1848.[12] This allowed riverboat traffic from Grafton, on the Mississippi, up the Illinois River and the Chicago

River to Lake Michigan. But the ninety-seven miles and sixteen locks of the Illinois and Michigan Canal quickly succumbed to the competition of the rail-roads. The "Illinois River Improvements," finally accomplished just before World War II, led to increased traffic from Grafton to Chicago, but from 1907 to 1940, Davenport's dreams, which also had led it to build a freight ter-minal on its waterfront, suffered a cropper.[13] Mighty New Orleans, not Chicago and Davenport, would continue to dominate a north-south axis of trade on the Mississippi.[14] Beiderbecke reputedly admired New Orleans jazz, but he still allowed the Crescent City's music to steam up the river to him in Davenport rather than traveling south in order to hear it on his own.

The Mississippi River easily caused Davenport as many problems as it ever solved. Among the most controversial of them were riverfront and river-boat cultures. From Memorial Day to Labor Day, the sounds of hot dance and jazz music drifted up from the riverbanks to titillate and scandalize the citi-zens sitting on their broad verandas.[15] Children like young Bix Beiderbecke, Charles and Agatha Beiderbecke's active second son, gravitated like Tom Sawyer to the riverfront, passing from rock-skipping, rowing boats, and fish-ing to memorizing the details of the various boats and, inevitably, their hot dance bands. Excursion steamers played their hottest music in their early evening calling concerts, and youngsters begged their parents to take them on board for the evening dance cruises. In turn, their labors completed, packet boat roustabouts found their ways to the Blue Bird Tavern in the black part of town. It would become known for its music, and it attracted youths such as Beiderbecke to after-hours jam sessions.

The huge Streckfus Line vessels brought their commercialized riverboat mythology and their more organized and powerful forms of popular musical culture to challenge the Tri Cities' vaunted musical traditionalism. The influ-ence of the river and its boats flowed directly through the young cornetist's mother Agatha, who was the daughter of Bleigh Hilton, a Mississippi river-boat captain.[16] Whereas Bix's father Charles bequeathed to him a cold, au-thoritarian version of the Germanic tradition, his mother entertained him with reminiscences about the adventure and wanderlust of the American Nile.

Streckfus Steamers directly linked the southern jazz ideal to the Missis-sippi. Fate Marable's Metropolitan Jaz-E-Saz Orchestra with Louis Armstrong steamed right up to Davenport's landing in early 1919 or 1920. Whether the young Beiderbecke actually heard the band in person at that time is not certain,[17] but the sounds of Armstrong's revolutionary riverboat jazz danced through the evening air in Davenport during the early summers of Beider-becke's youth.

Although the river, the excursion boats, and riverboat jazz all exerted major influences on Beiderbecke's involvement in jazz, it is easy to exaggerate Armstrong's direct influence on the sixteen-to-seventeen-year-old cornetist. It would not be correct to claim that the two musicians' styles showed much resemblance. Beiderbecke played in an urgent but declarative style that re-phrased melodies in a hot but burnished tone and with an original harmonic awareness. Bix was still in his teens when he first sat in with riverboat orches-tras. He gigged only briefly on the river. He would need more time to develop a controlled playing style and, in typical Davenport fashion, unthinkingly accepted his parents' decision to send him east to a Chicago suburb when his grades crumbled under the onslaught of jazz.

Moreover, Armstrong, whose improvisational style was far freer, more flamboyant, and more virtuosic than Beiderbecke's, maintained a very gener-alized, evasive diplomacy in his published comments about Beiderbecke. When asked, he could not recall when he met him. Although they were about the same age, he characterized the Davenport youth as "a cute little boy" and called his playing style "pretty," not necessarily a compliment among jazz mu-sicians. Moreover, in his most substantial autobiography, *Satchmo*, he signified on minstrel stereotypes when writing about Beiderbecke: "After the first trip to St. Louis (1919), we went up river to Davenport, Iowa. . . . It was there that I met the almighty Bix Beiderbecke, the great cornet genius. Every musician in the world knew and admired Bix. He made the greatest reputation possible for himself, and we all respected him as though he had been a god. Whenever we saw him our faces shone with joy and happiness, but long periods would pass when we did not see him at all."[18]

For his part, Beiderbecke reported in a revealing 1921 letter to his sister that he had heard "Faite Maribores bunch who use [*sic*] to be on the *St. Paul*— The talk of the river—why I tried to tell you about them—I heard 'em in Louisiana, Mo."[19] His precision about the location indicates that he had en-countered Marable's orchestra not in Davenport but rather in a chance meet-ing of riverboats in July 1921, when he was playing in Doc Wrixon's Ten *Capi-tol* Harmony Syncopators.[20]

Beiderbecke appears to have found Marable's chart-reading riverboat dance band pretty tame when compared to groups on Chicago's South Side, for he went on in the same letter to write: "But they can't carry water to Al Tearney's new nigger bunch at 35th and State nor at the sunset or entertainer[;] boy theres some real jazz niggers. Don't think I'm getting hard Burnie but Id go to hell to hear a good band so I made all these places in one nite." This, the com-mentary of an eighteen-year-old, reflects the 1920s cultural tendency, born of minstrelsy, to associate nightclub improvisations by black musicians with ex-ceptional urgency and excitement. His closing comment, moreover, suggests a lingering shame at consorting with what promoters liked to advertise as hellions of Hades.

Neither Beiderbecke's nor Armstrong's comments indicate deep mutual musical influences. Armstrong's remarks suggest that the young jazzman built a major reputation by playing "pretty." Although it captures an important ingredient of the most remarkable characteristic of Beiderbecke's playing style, the generic term "pretty" understates his mature style. It certainly is possible that when Armstrong heard Beiderbecke, the latter hadn't yet found the interesting harmonic notes or the deeply moving timbre that he would later develop. Armstrong may have had good reason to call his style "pretty," because it may then have relied too heavily on correct tone and melodic and rhythmic accuracy. Beiderbecke might well have seemed but a stripling to Armstrong. The two young men's early years had been, after all, about as different as could be, Armstrong maturing quickly in order to cope with his poverty, Beiderbecke luxuriating in a prolonged youth that he never fully put behind him.

Beiderbecke left no recorded comments about Armstrong's instrumental accomplishments. He reverted to racial stereotypes when speaking about Marable's band and Al Tearney's combo, to which he compared it. His use of the phrase "real jazz niggers" seems to me to express less malice than an ignorant reiteration of white racist stereotypes. On the other hand, the term does communicate a blatant racial slur. In the upside down world of jazz values, Bix, following the standard traditions of minstrelsy, appears to have attributed a special authenticity to black jazz musicians. But his brief comments do not suggest that he tried to increase his own reputation by claiming what the historian George Lipsitz has called "a psychic and spiritual connection" to them.[21]

In a pattern that would become common among many popular music stars, Bix Beiderbecke rarely acted as if he had taken the time to analyze the major themes of his life. Just as he slipped unthinkingly into alcoholism, so he reached briefly and clumsily across the racial barriers of the United States. He ended up hurting the feelings of the one African American musician he cultivated the most, Fate Marable, whom he had sought out and whose playing he studied, by introducing the black bandleader to some of his white friends as the boat's cook. According to one source, "Fate got sore at that idea of a joke."[22]

The Mississippi River and its excursion boats seemed mainly to sing a commercialized siren song of wanderlust, adventure, wild women, wild men, and wild music to Davenport's naïve young people. That spirit mixed with the sounds of records, radio, and vaudeville to lead Beiderbecke inexorably into a 1920s-style rebellion against bourgeois values. His older brother Charles mustered out of the army in November 1918, when the jazzman was fifteen years old, and soon thereafter bought the recordings of the Original Dixieland

Jazz Band's performances of "Tiger Rag" and "Skeleton Jangle" into the family home. Beiderbecke adored those recordings and studied Nick LaRocca's cornet work carefully, learning the songs note for note.[23] In addition, white musicians from the Catalano, Evans, and Wrixon bands played fall, winter, and spring gigs right in town, making the kind of music Bix had much more occasion to emulate.

Given the strong influence of the Streckfus family in Davenport, a number of ambitious white musicians naturally gravitated toward the Iowa river city much as black ones did to St. Louis. Three well-regarded hot riverboat dance bands played in Davenport during the off season: Tony Catalano and His Famous Iowans, Carlisle Evans's band, and Albert "Doc" Wrixon's band. Many of their musicians lived in the Tri Cities, some of them simply in order to stay close to the powers that controlled summer hiring on the excursion boats. These bandleaders also recruited musicians from Chicago, New Orleans, and St. Louis. Seasoned jazz musicians such as the clarinetist Leon Roppolo, the banjoist Lou Black, the New Orleans cornetist Emmet Hardy, and the trombonist George Brunies played in Davenport dance bands. The young Bix Beiderbecke pestered these bands to let him sit in, and he got most of his early performance experience with the drummer Bill Greer's Melody Jazz Band and Buckley's Novelty Orchestra.[24]

None of the top three hot dance bands in the city ever recorded, so one cannot know how they sounded. Tony Catalano's was by far the most long-lived of these riverboat orchestras, and his career offers a telling counterpoint to that of Beiderbecke. Catalano played on the Mississippi as a sideman and leader for twenty-three years. Born in Indianapolis, Indiana, the trumpeter early left home with a traveling show, landing in Davenport in 1905. He played in the city's first vaudeville orchestra in the Family Theater. In 1907, John Streckfus recruited him for his first excursion boat band on the old *J.S.* Marable joined the violinist Emil Flindt in a duo that grew over time to a quartet that included Catalano and Rex Jessup. Catalano later claimed that he hired Marable rather than the other way around.[25]

As a riverboat musician during the early years of World War I, Catalano played in St. Louis and New Orleans during the off-season. He was much impressed with Joe Oliver's cornet style, but, in the segregated Crescent City, he actually played with several of the musicians who would become famous as the Original Dixieland Jazz Band. By the time Beiderbecke began to beg Catalano to allow him to sit in aboard the *Capitol*, the bandleader was a tough, seasoned jazz and dance band professional who had played through the fads of ragtime and New Orleans jazz. Like several of those who had inspired him and like many of the trumpet and cornet men who played in and around Davenport, he became adept at hot rephrasings of the melody. This relatively limited conception of the cornet's role in jazz inspired Beiderbecke but would become increasingly removed from the new virtuosic freedom and daring of Armstrong. The musicologist Brian Harker demonstrates that the latter found his way to instrumental virtuosity by learning to play the elaborate clarinet runs of Sidney Bechet on the cornet.[26]

Beiderbecke had only a brief, decidedly checkered career as a riverboat performer. It began on June 21, 1921, when he joined the band as a replacement on the *Majestic* in what might have been an auspicious start. The *Majestic*, a 228-foot long steamer built in 1906 and converted to an excursion boat in 1919, provided major competition for Streckfus Steamers, Inc., on the Upper Mississippi. The craft's owner, D. Walter Wisherd, turned the transportation history of the Mississippi valley on its head by mounting a miniature scenic railroad on the main deck as well as a merry-go-round.[27] The boat was popular but, like many another excursion boat, it suddenly and inexplicably burned, in this case in May 1922 while in winter quarters on the Illinois River. During its last full year of life, this excursion boat took Beiderbecke and his music north to St. Paul and back to Davenport. He then departed, his role having lasted only two weeks. He quickly joined Doc Wrixon's Ten *Capitol* Harmony Syncopators but left that band only nine days later. During the next two summers, he performed on a Graham and Morton Line excursion boat that steamed from Chicago to Michigan City, a rough water trip on Lake Michigan. Thereafter, Beiderbecke played on land only.

Two important facts made his an unnervingly prophetic riverboat career. First, in 1921, he was not yet a strong lead cornetist. His first extended river gig left him with a large sore on his lip. His playing style would have been rudimentary and his repertoire would have been relatively limited, too. Unlike Armstrong, he neither sang nor created comedic turns during which to rest his lip. Beiderbecke became a victim of the notoriously long and rigorous riverboat playing schedules. As Catalano, well trained in the school of hard knocks, put it, "If you didn't have a few neat tricks of your own to contribute to a number, you just didn't fit." This lack of endurance would plague Beiderbecke for much of his career.

Second, and most ironically, since he would spend the last years of his life desperately pursuing formal musical knowledge in the Paul Whiteman Orchestra, the young Beiderbecke also ran afoul of the tradition of musical literacy in the hot excursion boat jazz bands. The A.F.M. Local 67 in Davenport denied him a union card when representatives discovered that he could not read music. They hounded him relentlessly when he went ahead anyway and gigged on the riverboats. Officials from the local came on in a remarkably ag-

gressive way when dealing with the local youngster who performed without a
union card, calling him and his fellows "this band of punk kids" and Beiderbecke "this goddam kid who can't read well enough to get a card."[28] The union
finally yanked him off the riverboats entirely.

Jazz historians, following ample testimony from his musical pals, have laid
the union's tough policies at the door of Germanic traditionalism in Davenport. Ultimately, however, this explanation also allowed ambitious young musicians to avoid criticizing the union. Obviously, the Davenport local, with the
active cooperation of the Streckfus family, worked to control the local economy of riverboat jazz in a way that would favor its members, likely the older,
most experienced players. The riverboat captains had turned to Beiderbecke
and his young friends as very temporary replacements when their regular
unionized groups gave notice. Long-term employment of local youth jeop-
ardized the national organization's profitable control of riverboat musicians all
along the Mississippi. Esten Spurrier could protect his own union card by
diplomatically blaming Germanic musical traditionalism rather than the union.

Beiderbecke quietly acquiesced and ultimately got his union card without
learning to read music swiftly or accurately. But he came to realize just how
much musical understanding he had missed because of this. In performance,
if not in his artistic ambitions, his still-unexplained inability or unwillingness
to master sightreading until late in his short career forced him to specialize
in hot improvisation. He therefore became exceptionally accomplished in that
musical domain. But this incapacity would remain a major professional weak-
ness as his career advanced. Louis Armstrong, three years his senior, had faced
the same crisis and, with the help and protection of Fate Marable and the segregated black local in St. Louis, went ahead and learned enough sightreading
to hold onto his riverboat job for three seasons.

Sometime in his youth, his education appears to have inculcated the ideals
of European concert music in Beiderbecke while failing to give him the skills
necessary to gain full control over them. According to a wide-eyed local newspaper article titled SEVEN-YEAR-OLD BOY MUSICAL WONDER, his mother Aggie
and his music teachers discovered that the youngster possessed an exceedingly
acute ear for music, one so perceptive that he naturally heard, recalled, and re-
played, without visual reference to the score, whatever she played for him on
the piano. Even more important, in doing so he naturally transposed his own
version into the key in which she had played it, even when he might have preferred to play that tune in an easier key.

In one sense, Davenport's musical tradition both failed the Beiderbecke
family and also provided Bix with the aural musical elements of an original
jazz sound. Touting a seven-year-old boy as a musical wonder though he could

not read music could only have encouraged everyone's tendency to treat him as a special case for whom traditional musical education did not apply. Many years later, long after a young German American lad should have learned all he needed to know in music theory, the saxophonist and bandleader Frank Trumbauer still had to work hard with him in St. Louis, trying to correct the problems that prevented him from reading the charts. He reported that Bix was very confused, so much so that teaching him was difficult:

> Bix had a screwy way of picking out notes from a violin part, playing them in the key of "C" on a Bb cornet. It was confusing to everyone, even Bix! We fixed up a book of regular trumpet parts and for hours on end I would work with Bix. I would teach him a tune, note for note, and then hand him the part and we would follow it. Bix was a brilliant boy and it wasn't long before he could follow new parts. No one but Bix and I shall ever know the hard work and patience it took to accomplish this. We would take down some of Bix's choruses, note for note, and then hand them to him to play in an ensemble. He would take one look at the notes and say, "Man, this is impossible!"[29]

Some children will not be taught, but there must have been some highly re-spected Tri Cities musician with impeccable union credentials who could have patiently persevered in order to explain to the boy wonder that learning to read music would ultimately strengthen, not weaken, his improvisational powers and his future instrumental control. His biographer, Richard Sudhalter, com-ments in a provocative footnote full of suggestive interpretative analysis of Beiderbecke's early experience and personality[30] that the youngster seems to have grown up on his own, eliciting little sustained attention from his father. Faced with his refusal to learn to read music and his utter academic indiffer-ence, his family seems to have given up trying to personally participate in his education. As a result, he grew up lacking the necessary confidence and knowl-edge onstage and in the recording studios. Did his family have difficulty men-toring their second son? The youngster's father responded to his son's 1921 failures in high school by abruptly shipping him off to a military boarding school outside Chicago the autumn after his first abortive attempts at river-boat performance. Sudhalter's description of Beiderbecke at that time seems to me to describe a gifted young man without the skills required to either play music professionally or express the music that he felt so intensely in his heart. He could not read music on either the piano or the cornet. He had not devel-oped a strong lip. From a very young age, he regularly drank to excess.

A good deal of the literature concerning Beiderbecke and other jazzmen such as Eddie Condon, Jimmy McPartland, Pee Wee Russell, and George

Wettling contains an unacknowledged admiration for wild, excessive youthful drinking. Such behaviors, neither explicitly praised nor directly explored in any way, have usually been presented in cherished casual anecdotes. The punch line inevitably concerns one of the subject's endearing drunken capers.

Beiderbecke's fame has been founded nearly as much on his wild drunkenness as on his musical achievements. In twentieth-century popular music, he was the first of many stars whose struggles with alcohol and drugs were glamorized as legendary. The 1922 popular song "Runnin' Wild" might have been inspired by him. Written by A. Harrington Gibbs with lyrics by Leo Wood, the song, usually interpreted by jazz artists at breakneck tempi, tries to evoke the feeling of youthful abandon:

> Runnin' Wild, lost control, runnin' wild, feelin' bold,
> feelin' gay, reckless, too, carefree mind all the time, never blue.
> Always goin', I don't know where, always showin' I don't care,
> ain't got nobody, it's not worthwhile, all alone and runnin' wild.

The song glamorizes a state of feverish excitement camouflaged by a cool exterior and provides a rationale in its verse for such manic agitation. The wild one has been jilted and wants his ex-girlfriend to know that he's not sitting at home weeping.

"Runnin' Wild," an anthem for the Roaring Twenties, evokes only the innocent side of what can also be understood, in Beiderbecke's case, at least, as a more complex state of abandon as well as abandonment. The youngster, banished from the family, learns to act in a solitary, uninhibited, immoderate, ultimately dangerous way, the music and alcohol cushioning against an underlying feeling of loss. He grows up to abandon himself to booze and dangerous behavior, thereby re-creating, in his treatment of himself, his father's earlier abandonment of him. Louis Armstrong and Jess Stacy both had youthful problems with their fathers, but neither had grown up with Beiderbecke's feeling of entitlement. They had learned much earlier than he that working people simply had to get down to hard, repetitive labor.

But armchair psychology aside, Beiderbecke persisted with a musically unusual and ultimately original approach to jazz. Sociology and cultural history cannot explain away his wonderful talent and his contribution to jazz. Davenport's dedication to the ideal of European concert hall music did bequeath to him a strong aural attraction to avant-garde, impressionistic composers of the early twentieth century such as Igor Stravinsky, Maurice Ravel, and, above all, the little-known American composer Eastwood Lane. He approached their music aurally, coming, for example, to Lane's Greenwich Village apartment to lie on the couch dressed only in his underwear while Lane, also a strong individualist, played his "Adirondack Sketches" for him. Beiderbecke brought to his improvisations on the popular music of his day a harmonic awareness drawn from his aural analysis of the recordings of Stravinsky, Ravel, and Lane.

Beiderbecke's original inclination to combine by ear harmonic elements of avant-garde classical music with improvisations on popular tunes worked itself out differently in his cornet work and his piano music. In the latter, he moved with exceptional harmonic freedom, chording without a strict regard for any particular key signature. This can be heard most clearly on his recording of "In a Mist": there his melodic theme is so fully integrated into the chord progressions that one cannot speak of separate melodic and harmonic elements. This "harmonic melody" moves unpredictably, briefly establishing and quickly abandoning new key centers before any one tonal center has been fully established. The lyrics to Walter Donaldson's *Changes* could have been inspired by Beiderbecke.

Beiderbecke's piano playing allowed him a rich harmonic and compositional palette beyond that offered by the cornet. Although he did achieve a parallel harmonic freedom in his lead work and solos on cornet, that instrument's role in the band obliged him to hew more closely to the melody. Within these limitations, he nevertheless created a fully original style. It seems to me that the most prominent ingredient in this new style was the hauntingly magnificent tone with which he played his hot but stately, poised, and beautifully structured improvisations. Whereas Nick LaRocca and Tony Catalano had contributed a hard, no-frills lead, Beiderbecke brought aural elements of art music into the raucous white jazz band tradition.

The earliest jazz recordings and the public attitudes about them that swirled through Davenport had encouraged him to assume that the new popular music did not require serious musical preparation. In an important newspaper interview, Beiderbecke defined jazz as "musical humor."[31] His most important musical influence, the Original Dixieland Jazz Band, enjoyed parodies of musical primitivism. They routinely made animal noises and produced other comic effects on their instruments on novelty recordings such as "Livery Stable Blues." But the pervasively negative reactions to jazz in Davenport's traditional musical circles also may have played a role in stereotyping jazz as low comedy. A surviving publicity photo portrays the musicians as cartoon figures, transforming the serious-looking players into clowns. As we will see, the pianist Jess Stacy's mother made clown outfits for her son's first jazz band, and their classmates named them the Agony Four, in honor of their limited instrumental progress.

Advertisement for an excursion boat band led by Tony Catalano and Carlisle Evans out of the Quad Cities. (Advertisement courtesy of Duncan Schiedt.)

Beiderbecke played through this era of impudent musical comedy but firmly ignored the clownish effects in his own playing, devices that would have qualified it for the soundtracks of movie cartoons. If his recordings reflect his performance style, he could whinny with the best of them but instinctively brought to jazz a more serious artistic sensibility, his leads and solos reaching for tonal, rhythmic, and harmonic originality. Even late in his career, when recording the novelty number "Barnacle Bill, the Sailor" with an all-star group, Beiderbecke pierced musical slapstick with a searingly hot solo.

Although he had made little headway as a performer on the riverboats, he soon managed to make his musical mark downriver in St. Louis. After Labor Day, 1925, he took up residence there in order to play with the German American saxophonist Frank Trumbauer's dance band in the Arcadia Ballroom at 3515–3523 Olive Street. In order to attract dancers to the band's opening, Beiderbecke played very briefly during the late summer of 1925 on the *J.S. Deluxe.* With several years of experience since his previous riverboat efforts in 1921, he now possessed a stronger embouchure and had become a quite original jazz improviser. In his fall, winter, and spring seasons with Trumbauer's dance band he further developed an exceptional rapport with the saxophonist, one that made a major mark in recorded jazz history.

Charles "Pee Wee" Russell played with Beiderbecke in the Arcadia band. The two went on to play together at Hudson Lake, as well. Russell's own raging case of steamboat fever strongly resembled that which had gripped Beiderbecke. Also addicted to alcohol while still in high school, Russell received an offer to play on an Arkansas River excursion boat that steamed from Muskogee to an amusement park twenty miles away. His experience provides a textbook example of 1920s-style jazz rebellion: Russell "borrowed" a pair of long pants from his father and hid them in the garage. "I got a ladder up near my window—sneaked out, got the pants, met the boys and went on the moonlight cruise."[32]

When Russell and Beiderbecke recorded together for the Okeh label in 1927 with Trumbauer and his orchestra, a handful of numbers with river themes emerged: "Riverboat Shuffle," "Way Down Yonder in New Orleans," "Blue River," "Mississippi Mud," and "Dusky Stevedore." Beiderbecke recorded the first of these, Hoagy Carmichael's first composition, one inspired by Beiderbecke's improvisations, twice: first in 1924 with the Wolverine Orchestra and then with Trumbauer's orchestra. Given the influence of the Original Dixieland Jazz Band on Beiderbecke, Carmichael, and the nation, "Riverboat Shuffle" began as and remained a jazz number. The up-tempo stomp opens with a sharply declarative, descending riff figure, one that seems to express the musicians' need to shout out their own heated claim to the riverboats' slower, slinkier dance music. Beiderbecke also performed on two river recordings with the Jean Goldkette Orchestra, waxing another version of "Blue River" as well as the much less distinguished "Slow River." With the Paul Whiteman Orchestra he later cut gussied-up arrangements of Jerome Kerns's "Ol' Man River," "Selections from *Show Boat*," by the same composer, and "Mississippi Mud."

In spite of all of his problems with riverboat employment, Beiderbecke's first recording of "Blue River" with the Frank Trumbauer Orchestra best expresses the spirit of white riverboat jazz on the Upper Mississippi and important psychological patterns in his tragically short, troubled life. Joseph Meyer, the composer of such 1920s jazz standards as "My Honey's Loving Arms" and "California, Here I Come," wrote "Blue River" for the 1927 stage show *Just Fancy*. The tune is actually very simply constructed, with a sixteen-bar verse, a four-bar interlude, and a thirty-two-bar chorus. The melody features short steps moving inexorably downward in a minor mode, and the performance merely reworks various arranged variations thereon.

The Trumbauer orchestra's recording of "Blue River" contains a number

A young Bix Beiderbecke with the Wolverines. (Photo courtesy of the Putnam Museum of History and Natural Sciences, Davenport, Iowa.)

of relatively minor flaws in addition to an unfortunate vocal. The main idea of the tune's lyrics fits the excursion boat scene well. A young man laments a failed romance and cannot shake the haunting feeling that something is wrong as he cruises down the river. All of the recording's musical power and achievement belong to Beiderbecke. He played as if he felt a personal connection to this tune. He was then involved in a serious romance with Ruth Shaffner, who lived just up Olive Street from the Arcadia Ballroom. He would create a happy, loving relationship with her, make her pregnant, encourage her to seek an abortion, and then quickly and permanently leave town.[33] His sharply declarative opening statement of the melancholy melody, taken at a moderately slow tempo, epitomizes his growing ability to express his conflicted or, as Sudhalter puts it, "layered" emotions in evoking river themes. An entire trumpet section was to play this part, to much lesser effect, on his later recording of it with the Jean Goldkette Orchestra. Here, however, Beiderbecke's unearthly ringing notes, played in what seems to me well beyond anything that could be called a "pretty" style, achieves instead what sounds like an unsurpassed mixture of beauty, longing, and regret that floats and then lifts the melody into a graceful flight worthy of one of the rare trumpeter swans that occasionally glided slowly downward toward cadential repose on the Blue Mississippi.

Beiderbecke also recorded several Broadway show tunes that inevitably carried him into the heart of minstrelsy's legacy to the twentieth century. Although his first "Blue Mississippi" and Henry Creamer and Turner Layton's "Way Down Yonder in New Orleans" offered him worthy melodies and the improvisational freedom to explore them, he makes only perfunctory contributions to the Paul Whiteman band's recordings of "Selections from *Show Boat.*" His renditions of "Dusky Stevedore" and "Mississippi Mud" find him surrounded by heavy-handed minstrel show stereotypes of the roustabouts. As always, he plays seriously nonetheless.

Many of the recordings he made with Trumbauer seem to me to lack sufficient rhythmic dynamism and fluidity. The rhythm sections play with a heavy, wooden beat. Trumbauer plays a floating saxophone line, virtually refusing to rhythmically subdivide his statements, and the other musicians seem to plod. Beiderbecke's rhythmic drive is the most pronounced in these recordings. His sharp attack seems to pull the others along with him while his tone and harmonic movement bring to the Columbia sides their musical stature. He was far and away the most original white jazz musician in the Mississippi valley.

Beiderbecke's iconoclastic approach to music included influences from the nineteenth- and twentieth-century British and American cultural tradition of the inspired amateur. Originally a French word, the idea of the amateur developed as a core value in the rise of private boys' schools in England (where they are called public schools), on the Eastern Seaboard of the United States, and in the Olympic games. Although the term has come to have negative connotations of a lack of professionalism in the United States since the 1960s, it originally indicated "action or consumption arising from taste rather than instrumental self-interest." Within this complex concept lay the idea of loving or liking an activity (and doing it because you love it or like it).[34] Amateurism came to represent an elitist reaction against the commercial and professional models of social organization. Championed by upper-middle-class white males, the ideals of amateurism represented a hegemonic reaction to major national developments in the organization of society and the economy.

Contrasting the life and career trajectory of pianist Jess Stacy with those of Bix Beiderbecke will help clarify the role of amateurism and professionalism in early jazz. Stacy, who went on to extensively record celebrated solo features with the Bob Crosby BobCats, the Benny Goodman Orchestra, and the Eddie Condon Gang, became the most accomplished white riverboat musician to come out of the Mississippi valley. He won popularity polls in the major music magazines during the 1930s and 1940s. He also became known as a musicianly "band pianist," a skilled sightreader who could also improvise with a steady, swinging rhythmic pulse. A taciturn, self-effacing individual and instrumentalist, Stacy stopped the show at Benny Goodman's famous Carnegie Hall jazz concert in 1938. He played five hauntingly lyrical solo choruses that expressed a wistful sadness lurking behind the brassy explosions of "Sing, Sing, Sing," that thundering, warlike jazz vehicle that seemed to foreshadow World War II.

Compared to Beiderbecke, Stacy never lived the middle- to upper-middle-class life and therefore never thought to rebel against it. Stacy seems to have survived his childhood very much intact and, despite a confused family life, somehow found the focus and determination to somberly and soberly pursue river music as a highway out of the grim realities of lower-middle-class white society in Missouri. He also had the good fortune to drink only in moderation.

Poverty and social discrimination hounded Stacy's childhood and youth. He was born Jesse Alexandria Stacy on August 11, 1904. His mother Sarah "Vada" Alexander, a seamstress of Scotch-Irish descent, and his father Frederick Lee Stacy lived with their new son, whom they called "Jessie," in a converted railroad box car in Bird's Point, Kentucky, a tiny settlement then located just across the river from Cairo, Illinois. They were "poor as Job's turkeys" and sat down to many a plate of squirrel. Fred Stacy worked for the Illinois Central Railroad ferrying railroad cars back and forth across the river from Cairo. According to Pat Stacy, the pianist's wife, Bird's Point issued no birth certificates, and, to make matters of identity more complicated, the Mississippi River flood of 1927 washed away both the town and the boxcar. Jess grew up with no proof of his birth and told everyone that he had been born in Cape Girardeau.[35]

The saxophonist Raymond F. "Peg" Meyer, who played riverboat jazz with Stacy and remained his lifelong friend, told the historian Frank Nickell, director of the Center for Regional History at Southeast Missouri State University, another version of Stacy's origins. According to Meyer, Vada, while married to Fred, had an affair with a carnival card sharp with unusually large hands and long fingers, and she subsequently gave birth to Jess. Vada's parents disowned her for this transgression. A few months after his birth, she took the baby from Bird's Point to live in Malden, Missouri, sixty-eight miles south of Cape Girardeau, in Missouri's boot heel. He grew up practicing the piano in that wild region, moving to Cape Girardeau only in 1918.[36]

The Mississippi Delta's northern limits begin eight miles south of Cape Girardeau. Between 1907 and 1940, a two-million-acre acre area called the Great Swamp was sold at pennies per acre and then drained by the same workers who had dug the Panama Canal. The area long remained wild, often without law and order or educational institutions. When, during the Great Migration, blacks moved into Missouri's boot heel, racial conflict followed and has yet to completely disappear. A few towns remain segregated.

When he was a youngster, Stacy's fascination with the piano served to isolate him from the worst of Malden's follies. A neighbor regularly played "Memphis Blues" and "Trail of the Lonesome Pine" on her piano, and Jess, as he would always wish to be known, learned to play by ear. He loved to practice, voluntarily running chords and arpeggios with the exceptionally large, long-fingered hands he had inherited from his father. "I had to pay that boy a quarter to keep him from practicing so his Uncle Will Duncan next door could rest," his mother later recalled. By the time the family moved to Cape Girardeau, on the bluffs of the Mississippi River 131 miles south-southeast of St. Louis, the young man could play well by ear and had a beginner's awareness of written music.

Vada and Fred had put their budding pianist in the right place and the right time to become a riverboat jazz musician. The year they arrived at that well-established river port, the Streckfus family had begun building their excursion boat empire in earnest, converting the huge *St. Paul* into a floating jazz dance hall. Less than a year later, Stacy, who had had trouble finding a piano teacher in Malden, began taking formal piano lessons from J. Clyde Brandt, professor of piano and violin at what was then called Cape Girardeau University. Brandt headed the growing institution's music department until 1957. The music building at Southeastern Missouri State University carries his name. Stacy could now find his way from untutored improvisation to the music of Bach and Mozart. More important, he was learning to swiftly and accurately read charts of all kinds. This was just the sort of jazz-crazy but well-trained young musician favored by the excursion boats.

Stacy, like Beiderbecke, was completely absorbed by music. Without much prior contemplation, the youngster wanted to make music more than anything else, preferably hot dance music on the piano. His friend Peg commented, "His great interest in life was always the piano and he pursued it in a quiet and hard-working manner. He was born with a natural talent and fingers that could span thirteen [white] keys." At fourteen, he took a job in Cape Girardeau playing for silent movies at the Orpheum Theater. "I would look at the picture and make up my own tunes—sort of instant music."[37] The managers liked his work but lost their underage pianist when the Missouri state labor agent cited them for breach of the child labor laws.

Stacy and Meyer put together a little band for high school dances. The other kids labeled them the Agony Four. They ruefully agreed with the name, but that little band took them all out of Cape Girardeau, where, according to Stacy, everyone was "square as a bear." Hot dance music gave him a glamorous and exciting ride out of his family's rural obscurity and poverty, and Peg Meyer became his first tour guide.

Without proclaiming social rebellion, the two budding musicians reveled in the adventure, excitement, and daring of road jobs, beautiful young women, and living and playing in motion. As the Agony Four improved, Meyer renamed them Peg Meyer's Melody Kings and started booking jobs in southern Missouri and across the river in Illinois. They traveled by car, struggling along the dirt roads that branched off from the famous north-south Route 61, the highway of so many black migrants, blues singers, and jazzmen. A ferry was required in order to cross the Mississippi, but it did not run during the winter months, leading them into painfully long detours. In between gigs they snuck back into Cape at odd hours of the morning, staggered into their high school classes in rumpled tuxedos, rehearsed new tunes after school, and earned a reputation for reliably good hot dance music with Jess Stacy's pulsing, exciting, always steady beat.

Stacy first heard Fate Marable on that famous steamer in 1920 when, three times a year, it visited Cape Girardeau. Stacy had been stunned to hear Marable's dance band with Armstrong: "You can't imagine such energy, such musical fireworks as Louis Armstrong on that boat. The music sounded so good out on the river. They'd go out in the middle . . . and the paddle wheel would be turning slowly to keep it from drifting downstream. People danced there. That band carried me away. When I heard that band, I said, 'That's what I want to be. I want to play on the riverboats.'"[38]

Marable's approach to playing deeply influenced the young jazzman's career. When the *Capitol* arrived in Cape Girardeau, Stacy went aboard to play for Marable and to listen to his advice on how best to play piano in a dance band. Afterward, during the excursion itself, Stacy stood behind Marable watching what he played and how he played it.[39] As he later told the pianist Marion McPartland, "He was one of the best band piano players I've ever known. I listened to him a lot." He told the jazz writer Whitney Balliett that he "marvelled at the way [Marable] held everything together."[40]Stacy went on to become more of a soloist than Marable, but he always focused on being a big band pianist, as well. Thanks to J. Clyde Brandt, he read music swiftly and accurately. Thanks to Fate Marable, he knew how best to contribute to a dance band's attack, rhythms, and harmonies.

Stacy and Meyer took to the river on the steamer *Majestic* during the spring of 1921, playing with a band from Davenport. Owned by the D. W. Wisherd

Jess Stacy at the keyboard. (Photo courtesy of the Institute of Jazz Studies, Rutgers University.)

Line, the famous *Majestic*, a stern-wheeler, tramped down the Mississippi from Davenport, up the Ohio to Paducah, Kentucky, and back to St. Louis. They played in a series of small valley towns such as Cairo and Metropolis, Illinois. The *Majestic* burned to the waterline in 1922, the year in which Stacy graduated from high school. Stacy and Meyer each played subsequently on several other boats including the *Capitol* and the *Cape Girardeau*.

Individual temperament led the young men in different directions through the number and variety of things to discover. The contrasting paths of the two friends created an archetype of a major drama in young male jazz culture. In 1923, Stacy landed a job with Tony Catalano's Famous Iowans. He played a lot of jazz tunes with Catalano but was also required to "play the damn calliope." On a stopover in Dubuque, Joe Kayser, a territory bandleader, dangling an offer to open at the Arcadia Ballroom in Chicago, offered Stacy a job. They played stock arrangements after the sweet style of Jan Garber, touring myriad small towns in Wisconsin, Iowa, and Illinois before actually moving to Chicago. Stacy would have preferred to play jazz but read the charts in order to get to the big time.[41] Once he got to the Windy City, he caught on with Floyd Town and his Midway Garden Band, which included such leading hot jazzmen as the cornetist Muggsy Spanier and the reed man Frank Teschemacher. Stacy lived the jazz life thereafter, playing in dance bands to pay his bills, performing and recording with the leading jazz musicians whenever possible. He got used to living on the road in innumerable cheap hotels in uncounted cities.

Meyer played on the river for only one year after his wonderful pianist and friend left with the Kayser band. Peg had fallen in love with a young woman who disapproved of the musician's life. She demanded that he choose between their relationship and the jazz life. He chose the former. Their marriage would slowly crumble, Meyer loyally hanging on in order to help care for his wife though her long, lingering illness. He secretly dreamt of the jazz life he had left behind but made sure he kept busy building the largest music retail outlet in Missouri and even wrote a book about woodwind repair. He remained a witty, optimistic, energetic man who admitted to only one regret.

Stacy, ever the band pianist, was destined to have a much less pronounced impact on the subsequent history of jazz and of riverboat jazz than did Beiderbecke. In fact, during his lifetime and afterward, Bix, according to the trumpeter Doc Cheatham, influenced everyone who played in a pre-bop style. The tenor saxophone star Lester Young went on record as having listened carefully to the Bix and Tram recordings. George Avakian of Columbia Records issued a long-lived, influential multidisc set of Beiderbecke's best recordings. Despite his demonstrated inability and unwillingness to play the riverboat gig, Bix became the primary inspiration for many of the small traditional jazz revival bands that played on the declining number of excursion boats and in the major river towns after World War II. Early recordings of William "Wild Bill" Davison document that before developing his hell-bent-for-leather lead, he played much like Beiderbecke. Jimmy McPartland also echoed some elements of that style, as did Bobby Hackett. During the 1950s, young white jazz musicians split between the Boppers and the Moldy Figs (bebop players and traditional or Dixieland players). The traditionalists often savored Beiderbecke's style and mystique, and Eddie Condon's Gang featured trumpet and cornet players such as McPartland and Hackett. Condon enjoyed emphasizing his own lack of professional training as a guitarist and included plenty of Beiderbecke drinking stories in his autobiography *We Called It Music*.

The midwestern cornetist Tom Pletcher has built an impressive regional career with his exquisite re-creations of Beiderbecke's recorded leads and solos in the Sons of Bix, a band that grew out of the 1973 Bix Beiderbecke Memorial Jazz Festival in Davenport. So too, the journalist, writer, and cornetist Richard Sudhalter kept the flame alive with his Classic Jazz Band, which also featured the guitarist Marty Grosz. The latter, in turn, organized and recorded with a number of different combos that featured Bixian sounds. Sudhalter, of course, also wrote the best biographies of Beiderbecke and his friend Hoagy Carmichael. The trumpeter Randy Sandke has been only the most recent major swing player to include Beiderbecke re-creations in his recordings.

Pletcher has adamantly championed the role of the gifted and accomplished amateur in the traditional jazz revival that began after World War II and has continued to this day. In recent interviews he has insisted, "I am not now nor have I ever been a professional musician, but I am known among jazz musicians as being good enough to play in the big leagues." He asserts that playing the cornet is "just a hobby." He denies that the widespread devotion to Beiderbecke's playing involves a "cultural infatuation" but admits that it amounts to about the same thing. When going on record about Beiderbecke's influence, he speaks of a "soulfulness below the beautiful tone—a deep, underlying sadness. It has the beauty of a butterfly or a daffodil—vulnerability and mortality. He could achieve that with a single note."[42]

Beiderbecke, as translated through his many devotees, became the single most important influence in the Dixieland and traditional jazz revival. His idiosyncratic approach, self-absorbed originality, and decidedly mixed attitudes toward careerism in jazz, in addition to his musical influence, opened up social and cultural space for hundreds of avocational traditionalists. These musicians have gathered in local jazz clubs and in regularly scheduled regional and national festivals and performed on expensive oceanic cruise ships and near the winter watering holes of Florida, Arizona, and California.

The line between the amateur and the professional in traditional and non-traditional jazz circles remains porous. Many musicians have followed Beiderbecke's trajectory of youthful amateurism growing into professional pride.

Chapter 6

Steamin' to the End of the Line:
Jazz On, Along, and Beyond the Ohio River

Melancholy, indeed, is the river-view when a rainy day dawns in dull gray light upon the levee—the view of a rapid yellow river under an ashen sky; of distant hills looming dimly through pallid mist; of steamboat smoke hanging sluggishly over the sickly hued current . . . the ancient fronts of weather-stained buildings on the Row, gloomy masses of discolored brick and stone with gaping joints and shattered windows. Yet on rainy nights the voice of wild merriment echoes loudest along the levee, the shout of the lithe dancers and the throbbing of bass viols and the thrumming of banjos and the shrieking of fiddles seem to redouble the volume.

—Lafcadio Hearn on the levee in Cincinnati, Ohio, 1876

On the train [from Atlanta, Georgia] to Pittsburgh [in 1915] we must have looked just awful with all the luggage tied with rope, our phonograph player with the megaphone and all the trunks, etc. but the noise of the engine and cross ties [was] like music to my ears.

—Mary Lou Williams

It's a dirty, greasy town and that's where I was born. I worked at the Carnegie Steel Mill, and that's one of the things I would like to forget in my life. I started playing music to get out of the coal mine and the steel mill. . . . I would leave music at six in the morning and be at the steel mill by eight. I would work all day, then go to the club at eleven in the evening and work. I finally left Pittsburgh. I never really had a childhood . . . I

missed out on everything a kid has. I was a grown man at fifteen, and I
was glad to get out of Pittsburgh.

—Art Blakey

With its great natural beauty, immense power, and impressive 981-mile
length, the Ohio River bore riverboat jazz from Cairo, Illinois, where the Mississippi and the Ohio meet, up to Pittsburgh, Pennsylvania, the end of the line
for the large Streckfus steamers. As a result, the history of jazz before on the
inland waterways before World War II arose in New Orleans and culminated
in Pittsburgh, where innovative, sophisticated, leading-edge jazz graced
Wylie Avenue in the Hill District overlooking the headwaters of the Ohio.
Owing to shallow river water at Pittsburgh and the Streckfus line's close association with New Orleans and St. Louis, only a few Pittsburgh jazz musicians—Lois Deppe, Earl Hines, and Erroll Garner—ever looked to the river
to build their lives and musical careers. The exceptional depth and creativity
of the Wylie Avenue jazz scene during the 1920s, 1930s, and 1940s, particularly its outstanding school of jazz piano, offered fresh styles for taking riverboat jazz into postwar America. But Streckfus Steamers had always hired its
musicians along the Mississippi, not the Ohio.

The company steamed up the Ohio in order to sell its riverboat jazz excursion packages to people in the Ohio River valley. From the 1929 stock market crash to the outbreak of World War II, the aging concern continued to
bring good hot dance music spiced by a small number of exceptionally creative get-off men to this region. Throughout this, its culminating period, the
company continued to trumpet riverboat jazz as its own invention and trademark. With an aged fleet of wooden vessels, the Streckfus family continued to
do a remarkably profitable business during those difficult years. With so many
people out of work, relatively inexpensive river cruises played an important
role in maintaining public and national confidence.

Although the year 1929 is known primarily for the terrible stock market
crash and the economic depression that ensued, that year actually marked a
milestone in opening the Ohio River to increased riverboat traffic. Major improvements to water transportation were completed during the 1920s and
greatly stimulated all boat traffic and riverboat jazz after 1930.[1] The canaliza-
tion project, begun in 1879, constructed a series of locks and dams along the
Ohio. Completed in 1929,[2] the project created a nine-foot depth of "slack water" over the 981 miles from Pittsburgh to Cairo. During the darkest years of
the depression, 1930–1932, Ohio river traffic still lagged, but it began a long
and impressive growth in 1933.

This opened a larger door of opportunity to excursion boats. Although only one-fifth as long as the Mississippi, the Ohio had always possessed natural advantages over the "Father of Waters."[3] As one Ohio River musician put it: "The Upper Ohio River is much more scenic than the lower part of the Ohio. . . . The lower stretch of the Mississippi is just from nowhere . . . once in a while you can see across the top of the levee."[4] Excursion companies sold the steep green scenic banks of the Upper Ohio, provided just the wooded hills needed to charm tourists and even a few of the musicians.

Moreover, riverboat traditions had long been strong in the Ohio River valley. Small towns near Pittsburgh, Cincinnati, and Wheeling, West Virginia, had pioneered the manufacture of wooden-hulled, steam-driven riverboats in the first place. In 1811, Robert Fulton's steamboat the *New Orleans* was built at Pittsburgh and steamed down the Ohio and Mississippi rivers to New Orleans. It was the first steamboat in western waters. In 1817, the *Zebulon Pike*, built at Cincinnati, was the first vessel designed exclusively for passenger service and the first steamboat to travel from Cincinnati to St. Louis. It was also the first boat in the Cincinnati-based United States Mail Line, which became the longest-lasting steamboat line.[5]

The nineteenth-century packet boats, so suggestive of the South, had actually been manufactured in the North. During the twentieth century, a large percentage of all riverboats continued to be constructed along the Ohio. Because that river and its tributaries were so shallow near Pittsburgh, that city's largest steel shipyards, such as James Rees and Sons, actually carried out much of their work further downriver in Marietta and Cincinnati. Other influential boatyards were located on the Ohio in Point Pleasant, West Virginia, and in Jeffersonville and New Albany, Indiana.[6]

Cincinnati also had been a major port for the nineteenth-century riverboats, a strategic point of departure for the thousands of immigrants looking for transportation westward. A strong levee culture dominated by African American roustabouts provided enduring traditions of hot dance music, a tradition that might have been passed on to twentieth-century Ohio had local riverboat captains so ordered. Such music had flourished after the Civil War when blacks took over the roustabout jobs from the white laborers who had dominated them up to that time. The famous newspaper columnist Lafcadio Hearn wrote extensively about Cincinnati's levee culture during the 1870s, creating images of black riverfront life colored both by the essentialist assumptions of his day and by the writer's obvious attempt to write fairly about his subject.

Hearn, born in Greece, had been raised in Ireland and schooled in France and England. Myopic, deeply insecure, and alienated from society by the loss of the sight in one eye in a childhood accident, he grew up to be a free thinker

who doubted the superiority of whites as well as the idea that "one's human-
ity grew greater as his wealth and station in life improved." His intellect struggled with his social origins and education, leaving him attracted to "the oc-
cult, the remote, the macabre" in Cincinnati and in literature.[7] As a result, the
remarkable even-handedness of the *Cincinnati Enquirer* columns he devoted
to black levee life vied with his tendency to dramatize what he saw as "gothic"
aspects of that life.

Hearn believed that roustabout life formed the dominant thread in black
life on the levee. In the large number of bars and dance halls where steamboat
and levee laborers gathered, Hearn discovered distinctive instrumental dance
music. He interpreted what he heard of that music as a cornerstone for the resilience of a downtrodden, poverty-stricken people. Roustabouts made their
dance music on guitars, banjos, upright string basses, and violins. In Kirk and
Ryan's Dance Hall at the corner of Culvert and Sixth Streets, for example,
Hearn found a "well-dressed, neatly-built mulatto" who picked the banjo and
"a somewhat lighter colored musician" who led the music with the fiddle,
"which he played remarkably well and with great spirit." A short, stout, poorly
dressed woman named Anna Nun played the string bass "with no inexperi-
enced hand."[8]

The poorer roustabouts danced barefoot, dressed only in shirt, pants,
and "shocking hats," while the women wore neat dresses; the more "wickedly
handsome" of them smoked stogies. One "gigantic" black woman with "an
immense head of frizzy hair" was known to be "an adroit thief" who picked the
pockets of those with whom she danced, hiding the money in her hair. Everyone, men and women, carried knives, but few quarrels arose. Instead, revelers
couldn't seem to dance enough. In describing the music, Hearn described the
origins of jazz on the river:

> The musicians struck up that weird, wild, lively air known perhaps to many
> of our readers as the "Devil's Dream," and in which "the musical ghost of a
> cat chasing the spectral ghost of a rat" is represented by a succession of "mi-
> auls" and "squeaks" on the fiddle. The dancers danced a double quadrille, at
> first silently and rapidly; but warming with the wild spirit of the music,
> leaped and shouted, swinging each other off the floor, and keeping time with
> a precision which shook the building in time to the music.[9]

Hearn's is one of a tiny number of firsthand accounts of nineteenth-
century black music and dance on the levees. Such nightlife was still a powerful force in Cincinnati by the onset of World War I. The Great Migration
brought a stream of blacks into the Ohio valley and other northern cities—as

many as 1.5 million by 1930, according to the historian Joe William Trotter Jr. Most black migrants arrived in Cincinnati by railroad, and they continued to arrive during the depression. By 1920 the black population of 30,079 amounted to 7.5 percent of the city's inhabitants, and, by World War II, this figure had grown to 15 percent. Most were confined to the deplorable slums: Bucktown in the Thirteenth Ward on the East End, Little Africa, along Front Street between Walnut and Ludlow near the docks (with subsections called the Levee, Sausage Row, and Rat Row), and Little Bucktown, which emerged above the river's bank in the city's West End.[10]

Among large numbers of white people, the swelling tide of African Americans created in Cincinnati, as in the other major urban industrial areas of the North, the social, cultural, and psychological conditions that created the jazz age in the 1920s and 1930s. The *Cincinnati Union*, the city's black newspaper, reported that members of Ohio's Democratic Party talked about "a steady stream of Blacks [that] has swollen into what appears to them to be a tidal wave."[11] Racial tensions fed whites' search for liminal experiences, stirring a fascination with the music of the very people whose arrival had provoked apprehensions in the first place. So, too, increased numbers of black migrants, on the move and restlessly affirming their right as free people to live in motion, looked for musical entertainment in nightclubs and dance halls.

None of them was wilder or more restless than the New York City jazz pianist Thomas "Fats" Waller. Waller took up residence in Cincinnati from the fall of 1932 to 1934 in order to perform on his own WLW radio show, "Fats Waller's Rhythm Club." This lengthy stay appears not to have moved Waller to play and sing about the Ohio River, but it did transform his performing and recording career by making him much more widely known as a singer and entertainer. While in Cincinnati he broadcast but did not record. When moving back east, Waller took the St. Louis riverboat tenor saxophonist and clarinetist Eugene P. "Honey Bear" Sedric with him to perform as part of Fats Waller and His Rhythm.

Gene Sedric, who became a mainstay in Waller's rise to fame, had been an integral part of the black St. Louis jazz and riverboat jazz scene. Born in St. Louis on June 17, 1907, the son of the ragtime pianist Paul "Con Con" Sedric, by ten years of age Gene played in the Knights of Pythias band,[12] and he landed his first paying job in 1922 with the great Charles Creath. He played for two years on the river for Streckfus Steamers out of St. Louis with the Creath, Dewey Jackson, Fate Marable, and Ed Allen orchestras. He always counted the riverboat clarinetist Thornton Blue as a major influence on his playing style.[13] In 1923–24, thanks in great measure to his riverboat jazz experience, he caught on with Julian Arthur's popular ten-piece band, part of Jimmy

Cooper's Black and White Review, which toured widely.[14] As a result of that job, Sedric signed on with Sam Wooding's Club Alabam Orchestra, which toured Europe and Latin America for six years from 1925 to 1931 with the "Chocolate Kiddies" Review, playing extensively in Germany, France, Spain, Russia, Romania, Hungary, Italy, and the Scandinavian countries. Sedric enjoyed an eight-year run with Fats Waller on his return to the United States and spent the last part of his career playing with the leading bands of the traditional jazz revival in New York City.

Cincinnati relied heavily on touring bands and visiting national stars such as Waller, the Duke Ellington Orchestra, the Fletcher Henderson Orchestra, and Bix Beiderbecke and the Wolverines in building its jazz history.[15] At the same time a variety of black territory bands, closely associated with St. Louis and its riverboat music, played in Cincinnati. Among them were Floyd Campbell's Singing Synco Seven, the Jeter-Pillars Orchestra, and Eddie Johnson's Crackerjacks.

The Queen City still did manage to produce a few local jazz musicians of stature. The richly detailed autobiographical memoir of the jazz trumpeter Bill Coleman, for example, serves, among other things, to document the survival well into the twentieth century of the active musical scene on Cincinnati's black levee. Born in 1904 in Paris, Kentucky, Coleman moved with his mother to Cincinnati in 1911 and spent most of the next sixteen years there. He lived with either his father or his mother in series of different apartments close to the levee in the segregated tenderloin that extended along George Street from Mound to John Street and on Central Avenue from Mound to Plum Street, up from Fifth Street: "Cincinnati was like New Orleans in many respects because the same boats that sailed up and down the Ohio River from New Orleans to Kansas City all stopped at Cincinnati which had a levee also. The ways and means of making a living in the parts of Cincinnati around the levee up to certain streets were exactly like in New Orleans, because there were saloons, gambling and prostitutes."[16]

After many long years of scuffling as a boy and young man, years during which he was reduced to living in abandoned buildings and to stealing in order to survive, Coleman began to take musical inspiration from the trombonist and bandleader Wilbur DeParis and his brother, the trumpeter Sidney DeParis. Both were playing at the Cotton Club in the Sterling Hotel at Sixth and Mound Streets.[17] The Sterling had been a white hotel, but as its neighborhood changed in racial complexion, the Sterling began to cater to a black clientele, becoming a major performance center for local bands led by Clarence Paige, Edgar Hayes, and Zack Whyte. Coleman worked his way into the best of these regional territory bands and then moved on to work in New York City and, for many years, in Paris, France.

Coleman later recalled the strong impression that Fate Marable's riverboat band made when they played in Cincinnati. Coleman omits any specific dates but recalls that Jelly Roll Morton had already been in town and that he returned not long thereafter with the Fate Marable Orchestra. "I never knew who the musicians were, but I and everyone that heard them knew that we had heard one of the best jazz orchestras that had ever come to town." To drive his point home, Coleman added that he had heard the Speed Webb and Alphonso Trent orchestras before catching Marable's band. While in Cincinnati with Marable, Morton let it be known that he would return with a much better band "that would wash Fate's away." When Morton did return, "it was the worst-sounding band I had ever heard."[18]

Coleman leaves no doubt of the vibrancy of Cincinnati's black music scene and its strong tradition of social dance music. Had the city's riverboat companies so desired, this tradition would have moved out onto its vessels. But elements of packet boat elitism greatly limited the amount of jazz played on Ohio excursion boats.

No one on the inland waterways did more to extend the packet-influenced excursion trade through the twentieth century than Cincinnati's Greene family. In 1890, Gordon C. Greene and his wife Mary bought the *H. K. Bedford*, the first boat in the Greene Line. Three years later, the family bought the *Argand*. Mary captained the *Argand*, thus becoming the only licensed woman pilot on the river.[19] The packet *Gordon C. Greene*, formerly the *Cape Girardeau* and rebuilt in 1923, was one of the most famous of the line's steamers, carrying through passengers and produce. This vessel did present a little jazz in the off season when it offered expensive Mardi Gras tourist packages from Cincinnati to New Orleans. Captained by Gordon Greene's son Tom, the *Gordon C. Greene* enjoyed a long and illustrious but marginally hip career before being retired in 1952.

The music offered on the Greene Line packet boats might at most be called a gentle relative of jazz. Musicians emphatically denied that they played jazz on these vessels during the halcyon days of riverboat jazz. John Ault, who worked as a musician on the *Island Queen* out of Cincinnati, insisted that they had only a small combo that played Broadway show tunes "and, perhaps, *a little* jazz, but not much."[20] Ault insisted that his combo played "landlubber dance floor music all the way [from Cincinnati to New Orleans]." No "gut bucket or New Orleans Jazz or anything like that."

Then as now, the sociology of boat trips out of Cincinnati worked against

a music policy that called for jazz. Riverboat jazz had been specifically designed to stimulate widespread popular appeal on the inland waterways. In
contrast to the relatively inexpensive short excursions of the Streckfus Line,
the expensive long-distance packet cruises that descended most of the Ohio
nd all of the Lower Mississippi were affordable only for wealthier individuals.
As Ault put it: "Wealthy people could afford the trip—taking a winter vacation, so to speak, so we played pretty much what we call now 'society music.'
We didn't play much wild music or anything like that." He reported that the
only time that he heard "any so-called riverboat jazz" was "out of St. Louis on
the Streckfus Line": "When we'd run into one of those boats . . . a lot of times
they would have pretty much of a jazz band on those boats, but more of a style
that was known as riverboat jazz. Most of the boats that worked the Ohio were
more or less . . . typical ballroom bands."[21] Here Ault notes the important
overlap between riverboat jazz and straight social dance music. But he still
thinks that there were significant differences between the two. One of those
differences was racial. According to the *Pittsburgh Courier*, Lois P. Deppe of
Pittsburgh was the only local black leader of an all-black riverboat band on the
Ohio River. A few less famous black musicians may have led black groups on
trips from Pittsburgh from time to time, but not often enough to make the
newspapers. For some reason, the famous Streckfus musical policy for excursion boats was not adopted on the Ohio. I have uncovered no record of any
black bandleader who steamed out of the port of Cincinnati.

At the same time, the lack of demand for hot dance band musicians on the
long-distance Cincinnati boats left the Queen City deep in the musical wake
of New Orleans, St. Louis, and Pittsburgh. The leading authority on black
music in the Queen City during the 1920s names only three local black musicians—the trumpeter Bill Coleman, the pianist Charles Alexander, and the
tenor saxophonist Edgar "Spider" Courance—among those who made it into
the Who's Who of Jazz.[22] This surely does indicate that a significant amount
of jazz was played in Cincinnati from the 1920s to the end of World War II.
Many touring jazz greats played in Cincinnati, but most chose not to work
primarily in that city for long periods of time, tending instead to pass through
while on regional and national tours.

Natural disasters further diminished riverboat jazz by periodically crushing Cincinnati's excursion boats, leaving the musicians with no vessel on
which to play. Just as the Streckfus family was launching and consolidating its
new jazz policy on the Mississippi in 1917–18, for example, the most destructive ice flow in memory on the Ohio crushed the *Princess*, one of Cincinnati's
two excursion boats. Then, in November 1922, a terrible fire destroyed two
more of the city's excursion boats—the *Morning Star* and the famous *Island*

Queen. In 1896 a second *Island Queen* had taken to the river, running a tightly regulated and limited summer schedule between Cincinnati and Coney Island, an amusement park ten nautical miles to the south. Both *Island Queens* tramped the Ohio and the Lower Mississippi in early spring and after Labor Day but spent the summer seasons on their domesticated short-haul loop.[23] In 1947 the third *Island Queen*, built in 1925, exploded at the Ward Street wharf in Pittsburgh.

With only intermittent and limited excursion boat service in Cincinnati, the Streckfus family kept at least one of its steamers tramping the Ohio during the summer seasons. The steamer *J.S.*, with Fate Marable and his orchestra on board, docked in Pittsburgh before that vessel burned to the waterline in 1910. Historians of the Ohio River scene consider Marable, who played during the winters in Paducah, Louisville, and Pittsburgh, a major influence in bringing ragtime and jazz to Pittsburgh.[24] The *Washington* worked the Upper Ohio River at Cincinnati and Pittsburgh, the two most lucrative excursion markets, from 1921 to 1937. The *J.S. Deluxe* tramped the Upper Ohio in 1934 and 1935.

The S.S. *Washington* tramped the Ohio River during the Great Depression with black dance bands led by Fate Marable and Walter Pichon. (Photo courtesy of Duncan Schiedt.)

The Streckfus boats vied with intermittent local excursion boat service in Pittsburgh. The *Julia Belle Swain* worked out of Smoketown from 1924 to 1931, and the *Greater Pittsburgh* sold excursions from that city from 1928 to 1931, when she, too, burned under suspicious circumstances. This opened another important urban market to Streckfus-style jazz excursions. Finally, in 1931, that company purchased the seven-year-old steel-hulled packet *Cincinnati*, converting it into the all-steel *President*, a boat that found great popularity with the public starting in 1933, one of the darkest years of the depression.[25]

Riverboat jazz, always a precursor of the big band era, found continued success, responding directly to the shaken sensibilities of the 1930s. Marable's orchestra featured skilled and innovative instrumentalists such as the string bassist Jimmy Blanton, the pianist Walter "Fats" Pichon, the reedman Tallmadge "Tab" Smith, the trombonist Nathaniel Story, the trumpeter Clark Terry, and the saxophonist and arranger Earl Bostic. Marable's men played well up the Ohio River during the 1930s, helping Joseph Streckfus extend his musical influence on the inland waterways.

The New Orleans bandleader, pianist, vocalist, and arranger Fats Pichon (1906–1967) played an important role on the Ohio River between 1931 and 1941. He played piano and led Pichon's Famous Mississippi Serenaders on the *Capitol*, the *Washington* (the refurbished *Sidney*), the *J.S.*, the *St. Paul*, and the *President*. Like Marable, Pichon came fully musically literate to Streckfus Steamers. As a youngster in New Orleans he studied piano for eight years and worked as second pianist in Armand J. Piron's orchestra. In 1922 he landed a playing job in Strunsky's Atlantic Hotel in Belmar, New Jersey. The owner-manager of this establishment was an aunt of George and Ira Gershwin. George Gershwin, impressed by Pichon's ambition, put up the money to send him to the New England Conservatory of Music in Boston. Pichon studied there for nearly four years, leaving before graduation in order to take a lucrative offer from the 11 Aces, a Dallas orchestra, to play throughout the southwest and in Mexico.[26]

Having earned his nickname in Mexico, Pichon returned to work in New York with Elmer Snowden's band alongside Rex Stewart and Roy Eldridge. Pichon recorded with Red Allen and with a trio called the QRS Boys. A photo of Pichon's orchestra finds him standing in front of the *Capitol* along with the trombonist Irving Douroux, the banjoist Sam Casimir, the trumpeters Clarence "Perch" Thornton and Jack Lamont, the saxophonists Harry Lang, Manuel Crusto, and Willie Casimir, and the trombonist Ray Brown. The highly regarded St. Louis pianist Burroughs Lovingood played second piano in Pichon's orchestra, although he was not present for the photo. He also played the calliope. Perch Thornton recalled in an interview that while working for Streck-

Walter "Fats" Pichon (standing fourth from left) and his orchestra pose in neckties with other black employees in front of the S. S. *Capitol.* Left to right, beginning with Pichon: trombonist Irving Douroux, banjoist Sam Casimir, unidentified, trumpeters Clarence "Perch" Thornton and Jack Lamont, saxophonists Harry Lang, Manuel Crusto, and Willie Casimir, and trombonist Ray Brown, along with other members of the ship's staff. (Photo courtesy of the Historic New Orleans Collection, accession no. 92-48-L, MSS 520.)

fus Steamers, Pichon was advertised as the Second Fats Waller. In the Streck-fus tradition, his, like the other riverboat jazz orchestras, never recorded. The bandleader Paul Whiteman is said to have introduced Pichon onstage at Carnegie Hall by calling his "the fastest left hand in show business."[27]

In addition to the orchestras led by Pichon and Marable that played up and down the Ohio River on various Streckfus steamers during the 1920s and 1930s, Eddie Johnson's St. Louis Crackerjacks played their way from Alton, Illinois, to Pittsburgh and back aboard the steamer *Idlewild,* a relatively small vessel 157 feet in length that belonged to Henry Meyer of Hardin, Illinois. From 1933 to 1936, the Johnson band included Harold "Shorty" Baker, Freddie and Walter Martin, Earnest Franklin, James Telphy, Lester Nichols, Bennie Jackson, and Singleton Palmer.[28] Palmer reported playing with the Dewey Jackson Orchestra up to Pittsburgh, as well, after 1936. When asked by the steamboat historian Irene Cortinovis what it had been like traveling on these

Walter Pichon at the piano. (Photo courtesy of the Historic New Orleans Collection, accession no. 92-48-L, MSS 520.)

boats, Palmer replied: "Well, it was almost like an army thing—breakfast at seven and rehearsal at twelve and we'd play at night."

Of all the traveling bands that played in Pittsburgh, Johnson's St. Louis Crackerjacks "took the city by storm."[29] An anonymous local newspaper reporter called Johnson's music "immeasurably good." The band developed a strong local following, winning staged battles of the bands against groups co-led by Harvey Lankford and Charles Creath from the *St. Paul* and vanquishing Dewey Jackson and Fate Marable's Harlem Steppers.

In contrast to Cincinnati, black Pittsburgh produced its own exceptionally strong and creative jazz scene, one stimulated by protean initiatives in drama, journalism, nightclub and sports enterprises, and a broad range of small business activities. Pittsburgh's contributions to jazz began just after World War I, when the Hill District assumed in a minor way some of the aspects of Harlem. Night spots, most of them small clubs where black musicians performed, sprang up. Whites frequented some of these clubs, including Derby Dan's, the Paradise Inn, and the Devil's Cave. Visits to these clubs were thought to offer a chance to "see Negro life" or "life on the Hill." Initially, some clubs did not welcome whites, but the number of such clubs declined with the years.[30] The

Hill District lasted well beyond the Roaring Twenties and contributed many of the major national stars of the years following World War II.

The Great Migration from the South fueled this brilliant, too often overlooked musical movement. The musicianly sophistication of black jazz in Pittsburgh surpassed that of any other river city including New Orleans. In some important regards, this impressive musical achievement took inspiration from riverboat jazz without becoming especially reliant on it. The list of exceptionally accomplished jazz musicians who lived for many years in Pittsburgh and who went on to build national and international reputations includes the drummers Art Blakey and Kenny Clarke, the vocalists Billy Eckstine, Maxine Sullivan, Lena Horne, and Dakota Staton, the trumpeter Roy Eldridge, the guitarist George Benson, the tenor saxophonist Stanley Turrentine, the string bassist Ray Brown, and a school of jazz pianists and composer-arrangers that included Earl Hines, Mary Lou Williams, Billy Strayhorn, Erroll Garner, Ahmad Jamal, Horace Parlan, and Shirley Scott. The piano had not played a major role in the birth of New Orleans jazz. Most of the early African American jazz band pianists had been women from more northerly cities. Pittsburgh rivaled New York City in its development of the piano in jazz.

As increasing numbers of black migrants began to arrive in Pittsburgh during World War I, they settled in many different parts of the city. This dispersal of black settlements into separate neighborhoods, among them the Hill District, East Liberty, Homewood, Homestead, Braddock, and Duquesne, had the predictable effect of weakening communications between new black settlers. Moreover, the increasingly black neighborhoods that emerged as a result experienced often painful struggles with the sons and daughters of the Germans, Italians, Russians, Slovaks, Armenians, Syrians, Lebanese, Greeks, Chinese, and Jews who had arrived earlier in the same neighborhoods.

For example, the neighborhood called the Hill District became the famous center of black jazz, but it housed many Italian, Polish, Russian, Syrian, Hungarian, German, Irish and Jewish residents when African American migrants moved in.[31] This both intensified economic and cultural conflicts between the new arrivals and the more settled inhabitants and also encouraged cultural give and take. Many of Pittsburgh's leading black jazz musicians noted daily struggles with racial prejudice in their changing neighborhoods. As the pressure of black migration continued, many of the settlers of European origin moved out to more rural, less crowded, middle-class neighborhoods. Such social and economic pressures pushed African Americans into what increasingly became all-black neighborhoods such as the Hill District,

East Liberty, and Homewood, located about six miles from downtown Pitts-burgh, and into the many separate blast furnace towns.[32]

The Hill District, a 1.4-square-mile cluster of neighborhoods perched above the downtown area between the Allegheny and the Monongahela Rivers, became the cultural center of black Pittsburgh. In "the District" one could find the offices of the *Pittsburgh Courier,* one of the nation's most influential black weekly newspapers. The Hill was also home base for the Pittsburgh Crawfords, the Negro National League baseball team that fielded Satchel Paige, Josh Gibson, and Cool Papa Bell and won the black National League championship in 1922, 1935, and 1936. Referring to its heyday from 1930 to 1950, the Harlem Renaissance poet Claude McKay called the District "the crossroads of the world"[33] since African Americans, Jews, and Italians lined the streets with mom-and-pop stores. The Hill's ethnic diversity encouraged left-wing politics.

Wylie Avenue, "The Street of 1,000 Sighs," according to a thoughtful city cop on the night beat,[34] acted as the commercial center of jazz in black Pitts-burgh. Just after World War I, clubs such as the Leader House, the Collins Inn, the Humming Bird, Derby Dan's, the Fullerton Inn, and the Paradise Inn took the lead. One had to reach Marie's and Lola's, an active after-hours spot for musicians who came up from the riverboats or over from the dance halls, "by many steps and along narrow hallways where the air was thick with cheap incense and dim with red or green."[35] Jam sessions continued all night long. As described in 1940, the two preceding decades had seen the rise such haunts as the Crawford Grills No. 1 and No. 2, the Hurricane Lounge, the Green Front, the Coobus Club, the Bamboola Club, the Center Avenue Elks, the Perry Bar, the Granada Bar, and the American Federation of Musicians Local 471 Musicians Club dotted the avenue. A hole-in-the-wall called the Subway also served as the hangout for networking musicians. In addition to the local musicians who got a start in these clubs, national stars played in them after their gigs downtown had ended.[36]

This profusion of nightclubs and bars relied on the relatively high wages that the steel mills paid to their laborers. Still, the great Billy Eckstine earned only $6.00 per week at the Harlem Show Bar. Jazz found additional support among the many private social clubs that sprang up in Smoketown, often to disappear just as quickly. The Coobus Club and the Frogs were two of the most famous Pittsburgh social clubs known for organizing invitation-only parties. The Sevilles (a young men's club), the Pierettes, Les Modernes, and Le Gaies Femmes (all women's groups) and the Swelegants, the Ducks, the Drakes, the Frogs, the Matrons and Maids, the Turf Riding Club, the Entre

Nous, the Junior Debs, and the Gay Hill-Toppers enlivened the long dreary winters with their parties, luncheons, and dances.[37]

These groups hired bands or smaller combos and solo pianists, helping to augment the parsimonious wages paid by the clubs. But for those still too poor to belong to a social club, "house socials" and "rent parties" provided ample occasion to sample the music of Pittsburgh's strong corps of pianists. On paydays crowds would gather "in little rooms lit with a single 25-watt red bulb. Strangers are not usually welcome. A piano player is engaged from 9:00 P.M. to 4:00 or 5:00 A.M., usually for all he can eat and drink: liquor, cut or bootleg, is sold. Chitterlings or barbecued pork sandwiches are served in the kitchen." In addition, "reefers" sold for fifteen cents or a quarter, depending on their strength, and dancers did the slow drag through the dimly lit night.[38]

A rich, quickly evolving jazz culture arose in the bright light districts of cities across the nation, and, in Pittsburgh, the Wylie Avenue clubs were no exception. "On the Hill at little bars, over sloe gin or beer, across wooden tables where chitterlings and turnip greens are the specialty, or at street corners or window-to-window," a dynamic vernacular was spoken. Called "Jive," it became the mother tongue of many. The Works Progress Administration described it as coming "rhythmically and vividly from the lips. It explodes and crackles and sings and hums . . . brilliant with racial imagery and prismatic with race moods."[39]

In Jive, a smart, aware person was "hipped" or "a hip cat" or a "hip chick." Hip cats, whether "fast blacks," "Jew Babies" (mulattos), "chalks" (white women), or "grey studs" (white men), might "feed the joy box" (juke box). No-account individuals, whether "frone guys" or "frone frails," were often "beat to the socks" (broke) and could only "case the pad" (sit in a corner and watch) while those who had "lead" fed the joy box.

Money played an important role in Jive's vocabulary: Those who had some were "holding." Those who wanted to borrow money said, "Let me hold." A quarter was a "rough" and a dime was a "deuce." Change of less than a "lamb's tongue" (one dollar) was "scratch." A five-dollar bill was a "fin." To spend money was to "knock oneself back some," and spending a lot of it was to "jump up" or "kick up a little light sport." Ignoring an acquaintance was to "play him cheap."

Because one often spoke Pittsburgh Jive in bars, nightclubs, and dance halls, many phrases dealt with alcohol and drugs. To get high on alcohol, you "blew your conk," but "blowin' reefer" or "gage" (marijuana) was to "bust your conk." Having a grand time in this manner was to "kill your fine self," for example, by "beatin' up your gums" or "layin' your gamble" (talking). Jivers were likely to meet a variety of characters such as a "soft" (a ready woman), a "mellow chick" (a desirable one), a "killer diller" (a playgirl), a "beat broad" (a woman worn down by life), or a "pink" (a white woman). Men could be "Lochinvars" (playboys), "solid drags" (always borrowing), "gay nineties" (older), "cream-puffs" (drunks), "double trouble" (beggars), "jokers" (no-good guys), or, per-ish the thought, "nabs," "bluebirds," or "Johnny Nabs" (policemen). If you ran into one of the latter, or if you had "fast mail" (a woman waiting for you), you could let it be known that you were "cuttin' out" or "blowin'" in order to "scarf" (eat), "cop a nod" (sleep), or even "weave" (pray) on your "double deuces" (knees) to "the Big Jeff" (God).

Nightlife vernacular changed swiftly and, during the Great Depression, found its own ways to describe the welfare state. A Works Progress Adminis-tration worker was a "G-man," welfare relief day was "international pay day," a relief check was "wrapping paper," and an informer was "a sitting squawk" or "Quawker." Digging with a shovel on a WPA project was "usin' a spoon," and being unemployed was "working for Pat and Turner."[40]

Pittsburgh's jazz movement opened with some very promising riverboat jazz. During the 1920s the singer, saxophonist, and bandleader Lois P. Deppe led his ten-piece dance band for moonlight cruises on the relatively small steamer *East St. Louis*, promoted as "The Palace of the Rivers," which left on Monday evenings from the foot of Federal Street not far from "the Point," where the Allegheny and the Monongahela rivers met to form the Ohio. This choice of a downtown wharf would not have been convenient for Pittsburgh's black passengers, who lived in other parts of the city. The cruises on the *East St. Louis* were "strictly invitational," after the manner of black cruises on the Streckfus Line.[41] Deppe's Serenaders also played "jazz as it should be played," that is, for dancing, at Duquesne Garden.[42]

Deppe's early life and subsequent career indicate that before jazz came to Pittsburgh, music influenced in part by European concert traditions played a strong role in local black musical culture. Deppe's protégé, the pianist Earl Hines, would be similarly oriented in his own musical development. Born in 1897 in Horse Cave, Kentucky, Deppe moved with his parents to Springfield, Ohio, in 1903, where, as a very young boy, he sang concerts in churches and white country clubs. At age sixteen he wrote to the entrepreneur, activist, and philanthropist Madame C. J. Walker, who was scheduled to speak in Indi-anapolis, Indiana, offering to sing as part of a program she was organizing in honor of Paul Laurence Dunbar. Walker took Deppe to New York City with her and had a couple of lessons with Buzzi Pecci, Enrico Caruso's vocal coach. Under her auspices Deppe also met such black composers as Harry T. Bur-leigh, Joe Jordan, and J. Rosamond Johnson, all of whom hoped to develop an active urban black movement in musical theater.[43]

In 1916, the black songwriters Henry Creamer and Turner Layton helped Deppe begin a career as a nightclub singer. He continued to sing concerts of operatic airs and spirituals in churches but saw that popular music would provide his only avenue toward financial solvency. As he turned to organizing his nightclub act, Deppe recognized the originality and professional versatility of the pianist Earl Hines. Hines could accompany Deppe but also fascinate audiences with his own piano solos.

Hines, a native of Pittsburgh, became the key instrumentalist in Deppe's orchestras. He made an extraordinary place for himself as the first and arguably the greatest of a long line of fine pianists who began long national and international careers there. He was the first in the Pittsburgh school of jazz piano to establish that a solid foundation in traditional European and American musical concepts and techniques should be mixed with elements of African American vernacular to make authentically creative jazz music. Fate Marable had brought a similar confidence in musical knowledge and keyboard mastery to the city as early as 1907 and ultimately settled his family there while he steamed the inland waterways. Marable first arrived in Pittsburgh during the ragtime era and came back yearly throughout the initial rise of jazz and the evolution of swing.

The 1940 WPA survey titled "The Negro in Pittsburgh" emphasizes Marable's musical influence on the s earliest stages of jazz's development there: "Fate Marable carried jazz up the Mississippi and Ohio to every town along the banks. He himself played it. He picked up one man after another, trained him soundly in musical technique, and watched him leave the river to carry the gospel into cities inland, on lake shore, prairie, and mountainside from coast to coast."[44]

In the off seasons, Marable drifted between St. Louis, Paducah, and Pittsburgh. When in Pittsburgh he performed regularly in the Crawford Grille, in the Bailey Hotel, and in a number of clubs along Wylie Avenue. Pittsburghers saw Marable as a "small, slender man, light coffee-with-cream colored," wearing "expensive suits, slightly bald, nice eyes, long arms and hands, and always smoking a cigar. He has a strange manner of speech—runs his words quickly and obscurely together, but breaks into long pauses. He is notoriously reserved on all subjects but music, slightly touched by arrogance, used to telling people what to do."[45] Sitting, drinking, and talking with musicians between sets, Marable favored water glasses full of straight gin washed down with whiskey or beer. He rarely went to bed and preferred to doze as needed right there in his chair.

To the author of "The Negro in Pittsburgh," Marable was the founding father of the city's school of jazz piano. Although Smoketown jazz encompassed the full variety of instruments, an unusually large number of major pianists graced the city's clubs and concert halls. Beginning with Marable and continuing with Hines, Williams, Strayhorn, Garner, and Jamal, black Pittsburgh's involvement with the piano was a major cultural phenomenon stimulated by the Great Migration's thirst for cultural advancement and the traditional respect accorded harmoniums and pianos in southern black life.

Hines became the first native of the city to champion artistically crafted piano jazz. Born on December 28, 1905, in Duquesne, Pennsylvania, then an industrial suburb of Pittsburgh, Hines commented extensively on the disturbing social changes that accompanied the arrival of black migrants in the Pittsburgh area.[46] Before World War I, neighborhoods such as Duquesne were predominantly white. Two generations of the Hines family lived in a twelve-room house on a hilltop with plenty of land for extensive gardens and farm animals. They represented an older Pittsburgh, where a more limited number of urban pioneers had settled well before the war. As migration from the South proceeded, the newer arrivals were perceived as dangerous. They were increasingly segregated in all-black neighborhoods across the railroad tracks, closer to the major steel mills located between the Monongahela and the Allegheny rivers. The Great Migration, according to Hines, stimulated increased racial prejudice that he had not experienced as a younger child.

Hines's parents created a strong, musically active family, something that many migrant jazz musicians from Pittsburgh would have appreciated. His father worked hard to organize groups that would bring together black people forced to live close to the scattered steel mills surrounding Pittsburgh. For example, he headed the Eureka Brass Band and organized summer picnics for people from McKeesport, Braddock, Duquesne, and Homestead. Earl Hines acutely observed that Pittsburghers of his acquaintance highly valued piano lessons for their children. Throughout his own youth, Hines took piano lessons from a series of teachers, including one very authoritarian German American by the name of Von Holtz, who led Hines through the literature of the major European composers. The young pianist played in a series of concert competitions organized by Von Holtz in the surrounding towns. All the while, however, Hines played the popular songs of his day by ear, earning a reputation as a party pianist among his peers.

When Hines reached fifteen years of age, one of his older friends took him to Wylie Avenue: "This Phil Windear who lived across the street from us was a sort of playboy. He and Pat, my oldest cousin, were both working by now, and their greatest thrill was to drive into Pittsburgh to a nightclub. It was a wild town at that time, especially on Wylie Avenue." Hines describes the power of the bright-light district in bringing him to jazz for the first time:

"We were sitting in a restaurant eating big steaks like I'd never had before, and I was reacting to the glamour of the waitresses, when I heard this music upstairs. It had a beat and a rhythm to it that I'd never heard before, and everybody seemed to be enjoying themselves. 'Oh,' I said, 'if only I could just get upstairs and see what they're doing—see what kind of music that is!'"[47]

Not long thereafter, Lois Deppe asked Hines to join his band at the Leader House (which eventually became the Crawford Grille) on Wylie Avenue, and Hines soon rented a room on Wylie in order to stay close to the action at such nightclubs as the Leader and the Collins Inn.[48] On hearing Hines, the *Pittsburgh Courier* concluded, "There may be some better, but we doubt it. The Best In Town."[49]

Into the male-dominated jazz culture came a five-year-old from Atlanta, Georgia, who would come to call herself Mary Lou Williams, who migrated with her family in 1915 to the East Liberty neighborhood of Pittsburgh. According to Linda Dahl, Williams's biographer: "One can only imagine the family's culture shock at arriving in cold, smoggy Pittsburgh after the hot, small-town ways of Edgewood [Georgia]. An army of smokestacks lined up along the Allegheny and Monongahela rivers, belching coal and steel fumes. By noon the sun would have dimmed to premature night, blotted out by thick black smoke. Air pollution was not curbed until the 1960s, and Pittsburgh had one of the highest tuberculosis rates in the nation."[50]

More settled residents of the neighborhood into which Williams moved felt as if they were "under siege" due to the increase of black residents. White families lived all around her family, and people living in nearby Germantown threw bricks, threatened black children with knives, and wielded a variety of racial epithets. Despite (or because of) terrible childhood deprivation, unimaginable family trauma, and daily fear, she grew up practicing the piano all day to become a major jazz piano stylist and composer. She explained: "I began building up a defense against prejudice and hatred and so many other miserable blocks by taking my aching heart away from bad sounds and working hard at music. Looking back, I see that my music acted as a shield, protecting me from being aware of many of the prejudices that must have existed. I was completely wrapped up in my music. Little else mattered to me."[51] As her family experienced long periods of severe poverty, the teenaged Williams worked as a pianist.

At Lincoln Elementary School and at Westinghouse High Williams sometimes lashed out at her teachers. At that time, no African Americans taught in those schools, and Williams saw teachers through the eyes of family members whose stories of racial prejudice had painted all whites in threatening hues. The principal of Westinghouse recognized her talent, however, and took her to the opera, arranged concerts for her at the University of Pittsburgh, where she played for professors and students, as had Hines before her, and arranged for her to play for Pittsburgh's leading socialites.

Musical development acted as a fascinating world of growing awareness, an activity and aesthetic experience in which hard work brought a growing sense of mastery of great beauty and power. For Williams, as for the impressive number of great pianists who followed her, music also served as a "passport" into brighter worlds where hard work and concentration found aesthetic rewards.[52]

Thanks to her tireless practice as a youth, Williams caught the attention of her teachers. As the WPA survey noted in 1940, in addition to African American musical traditions, "the introduction of music into the segregated black schools in 1869 and the teaching of music in public schools after segregation was abandoned developed a wide range of music ability and appreciation." Budding young musicians of any skin color had respectful, dedicated allies in the music teachers Carl McVicker and Jane Patton Alexander, who insisted that their students learn the fundamentals of music and grow in control and mastery. In 1927, McVicker instituted a radically innovative, racially integrated educational program at Westinghouse High, two miles from East Liberty. All students, regardless of racial or ethnic identity, were encouraged to experiment with any musical instrument that attracted them. Moreover, according to Ahmad Jamal, McVicker "instilled self-respect in those of us who were his students, because he respected us regardless of our background."[53] McVicker and leaders of local churches made contacts with music teachers at the University of Pittsburgh and with those among the city wealthiest white families who were dedicated to *soirées musicales.* Outstanding Westinghouse music students accepted invitations to perform and entertain in the leading homes of the city.[54]

Mary Lou Williams was taken to the Saturday afternoon dances at the Arcadia Ballroom, where Lois Deppe was playing. Such gatherings could be dangerous. "These dances ran from noon until 4 P.M., and shortly before break-up time the biggest fight would invariably commence. Half the kids in Pittsburgh could be seen running from the hall, grabbing the backs of streetcars to get away. We had groups of kids from the different districts—East Liberty, Soho, the downtown district, and so on—who were considered very tough. If an East Liberty kid was caught in Soho, or downtown, he would either be assaulted or chased back to his own district."[55]

Williams broke free of her alcohol-soaked family in 1924 when she got a job playing piano with the Memphis-born saxophonist John Overton Williams in a modest group called Buzzin' Harris and His Hits and Bits, which toured on the black vaudeville circuit run by the Theater Owners' Booking Association in Pennsylvania and Ohio. Their touring finally took them to Chicago, where Williams made sure she looked up Earl Hines, her early inspiration at the piano. Hines introduced her to Louis Armstrong and his accompanist, Buck Washington.

The experiences of the pianist and composer Billy Strayhorn paralleled those of Williams. In 1920 his family moved to Braddock from Hillsborough, North Carolina. In 1926, they moved to Pittsburgh's Homewood district. This, too, was then an ethnically diverse neighborhood in which 15 percent of the citizens were African American. Homewood, however, was diverse without becoming a melting pot. Black children learned quickly to hold their tongues with whites, even with children of their own age. If racist insults ever escalated to violence, the police always sided with the whites.[56] White families lived along the main streets of Homewood while black ones had to be satisfied with the back alleys. Such was 7212 Tioga Street Rear, where the Strayhorns lived.

For five years Billy Strayhorn went to Westinghouse High, only a half-mile from his home. The school, which was only 20 percent African American, gave Strayhorn a first-class education, particularly in music. His wonderful biographer, David Hajdu, quotes McVicker as saying: "We were a factory-town school, so we had a lot of kids like Billy, kids who needed an outlet of one kind or another but had a hard time because they were black."[57] McVicker later recalled that Strayhorn showed little interest in the swing band that he had instituted at Westinghouse High, the innovation that had caused such an uproar in 1927. Rather, under the strict but unstinting tutelage of Alexander in piano and harmony, he, not unlike Fate Marable before him, had determined to become a serious pianist who specialized in the European concert repertoire. In 1934, with the Westinghouse student orchestra, Strayhorn performed Edvard Grieg's Piano Concerto in A Minor, opus 16. McVicker remarked: "I never heard a student play that way before or after. The orchestra may have been a group of students, but Billy Strayhorn was a professional artist."[58]

Pittsburgh's Jane Patton Alexander and Carl McVicker, like St. Louis's Jesse Gerald Tyler and Nathaniel Clark Smith, gave their students a systematic grounding in music theory and orchestral practice that went far beyond the question of how well a musician could read music. Gifted students such as Strayhorn could learn to read swiftly and accurately at sight and also to compose and arrange music. They left high school ready to manipulate and blend the many different instrumental parts in their varied key signatures. Mary Lou Williams, in her rebellion against white authority figures, learned to read and write music much later while on the road with Andy Kirk. She went on to compose and arrange for swing bands, while, of course, Strayhorn would do the same for Duke Ellington.

For both of these musicians, Pittsburgh's raging racism and sexism made careers in the leading theater pit bands or the symphony orchestra out of the question. Both had first to perform in the joints of the Hill District, East Liberty, and Homestead, seeking contacts with passing musicians and bands that needed a pianist who could compose and arrange.

Next Erroll Garner, who enjoyed a career of unsurpassed national, international, and critical acclaim, followed his own path into black Pittsburgh's school of jazz piano. Garner was born in Pittsburgh on June 15, 1921, and grew up with his family at 212 North St. Clair Street in the East Liberty neighborhood. Garner's mother and father had come to Pittsburgh from Virginia and North Carolina, respectively. The Garners' neighborhood was mostly white and, compared to those of Williams and Strayhorn, without notable racial conflict. Saint James African Methodist Episcopal Church, close by 212 North St. Clair, proved one of two cornerstones for the Garners. The other was music. Every person in the family played an instrument, and most of them sang. Erroll's father had his own band and sang in the church choir in addition to holding down two full-time jobs.

In stark contrast to Hines, Strayhorn, and Jamal, Garner remained, from the beginning to the end of his brilliant career, an intuitive improviser who did not read music. Like Bix Beiderbecke, he played anything he heard from an early age and, unlike him, enjoyed playing piano so much that he would happily play all day long. In grammar school, Garner played so well that he performed daily at recess for his schoolmates. After school, his friends took him to their homes to perform for them. He was a shy but high-strung, sensitive, energetic youngster who tried hard to please everyone. He found that difficult but never complained.

Garner like Williams and , went to Westinghouse High, where he was taught tuba by McVicker in 1935 or 1936.[59] McVicker recalled being "very close" to his pupil. A biographical profile written of Garner by Whitney Balliett in the *New Yorker* quoted McVicker as saying that the pianist "had a low I.Q. so he was put in an upgraded class run by Mrs. Lyons—naturally, we called it the Lyons Den."[60] McVicker later insisted that his words had been taken out of context. Without denying the low scores Garner achieved on his intelligence quotient tests, he insisted that Garner possessed exceptional musical intelligence: "My point is this: an IQ does not determine or show musical talent like Erroll had. It was misrepresentative of him because he was able to memorize thousands of tunes, thousands of rhythms and was able to play them perfectly."[61] Garner sneaked out of his other classes to watch and listen to his teacher working with his bands. He did this so often that he was ulti-mately allowed to spend half the school day in McVicker's classroom. Despite his persistent unwillingness and inability to read music, Garner flawlessly played by ear even the most difficult piano parts.

Garner was the only jazz musician from Pittsburgh to be on record as hav-ing performed on the Streckfus excursion boats. His sister Ruth remembered his talking about riverboats but insisted that she knew nothing else about them. Erroll's close friend Allen Carter revealed, "We weren't allowed on the riverboats."[62] By "we," Carter seems to have meant African Americans from Pittsburgh, but other sources make no mention of such a racial ban, which would have contradicted Streckfus Streamers' separate and unequal policy elsewhere. In 1926, a Monday evening cruise for black people was sponsored by an organization called "The Forty Thieves" aboard the *Verne Swain*. Two bands played for eight hundred passengers. The cruise ended in violence as a policeman opened fire.[63] The *Pittsburgh Courier* subsequently fell silent about riverboat cruises, carrying only one or two notices for Streckfus Streamers in May 1931, when the Church of the Holy Cross organized an outing aboard the steamer *Washington*.[64] Although that cruise appeared to proceed smoothly, the newspaper again felt silent about riverboats. In addition to the ban on blacks as customers, the cruises departed from the foot of Wood Street, in downtown Pittsburgh, at least 5.5 miles from East Liberty. The WPA history of African Americans in the city flatly declares that riverboat cruises were a regular part of summer life in black Pittsburgh.

Garner nevertheless became one of the very few black musicians from Pittsburgh to perform for riverboat cruises. He gained great fame for his pi-ano playing while still at Westinghouse High. As Allen Carter put it: "Fate Marable was, at that time, one of the leading musicians that came out of St. Louis on the riverboats. We weren't allowed on the riverboats, but when Fate came to town, by that time Erroll had built up quite a following, and it was the thing to do to put out a sign saying that Erroll Garner would be playing the piano. Marable was assured of huge crowds. . . . Erroll brought more attention to Westinghouse than the football team. When Erroll started swinging, that was it."[65]

In the mid-1930s Marable's musicians were dazzled by Garner's ability to handle by ear the most challenging passages in their arrangements. Vertna Saunders played his way north to Pittsburgh and back aboard the steamer *President* during the summer of 1935. He reported that Marable had tooth trouble one day and wasn't able to play. They asked the union to send a sub-stitute, and the twenty-four-year-old who turned up did not at first look very promising. Charles Creath asked the youngster if he would like to rehearse a bit before the cruise. Garner replied in the negative!

> [We were to] just give him all the guitar parts. He didn't want the piano parts because he couldn't read piano music. On the boat, we would play the intro-duction and a couple of choruses and a solo. Then [the arrangement called for] a modulation, because the last chorus was always in a different key. . . . So they explained that to this guy, so he said, "Well, no problem!" There wasn't! There was no problem. I don't care what key you wanted to play in, I don't care what key it was, you just called the key. He played and he sounded as though he'd played with the band another time. After the first day, the guys found out that it was a fella named Erroll Garner.[66]

Garner epitomized black Pittsburgh's drive toward technically sophis-ticated jazz piano styling before World War II. In Marable, Hines, Williams, Strayhorn, and Garner, as in so many other black musicians, the experience of the Great Migration involved a thrust for keyboard virtuosity. Why wouldn't a northeastern industrial city with relatively high wages available for black la-borers produce such an aesthetic? In a psychological sense, the combination of technical ability, growing awareness of music theory, intensive experimen-tation in arranging and composing, and creative exploration of improvisation expressed the spirit of the Great Migration's drive for greater freedom and op-portunity, a chance to build careers in music and the hope for a fuller in-volvement in American musical life.

Moreover, African American piano culture of the interwar years also con-tained a deep ambivalence that helped drive jazz pianists toward brilliant key-board mastery and international renown after World War II. This cultural ambivalence emerges most clearly in the play *The Piano Lesson* by August Wil-son. Wilson lived in postwar Pittsburgh and listened to the swan song of Wylie Avenue. He had been born Frederick August Kittel in that city in 1945 to Frederick August, a baker, and Daisy Wilson Kittel, a cleaning woman. At least four of his plays—*Ma Rainey's Black Bottom, The Piano Lesson, Joe Turner's Come and Gone,* and *Fences*—evoke "the effects of separation, migration, and reunion on the descendants of slaves who migrated from the rural South to the northern urban centers like Pittsburgh." Wilson's plays draw on the migrants' "dreams, restlessness, and struggle to find practical and spiritual havens in an essentially hostile society."[67] In their struggles, his characters, beset by racist restrictions, confront in different ways a highly symbolic cultural identity as diasporic Africans.

The Piano Lesson (1990) provides a compelling exploration of the complex role of the piano in this process. Without portraying the worlds of Pittsburgh's great jazz pianists, this play nonetheless dramatizes lives and cultures in which the piano played a deeply ambivalent role. Although music-making provided a vehicle for memories of Africa and life in the southern United States, thus playing a key role in African American cultural identity, it also led blues musicians into yet another racially segregated, exploitative business run by whites.

The principal characters in the play, the brother and sister Boy Willie and Berniece Charles, feud over the particularly symbolic piano that Berniece has brought all the way from the South to her Pittsburgh home. An unhappy but resilient individual whose husband and father both died violently in the South, Berniece learned to play on this instrument at her mother's insistence. She interprets the piano as a relic and a totem of her family's tragic past, and, since her mother's death, has refused to play it at all. She understands the instrument's symbolic power and therefore cannot relinquish it. She provides lessons and practice time in a family environment for her young daughter Maretha.

Boy Willie still lives in the South and has determined to buy the land that their family had been forced to work under slavery and Jim Crow. He hopes to sell the piano to help finance his plan to fully free the family for the first time from southern slavery and peonage. Berniece both empathizes with and rejects her brother's plan to sell the piano, clinging unhappily to the family's musical history.

As the play unfolds further, we discover the particularly poignant nature of the Charles family's struggle over the piano's power to simultaneously evoke painful memories and express their drive for freedom. In slavery times, Robert Sutter, the family's master, had bought the piano for his wife, paying for it by selling down the river two of his slaves, both direct ancestors of Berniece and Boy Willie. When Sutter's wife subsequently complained about the absence of two of her prized household domestics, her husband had ordered Berniece and Boy Willie's grandfather to carve images of those individuals into the piano's large legs. Instead, he went ahead and carved powerful images of many family members. The playwright describes these figures as conveying, "in the manner of African sculpture, mask-like figures resembling totems."[68]

Believing that if the old white master and his descendants continued to own the piano, they would effectively own an important part of the Charles family's history, they steal the instrument from Sutter, unleashing a series of mortally violent clashes in which still more family members die. Exiled from the South and persecuted in the North, the brother and sister struggle over the future of the piano in their family. Berniece finally triumphs by playing and singing a prayerful chant for help. The piano, a symbol of one family's African American history, remains where the coming generation may play on it as did their parents, grandparents, and great-grandparents.

Supporting characters in *The Piano Lesson* reveal further examples of the migrants' ambivalence about their involvement with the piano. Wining Boy, uncle of Boy Willie and Berniece, made a career as a gambler and blues pianist. Gambling and performing from town to town for more than twenty-five years, Wining Boy came to find the instrument and his involvement with it an intolerable burden. What seemed to bring spiritual freedom became a ball and chain as customers, often white ones, kept him laboring at the keyboard well past the point of exhaustion. Wining Boy loses the spiritual identity that he had earned with his piano blues and turns to African American history in search of his identity. He is portrayed as a blues pianist, but most of Pittsburgh's jazz pianists surely came to a similar crossroads in their own careers as musical entertainers. Levee, another character, had to court a white man in order to secure a recording contract—which turns out not to have been worth the moral compromises required to secure it.

Most jazz writers have assumed, and one can still argue, that Pittsburgh's famous jazz pianists became so accomplished, so artful in their playing, that their experiences at the keyboard far surpassed the relatively simple, repetitive hammering of juke joint piano laborers. Performing nationally and internationally brought a greater measure of pride and control over performances. This drive for artistic growth and major careers surely helped create and maintain the impulse to create jazz in the first place. Yet no matter how often and enthusiastically celebrated, jazz careers could not, in themselves, provide a solution to the spiritual and psychological consequences of enduring racial discrimination and white dominance in the jazz world.

The life histories of Earl Hines, Mary Lou Williams, Billy Strayhorn, and Erroll Garner reveal that even musicians of their stature could have made at best only a modest living playing in Pittsburgh. Too many local clubs paid only in drinks and meals. One reason that all of them left Pittsburgh had to do with the musicians' local, which reserved all of the more lucrative professional performance opportunities for white musicians. Although the *Courier*, the city's famous newspaper, provided a wonderful array of news from around the nation and dutifully reported the arrivals and departures of major jazz stars in Pittsburgh, the paper tended to report little on the activities of local musicians.

The *Courier*, however, did illuminate the plight of the city's unionized black musicians. It reported that Local 471 of the American Federation of Musicians was not permitted to broadcast from a certain local radio station unless payment for their services moved through the office of the white local before getting to the black musicians.[69] The *Courier* sharply criticized the local as "Jim Crow" and as "run by those who follow the will of the white local's President." Consequently, in Pittsburgh, blacks played mostly for black affairs. An inner circle of local African American musicians obtained just enough of the higher-paying jobs to entice a general compliance by blacks with a discriminatory system.[70]

The newspaper, moreover, concluded that the problem was regional in scope because in Washington, D.C., Cincinnati, Cleveland, and Dayton white musicians on the Columbia burlesque circuit refused to perform with traveling black musicians. Unionized white musicians wanted to retain control of the theater pit bands and therefore insisted that they had the right to grant permission to black orchestras to play in the pits of vaudeville theaters. As usual, the national organization of the A.F.M. refused to do anything to help its own (black) members.[71]

Relations between the segregated locals of the A.F.M. formed just one facet of a racially discriminatory musical world that also included white domination in the band-booking business, the recording business, radio broadcasting, and music publication. No matter how far or often they moved within the United States, African American jazz musicians discovered only more of the deeply painful and frustrating limitations that had set them in motion northward from the South after World War I. This maddening reality made a mockery of the Great Migration and ultimately provoked many jazz musicians to new forms of social, political, and psychological rebellion that would reveal the vulnerability of jazz as a form of interracial enterprise and communication.

The ambivalence of the jazz experience in general and within the lives of Pittsburgh's great piano improvisers often found expression in their strained relations with the Jewish promoter and booker Joe Glaser. The breathtaking professional careers of many jazz stars stemmed as much from this promoter's influence as from a spontaneous popular recognition of the musicians' keyboard command. In fact, the American public had to be wheedled by means of myriad manipulations into opening its ears and its pocketbooks. Glaser knew how to make popular stars out of great black musicians, but he, and he alone, decided which ones would receive the necessary promotion.

A comparison of the careers of Erroll Garner and Mary Lou Williams makes the point: Garner, like Louis Armstrong, got Glaser's star treatment and went on to national and international fame; Williams did not and went on to a bitter and unavailing struggle with Glaser. Williams's frustration with the Man's absolute power led her into some of the more radical black political movements of the 1940s and 1950s. Garner's good fortune led him into an exhausting touring schedule, relative wealth, and enormous popularity.

World War II brought further black outrage at the hypocritical way in which the United States treated its black fighting men and military nurses who risked their lives in the war against European fascism only to suffer from racial discrimination back home. African Americans who played jazz in the United States Navy at its Great Lakes Training Station, for example, experienced rigid racial segregation and abuse from their white officers as they learned about military music. The St. Louis riverboat trumpeter Clark Terry was among those who suffered this ongoing, official maritime racism.[72]

In the 1940s, just as the old Streckfus riverboats steamed to their last excursions, African national independence movements and black Islam began to stimulate a new awareness of black nationalism and Pan-Africanism among black American jazz musicians in general and those living in Pittsburgh in particular. In looking back on the riverboat jazz era from this new political and cultural point of view, jazz musicians could not help but be struck by the limits that had constrained their voyages of discovery on the inland waterways of the United States. The riverboat experience had been a wonderfully steady, long-lasting gig. The pay had been dependable. The opportunity to learn to read music had been invaluable. But the bitterness and disappointment felt by the excursion boat trumpeter Clarence Thornton and by the St. Louis jazz promoter and journalist Bennie Rodgers, editor of the *St. Louis American*, all the silences and diplomatic evasions of Louis Armstrong and Fate Marable concerning their respective struggles with Carl Mangan and the Streckfus brothers, the silence in Baby Dodd's autobiography about his brutal treatment at the hands of John Streckfus—all of the bravely borne bruises suffered while playing in the white man's riverine parade of power led the musicians into further, far longer, and far-flung journeys of discovery.

A sizeable group of jazz musicians who began their careers in Pittsburgh took an early lead in adopting new patterns of thought and sensibility that helped them travel physically, psychologically, intellectually, and aesthetically across the ocean waters to bring the African diaspora full circle back to West Africa. Among those who involved themselves to varying degrees in anticolonialism, Pan-Africanism, and Islam as these movements first swept African American communities in the United States during World War II were Mary Lou Williams, the vocalists Dakota Staton (Aliyah Rabia) and Billy Eckstine, the drummers Art Blakey (Abdullah ibn Buhaina) and Kenny Clarke (Liaqat Ali Salaam), and the pianist Fritz Jones (Ahmad Jamal).

Paul Robeson, whose outstanding musical career had received a major boost from his work in the theatrical and film versions of *Show Boat*, brought to Pittsburgh musicians a much greater awareness of African anticolonialism. Robeson's involvement with several future leaders of African and Indian independence movements while in England combined with his immense professional prestige among jazz musicians to draw Williams and a number of national stars to the anticolonialist, international perspective.[73] Many Pittsburgh musicians also responded to the new wave of Islam sweeping urban African American population centers. The Ahmadiyya movement, which in 1921 established the first North American Muslim newspaper, *Moslem Sunrise*, proselytized in Pittsburgh, Cleveland, Chicago, Kansas City, and Washington, D.C., and during the 1940s and 1950s drew increasing numbers of musicians into its fold.[74] For example, in becoming Ahmad Jamal, the young Pittsburgh pianist Fritz Jones took part of the name of Hazarat Mirza Ghulam Ahmad, the founder of the Ahmadiyya movement.

Local developments also spurred more embittered expressions of political awareness. The City of Pittsburgh's federally funded "urban renewal" of the Hill District became perhaps the most powerful of all the forces that brought major changes in the politics of jazz musicians. In the 1940s and early 1950s, the city, without consulting the residents involved, decided to raze the sooty and often decrepit buildings in the Lower Hill that had housed thousands of African Americans, later targeting all of the structures that had made up the cultural district of the Hill for more than thirty-five years. The decision took on a nasty racist coloration when, in 1943, City Councilman George E. Evans wrote that "approximately 90 per cent of the buildings in the area are substandard and have long outlived their usefulness, so there would be no social loss if they were all destroyed."[75]

Better reasons existed for the urban renewal of the Hill District: deteriorating neighborhood infrastructures and a highly publicized desire to build a world-class center for the arts were used as justifications. The district did, it was claimed, house the greatest tax delinquency in Pittsburgh and required the greatest portion of the city's tax funds to service and maintain.[76] As the 1950s rolled on, planners would increasingly concentrate their urban renewal efforts on Pittsburgh's serious lower-income housing shortage, a major problem aggravated by the redevelopment itself. City planners began by razing the Lower Hill residential district and thereby dispossessing thousands of blacks, who then crowded into the Upper Hill. This redevelopment displaced 1,239 African American families, 312 white families, and 16 businesses. In the face of racial discrimination, poor and dispossessed black people had little choice of new housing.

A glamorous center for the arts, a complex that was to have included two grand theaters, a combination opera house and symphony hall, and an arts museum that might in some measure have justified the loss of so many jazz clubs, was supposed to have been built behind the new Civic Center and to have brought to the city a cultural center of national stature. All such plans were abandoned. When, in the aftermath of the 1968 assassination of Martin Luther King in Memphis, a weeks' worth of major riots broke out in Pittsburgh's Hill District, the remaining residents declared Crawford Street the limit of any further redevelopment.

The destruction of the District and its Wylie Avenue jazz scene and the rise of Pan-Africanism, Islam, and black nationalism destroyed much of the remaining cultural confidence in the Great Migration, cast doubt on the efficacy of jazz in general as a way of life, and shone a harsh new political light on the segregationist politics and aesthetics of riverboat jazz. In the 1960s and 1970s world of interracial bitterness and recriminations, efforts to resurrect the excursion boat era on the Mississippi and Ohio rivers could only be seen as a step backward into an age of music, movement, and migration that had produced for black Americans false promises and broken dreams.

Epilogue

The Decline and Fall of Excursion Boat Jazz in St. Louis

The deaths of the major figures in riverboat jazz and accelerating cultural change in the United States put an end to the excursion boat era and its hot dance music. Fate Marable became ill in 1941 and, for the first summer in twenty-two years, did not play on a riverboat.[1] On February 10, 1941, Nat Storey organized a group of his former musicians that included Red Allen, Harry Dial, Zutty Singleton, Bob Bell, Jimmie Jones, Wilbur Curt, Kaiser Marshall, Earl Bostic, Al Snaer, Mouse Randolph, and Vernon King to hold a benefit for Marable in St. Louis.[2] Marable continued to play in St. Louis clubs but ultimately died of pneumonia in Homer G. Phillips Hospital on January 16, 1947. He had been the premier musician in riverboat jazz. Louis Armstrong passed away on July 6, 1971. He had been this idiom's greatest improviser. Joseph Streckfus left this earth on January 15, 1960. He, with his father, had ordered riverboat jazz into life; he promoted it for forty-two years.

But riverboat jazz also succumbed to vast changes in technology, race relations, cultural values, politics, governmental policies, and aesthetics. The era was swept away, leaving only a few isolated excursion and passenger boats on the Mississippi and the Ohio. As is so often the case with historical developments, this one can look inevitable. The Jim Crow racial policies of the riverboats that had seemed central to their symbolism had to go, and they did. The technological revolutions in land and water transportation as well as in heating and air conditioning combined with changing styles in popular music and jazz to leave the *Admiral* empty and silent, without motors to propel it, an old art deco ghost of the 1930s still tied up to the levee in St. Louis as this is written.

The invention and marketing of air conditioning in the 1920s led the way to the creation of a thoroughly artificial environment on board the *President* and the *Admiral*. The odors and warm, humid river breezes had always marred the idyll of the cooling river experience, but open-sided excursion boats had left passengers in much closer touch with the elements, their reveries of water, air, earth, fire, and music animating the river experience. The floating "pleasure palaces" became closed, air-conditioned amusement centers filled with every imaginable kind of arcade game, flight simulator, slot machine, bar, and restaurant, the old dance floor animated by blandly generic dance bands or increasingly highly amplified rock'n'roll combos. In this last regard, Streckfus Steamers held out against rock'n'roll for many years, indicating thereby that the more decorous, increasingly old-fashioned dance music of the 1920s, 1930s and 1940s had played an important role in generating the ambiance they imagined for river excursions.

At the same time, the steady development of the automobile and the spread of the highway system offered the public another, more individualistic technology for finding cooling breezes. Cars, moreover, solved the major complaint that youngsters had always made about the unbearable slowness of the excursion boats. A car allowed each driver to be the captain of his own errant land adventures. Television, moreover, brought entertainment into private homes that were, in their turn, increasingly air-conditioned in the 1950s and 1960s. As middle-class homes became entertainment centers, fewer people bothered to take river cruises.

The automobile, of course, also encouraged the creation of suburban living far from the sewage-filled rivers. What had once been vibrant downtown nightlife centers close to the rivers became office areas by day and deserted canyons by night. The history of St. Louis since 1920 has seen the steady movement of the population westward, away from the Mississippi. Even the Mercantile Library, formerly housed in a marvelous, stately old building in the downtown area, moved west to the University of Missouri's St. Louis campus, which is under the major glide paths of commercial, military, and private airplanes.

In the name of safety, the United States government ultimately put an end to the converted wooden packet boats that made up the majority of Streckfus Steamers' vessels. In 1934, the well-known oceanic excursion steamer *Morro Castle*, plying the Atlantic and the Caribbean between major eastern seaboard cities and Cuba, burned to the waterline with major loss of life. Subsequent investigations concluded that profit-driven inattention to basic safety procedures had accounted for the disaster.[3]

Echoes of this tragedy quickly made their way into the yearly minutes of Streckfus Steamers.[4] President Joseph Streckfus predicted that the Bureau of

Steam Boat Inspection and Congress would demand such expensive new safety measures as sprinkler systems. He admitted that their own company in particular would attract the government's attention because they carried passengers on no fewer than four wooden vessels, all well over twenty years old. The Bureau of Steam Boat Inspection had specifically mentioned that all such obsolete vessels should be junked. By 1938, the Bureau of Maritime Inspection and Navigation Service in Washington had instituted rigid new rules to rid the waters of old wooden vessels.

Several factors hastened the shrinkage of the company most responsible for promoting riverboat jazz. In 1933, the refitting of the passenger steamer *Cincinnati* as an all-steel excursion boat renamed the *President* had been completed, and this vessel went into operation the same year, affording a healthy profit in that dark depression year. In 1936, Streckfus Steamers purchased the steel-hulled railroad car transfer vessel *Albatross* from the Yazoo and Mississippi Valley Railroad Company. During the following years, at major expense, the company rebuilt the vessel into the *Admiral*, a 374-foot, all-steel excursion steamer that was to carry the company's flag for more than forty years. This boat was the first ever built under the stringent safety regulations of the Steamboat Inspection Service.[5] The *Admiral* went into operation on June 12, 1940.

Once the wooden boats had been retired, instead of deploying five of the largest vessels on the inland waterways, they now had only two such behemoths, the *President* and the *Admiral*. They also still had the cherished but increasingly waterlogged *Capitol*. As time went on, the company did create several much smaller excursion vessels such as the *Huck Finn* and the *Samuel Clemens*, which plied the waters of St. Louis and New Orleans.

With the end of World War II, a variety of new federal regulations and taxes cut into the old ways of making a profit. The Interstate Commerce Commission, the United States Fair Labor Standards Act (which mandated higher wage levels for all employees), Social Security taxes, sales taxes, franchise taxes, state income taxes, union difficulties, and the National Labor Relations Board all appeared to overburden Streckfus Steamers.[6]

At about the same time, the solidarity of the Streckfus brothers began to fall apart. The neo-Germanic immigrant tradition had favored the powerful Joseph Streckfus, who had inherited leadership of the family corporation on his father's death. Joseph so deeply entrenched himself both at the head of the company and in the civic life of St. Louis that his brothers Roy and Verne moved to New Orleans. By mutual consent, they took the *President* and the *Capitol* with them. Legally, however, their brother Joseph retained control of the company, and, of course, of the *Admiral* and the smaller vessels. When, by 1943, it became clear that the old *Capitol*'s hull had rotted out and that the superstructure presented an ever-increasing fire hazard, Roy, who captained the vessel in New Orleans, applied to Joe for help in paying for the necessary repairs. Joseph refused. Roy and Verne then threatened to split their New Orleans operations off from Streckfus Streamers, Inc. While ignoring their threats and demands, Joseph urged them to remember and to bless their father and mother, whose infinite wisdom had placed him, not his brothers, in control of a company that had always presented a united front to the world.[7]

In scolding his brothers Joseph also admitted that the company was in trouble with the Internal Revenue Service because of its financial practices. When incorporation had created Streckfus Steamers, Inc., the four brothers had become the chief officers of the company and had limited the number of its shareholders to members of the family, their close friends, and merchants and shippers from St. Paul and St. Louis. During its first thirty-eight years, the company's stockholders had invested only $179, 975 in Streckfus Steamers. In addition to the ownership of company stock by family members, the enterprise had fashioned a profit-sharing plan by which Joseph and his three brothers accepted low salaries supplemented by a percentage of the company's profits. Thus, in most years, each brother earned a salary, a percentage of the profits, and dividends. The company thus limited its overhead expenses during years of economic depression and drought.

Joseph wrote to his brothers in 1943: "U.S. Tax Court [is] investigating that all four brothers are in one and the same family, and all are directors of the company, and I have been advised by more than one attorney that our set-up was wrong in that respect, that should we have difficulty such as we are now having in the Tax Court, our corporation will be considered a family affair operating under the cloak of a corporation."[8] Using this pretext, Joseph then fired Roy and Verne. In subsequent family negotiations, Roy and Verne took over as masters of the *President* and the *Admiral*.

Years afterward, Roy became head of Streckfus Steamers. When he died, Verne became president but refused to live in St. Louis. He turned the company over to Roy's son William S. Streckfus. William S. and his brother John Curran Streckfus captained the *Admiral* and the *President*, thereby becoming the third generation of the family to captain family-owned excursion boats. William S. Streckfus, said to be a dictatorial personality, was pushed out of the company in 1979 in a dispute with William Carroll, son-in-law of Joseph Streckfus. Carroll remained in charge of the company's St. Louis operations thereafter, also becoming the custodian of the family's papers.[9]

But in the period after the Korean War, as air conditioners on land radically diminished the public's need for river breezes and air conditioning on board the *Admiral* traded much of the contact with the elements for artificial refrigeration, a movement to correct the fundamental racial injustice of re-fusing to admit African Americans to restaurants, theaters, and excursion boats grew into a powerful political movement too insistent to be ignored. The intertwined cultural patterns of the swan complex and riverboat jazz would never be the same.

African American protests against segregation in public places included excursion boats in a broad range of public accommodations that included ho-tels, motels, theaters, taverns, beauty parlors, barbershops, nursing homes, and bowling alleys. Such protests were generated by the formation of the Committee of Racial Equality, organized in 1942. Bernice Fisher, a young Chicagoan, brought information to St. Louis about CORE's work to end seg-regation there in public accommodations. She inspired a small group led by Irv and Maggie Dagen to organize the St. Louis chapter of CORE in 1947.[10] Following Mahatma Gandhi's principles of direct nonviolent resistance to injustice and inhumanity, the St. Louis chapter of CORE staged a long fight to open public accommodation to minorities. Their peaceful but insistent public demonstrations lasted for thirteen years (1949–1961), during which the *St. Louis Post-Dispatch* reported nothing about them.[11] In 1949, efforts were made to get the Board of Aldermen to pass a Public Accommodations Act. Those efforts failed that year and every year for twelve years thereafter before segregation was finally outlawed in the city on July 1, 1961.[12]

In the name of continued racial segregation, in 1961 Streckfus Steamers filed suit to enjoin enforcement of the new law. The company argued that its services to the public extended beyond the city limits of St. Louis into St. Louis County and Jefferson County.[13] The company also claimed that allowing en-trance to large groups of blacks and whites would promote violence on board, where no police force existed to restore order. Small numbers of black citizens led by Eugene Davenport of 5373 Wells Avenue in St. Louis tested the com-pany's sincerity by standing in line for admittance to a moonlight cruise on Sat-urday, July 8, 1961. They were refused admittance to the excursion boat. Roy Streckfus was quoted as saying that company policy remained one of "contin-uing to refuse admission to Negroes."[14] He insisted that his main concern in-volved the danger of "rowdyism." On August 16, 1961, three more young African American citizens were refused admission to an evening cruise.[15]

In April of the following year, however, Streckfus Steamers dropped its suit for an injunction declaring the Public Accommodations Law unconstitutional, and Roy Streckfus let it be known that any person "presenting himself in an orderly manner" would be admitted aboard the *Admiral* as soon as the excur-sion season recommenced in June. The City of St. Louis had opposed the Streckfus family's position on racial discrimination, arguing that the *Admiral* was a common carrier in interstate commerce and was prohibited by federal law from denying services on racial or religious grounds.[16] In St. Louis, at any rate, the old hidden transcript of riverboat jazz had come to an end.

The long fight for equality in public accommodations and Streckfus Steamers' determined resistance to such democratic reforms left the company in a far weaker position when the time came to apply to the City of St. Louis for help. That time arrived in 1979–1980, when the excursion boat company announced that the riveted steel seams of the *Admiral*'s hull had rotted out, requiring more expensive repairs than it could sustain. The Boatman's National Bank of St. Louis and the city's First National Bank refused to loan the necessary money, saying that the problem was far more extensive than announced.[17] The old argument that excursion boats played a major role in the cultural and civic life of river cities was harder to sustain when so many members of the Board of Aldermen recalled the long history of racial segregation on the riverboats. No city bonds were floated to save the *Admiral*. For a time, the art deco steamer was converted into a shopping mall, but it has since remained empty. In 1991, the *President* was converted into a casino and tied up in Davenport. In 2001 it was removed to Vicksburg, Mississippi, and moored in a diversion canal. Like the *President*, the following generation of Streckfus captains also moved south of St. Louis. Robert Streckfus Sr., Robert Streckfus Jr., and Steven Streckfus became ship pilots between Baton Rouge and New Orleans.

For the past twenty-five years, the sounds of hot dance music as played by Fate Marable, Charles Creath, Dewey Jackson, and Walter Pichon have been gone from the river. Riverboat jazz, however, reappears in the form of small traditional jazz combos that perform on the Greene Line and also on the *Natchez*, which runs excursions out of New Orleans. The *Natchez* is 265 feet long and 44 feet wide, and the United States Coast Guard and the American Bureau of Shipping approved her construction. She can accommodate sixteen hundred passengers.

Whether the limitation of riverboat jazz to New Orleans as a regular phenomenon is a cause for sorrow or satisfaction involves complex questions. On one hand, the rivers were far more beautiful when the old stream paddle wheelers plied them. Coal barges keep a lower profile, but ballroom dancing would seem inappropriate on such vessels. In beautifying the inland waterways with historical superstructures and jazz, the return of excursion boats might unleash a clean-up campaign to honor the country's great rivers. The possibilities are there.

But on the other hand, the excursion boats and their racial policies left many African Americans and their allies fearful and disgusted. It bears remembering that the trumpeter Perch Thornton cherished awards he had received from a black jazz society and unequivocally denied that he ever played what he considered jazz on the Streckfus excursion boats. One should not forget W. C. Handy's anecdote about the "strange tortured sounds" that William Malone, a Streckfus musician, emitted during his sleep every night, as if the woe of the entire world had rolled upon him. The interstice of riverboat jazz was caught tellingly by Ralph Ellison in his classic novel *Invisible Man*. His character lies in bed deep into the night listening to the call of a whippoorwill. He recalls his childhood home "longside the river," where he often looked at the "lights comin' up from the water" and listened to the sounds of the boats movin' along. In his recollection, the music of the "musicianers on them boats" melded with the night calls and whistles of birds: "Well that's the way the boats used to sound. Comin' close to you from far away. First one would be comin' to you when you almost asleep and it sounded like somebody hittin' at you slow with a big shiny pick. You see the pick-point comin' straight at you, comin' slow, too, and you can't dodge."[18]

Just as he is about to be stabbed, the dagger of riverboat music turns into the sound of somebody "breakin' little bottles of all kinda colored glass." That breaking sound still advances on him but begins to look like "a wagonful of watermelons, . . . one of them young juicy melons split wide open a-layin' all spread out and cool and sweet . . . like it's waitn' just for you. . . . And you could hear the sidewheels splashin' like they don't want to wake nobody up; and us, me and the gal, would lay there feelin' like we was rich folks and them boys on the boats would be playin' sweet as good peach brandy wine. Then the boats would be past, and the lights would be gone from the window and the music would be goin' too."[19]

The passing of the riverboat and its music seemed like the titillation of a plump woman in a red dress "kinda switchin' her tail" at you before disappearing from sight. The boat, the music, the watermelon, and the woman were bewitching dreams that hid a terrible shiny dagger plunging toward your eyes. The boat and the music contained a threatening power, and one would want to think twice about bringing back something like that.

Appendix A

Excursion Boat Musicians

Musician's Name	Instrument	Band/Leader	Excursion Boat
Alvin Alcorn	Trumpet	Marable	Streckfus Line
Ed Allen	Trumpet	E. Allen	*Capitol*
Henry "Red" Allen	Trumpet	Marable	Streckfus Line
James Allen	Trumpet	M. Bruckmann	*President*
Harry Amidon	Tenor saxophone	Burke and Webb	*Capitol*
Louis Armstrong	Trumpet	Marable	*Sidney*
John Arnold	Piano	Washington	*St. Paul*
Boyd Atkins	Violin	Marable	*Capitol*
Bert Bailey	Tenor saxophone	Marable	Streckfus Line
Howard Baker	Trumpet	Marable	*Washington*
Richard Baltz	Trumpet	M. Bruckmann	*President*
Danny Barker	Banjo, guitar	Marable	Streckfus Line
Dave Bartholomew	Trumpet	Pichon, Bartholomew	*Capitol*
Bix Beiderbecke	Cornet, piano	Plantation Jazz Orchestra	*Majestic*
Harvey Berry	Violin	Berry	*Majestic*
Druie Bess	Trombone	Marable	*St. Paul*
Bill Bieberback	Cornet	Plantation Orchestra	*Capitol*
Cliff Birdlong	Alto saxophone	Campbell	*St. Paul*
James Blanton	Bass viol	Marable	*Washington*
Thorton Blue	Piano, reeds	Creath, Marable	*St. Paul*
Peter Bocage	Trumpet, violin	Marable	*Capitol*
Earl Bostic	Alto saxophone	Creath, Marable	*Washington*

Musician's Name	Instrument	Band/Leader	Excursion Boat
Barnet Bradley	Violin	Marable	*St. Paul*
George Brashear	Trombone	Marable	*Capitol*
Wellman Braud	Bass viol	Marable	Streckfus Line
James Brecheur	Trombone	Marable	*Capitol*
Don Brink	Alto saxophone	M. Bruckmann	*President*
Arnold Brown	Banjo	Marable	*Capitol*
Ray Brown	Trombone	Pichon	*Capitol*
Red Brown	Banjo	Campbell	*St. Paul*
Ronald Brown		Witherspoon	*Avalon*
Sidney Brown	Bass viol	S. Morgan	*Capitol*
Len Bruckmann	Bass viol	M. Bruckmann	*President*
M. Bruckmann	Tenor saxophone	M. Bruckmann	*President*
Walter Brudy			
Polk Burke	Drums	Burke and Webb	*Capitol*
Floyd Campbell	Drums, vocals	Marable, Creath	*St. Paul*
Jimmy Cannon	Clarinet	Berry	*Majestic*
Earl Carruthers	Reeds, vocals	Jackson, Marable	Streckfus Line
Robert Carter			
Floyd Casey	Drums	Marable, Jackson	Streckfus Line
Sam Casimir	Banjo	Pichon	*Capitol*
Tony Catalano	Trumpet	Catalano, Marable	*Capitol*
Eddie Cherie	Tenor saxophone	Perez	*Sidney*
Cliff Cochran	Sop. and alto sax	Jackson	*Capitol, St. Paul*
Hal Conger	Banjo	Wrixon	*Capitol*
Grant Cooper	Trombone	Creath	*St. Paul*
Larry Covell	Tenor saxophone	M. Bruckmann	*President*
Charles Creath	Trumpet	Creath, Marable	*St. Paul*
Manuel Crusto	Saxophone	Pichon	*Capitol*
Ed Culligan	Saxophone	Elde	*Washington*
Johnny Dave	Banjo	S. Morgan	*Capitol*
Leonard Davis	Trumpet	Marable	*St. Paul*
Sidney Desvignes	Trumpet	Marable, Piron	Streckfus Line
Harry Dial	Drums, vocals	Marable	*J.S. Deluxe*
Kimball Dial			
Johnny Dodds	Clarinet, saxophone	Marable	*St. Paul*
Warren Dodds	Drums	Marable	Streckfus Line
Irving Douroux	Trombone	Pichon	*Capitol*
Albert Ducange			

Musician's Name	Instrument	Band/Leader	Excursion Boat
Honore Dutrey	Trombone	Marable	Streckfus Line
Sam Dutrey	Reeds	Marable	Streckfus Line
Clarence Elder	Banjo	Elder	*Washington*
Harold Estes	Saxophone	Six Aces	*St. Paul*
Horace Eubanks	Clarinet	Creath	*St. Paul*
Carlisle Evans	Piano	Evans, Catalano	*Capitol*
Laddie Fair		Witherspoon	*Avalon*
Wilbur Fisher	Trombone	M. Bruckmann	*President*
Willie Ford	Reeds	Marable	*Capitol*
Abbey Foster	Drums	Celestin	*Capitol*
George Foster	Bass viol, tuba	Marable, Creath	*Sidney, St. Paul*
Willie Foster	Banjo	Marable	*St. Paul*
Earl Fouche	Saxophone	S. Morgan	*Capitol*
Leon Goodson	Alto saxophone	E. Jefferson	*Idlewild*
William Guer	Drums	Imperial Aces	*G.W. Hill*
Clarence Hall	Saxophones	Celestin	*Capitol*
Cranston Hamilton	Piano	Creath	Streckfus Line
Grant Harris	Clarinet	Wrixon	*Capitol*
William Harris	Saxophone	Six Aces	*St. Paul*
Jane Hemenway	Piano	Jackson	Streckfus Line
Gerald Hopson			
Joe Howard	Trumpet	Marable	*Sidney*
Willie Humphrey	Clarinet	Marable, Pirson	Streckfus Line
Eugene Hutt	Trombone	Marable	*J.S. Deluxe*
Dewey Jackson	Trumpet	Matable, Jackson	Streckfus Line
Ike Jefferson	Tenor saxophone	Marable, Allen	*Sidney, Capitol*
James Jeter			
Eddie Johnson	Piano	Johnson	*Idlewild*
Jimmy Johnson	Bass viol	Perez	*Sidney*
Cliff Jones	Banjo	Marable	*Capitol*
David Jones	Mellophone	Marable	*Capitol*
Henry Julian	Saxophone	Desvignes	*Island Queen*
Gus Kelly	Trumpet	Celestin	*Capitol*
Paul Kenestrick	Piano	Elder	*Washington*
R. Kerschner		Elder	*Washington*
Henry Kimball	Bass viol, tuba	Marable	*Capitol*
Jeanette Kimball	Piano	Celestin	*Capitol*
Narvin Kimball	Banjo	Piron, Celestin	Streckfus Line

Musician's Name	Instrument	Band/Leader	Excursion Boat
Leon King	Trombone	Jackson, Marable	*St. Paul*
Al Knappe	Violin	Knappe	*East St. Louis*
Ransom Knowling	Bass viol	Desvignes	*Island Queen*
Red Koppman		Koppman	*Island Queen*
Jack Lamont	Trumpet	Pichon	*Capitol*
Tom Landfear	Violin	Burke and Leins	*J.S.*
Harry Lang	Saxophone	Pichon	*Capitol*
Harvey Lankford	Trombone	E. Allen	*Capitol*
Rex Leins	Saxophone	Burke and Leins	*J.S.*
Tick Leins	Piano	Burke and Leins	*J.S.*
Sammy Long		Marable, Jackson	*Streckfus Line*
Chuck Lotspeick	Piano	Imperial Acts	*G.W. Hill*
Burroughs Lovingood	Piano	Marable	*Streckfus Line*
James Madison		Witherspoon	*Avalon*
Simeon Marrero	Brass bass	Celestin	*Capitol*
Earl Martin	Drums	E. Jefferson	*Idlewild*
Ed Martin			
Norman Mason	Reeds	Marable, Allen	*Sidney, Capitol*
Bill Matthews	Trombone	Celestin	*Capitol*
Charles McCurdy			
Al Morgan	Bass viol, vocals	Desvignes, Marable	*Island Queen, Capitol*
Albert Morgan	Bass viol	Marable	
Andrew Morgan	Saxophone	S. Morgan	*Capitol*
Isaiah Morgan	Trumpet	S. Morgan	*Capitol*
Sam Morgan	Trumpet	Morgan	*Capitol*
Jelly Roll Morton	Piano	Morton	*Washington*
Robert Muse	Drums	Creath	*St. Paul*
Myron Neal	Saxophone	Evans, Catalano	*Capitol*
Louis Nelson	Trombone	Desvignes	*Island Queen*
Joseph Nevils			
Singleton Palmer	Bass viol	Jackson, Jefferson	*Idlewild*
Jerome Don Pasquall	Reeds	Marable	*Streckfus Line*
Pat Patterson	Banjo	Creath	*St. Paul*
Manuel Perez	Cornet	Marable	*Capitol*
Gus Perryman	Piano	Lankford	*Capitol*
Walter Pichon	Piano	Pichon	*Washington*
Alphonse Picou	Clarinet	Celestin	*Capitol*

Musician's Name	Instrument	Band/Leader	Excursion Boat
Hayes Pillars	Saxophone	Jeter, Pillars	Streckfus Line
Ralph Porter			
Irving Puggsly	Piano	Creath	*St. Paul*
Teddy Purnell	Alto saxophone	Desvignes	*Capitol*
Irving Randolph	Trumpet	Marable, Mason	Streckfus Line
William Ridgley	Trombone	Marable	Streckfus Line
William Rollins			
Robert Ross			
Joe Rouzan	Saxophones	Celestin	*Capitol*
John St. Cyr	Banjo	Marable, Allen	*Sidney, Capitol*
Vertna Saunders	Trumpet	Marable, Creath	*President*
Emmanuel Sayles			
Al Sears			
Eugene Sedric	Reeds	Marable, Allen	*Sidney, Capitol*
Percy Sevier	Saxophone	Desvignes	*Island Queen*
Elijah Shaw			
Robert Shoffner	Trumpet	Creath	*St. Paul*
Zutty Singleton	Drums	Marable, Creath	Streckfus Line
Talmadge Smith	Saxophones	Marable, Johnson	*Washington*
Albert Snaer	Trumpet	Jackson, Marable	Streckfus Line
Walter Stanley			
Thomas Starks			
Nathaniel Storey	Trombone	Marable	*Capitol*
Clark Terry	Trumpet	Marable	Streckfus Line
Joe Thomas	Vocals	Celestin	*Capitol*
Walter Thomas	Reeds	Allen, Marable	*Capitol*
Clarence Thornton	Trumpet	Pichon	*Capitol*
William Tomlin			
Alphonso Trent	Piano	Trent	Streckfus Line
Gene Ware	Trumpet	Desvignes	*Island Queen*
Bennie Washington	Drums	Six Aces	*St. Paul*
Frank Watkins	Saxophone	Creath	*St. Paul*
Andrew Webb	Cornet	Six Aces	*St. Paul*
Amos White	Trumpet	Marable	Streckfus Line
Cecil White	Bass viol	Campbell	*St. Paul*
Marcellus Wilson			
Carl Woods			
John Young			

Appendix B

River Songs and Tunes

Across the River
Across the Wide Missouri
All Along the River
Along the Mississippi Shore
Anything Is Nice If It's from Dixieland
As Long as the River Flows On
As the Wild River Rises
At the Levee on Revival Day
At the Mississippi Cabaret
At the River Front

Beale Street Blues
Beale Street Mama
Beautiful Ohio
Bend of the River
Big River
Black Bottom
Blue River
By an Old Southern River
By a Quiet Stream
By a Rippling Stream
By the Bend of the River
By the Millstream
By the Mississippi

By the River
By the Stream

Cabin on the Mississippi Shore
Cincinnati
Cincinnati Dancing Pig
Cincinnati Lou
Cottage by the River
Cry Me a River

Dancing on the Mississippi Landing
Davenport Blues
Deep River
Deep River Blues
Do You Know What It Means to Miss New Orleans?
Down Around the River at the Dixie Jubilee
Down by the Old Mill Stream
Down by the River
Down by the Riverside
Down the Mississippi
Down the River
Down the River of Golden Dreams
Down Where the Rivers Meet
Down Where the Swanee River Flows
Dream River
Dreamy River
Drifting Down the Dreamy Ol' Ohio
Drifting Down the River of Dreams
Dusky Stevedore

East St. Louis
Echoes from the Mississippi

Float Me Down the River
Floatin' Down That Ol' Green River
Floating Down a Moonlight Stream
Floating Down the Ohio
Floating Down the River
Floating Down to Cotton Town

Floating Slowly Down the River
The Four Rivers

Gently Lead Me by the River
Goin' from the Cotton Fields
Golden River
Green River
Gulf Coast Blues

I've Been Floating Down the Old Green River
I Want to Be in Dixie

Jazzin' the Cotton Town Ball

Lazy Mississippi
Lazy River
Lazy River Croon
Lazy River Reverie
Let's Go down the River
Levee Blues
Levee Camp Moan
Levee Lou
Levee Low Down
Levee Lullaby
Little River
Loadin' Up the Mandy Lee
Lonely River
Lonesome River
Love Songs of the Nile

Ma Mississippi Belle
Market Street Blues
Meet Me by the River
Meet Me in St. Louis
Memphis Blues
Memphis Bound
Memphis by Morning
Memphis Guide
Memphis in June
Memphis Mamie

Memphis Man
Memphis Maybe Man
Memphis Shake
Memphis, Tennessee
Memphis Yodel
M-i-s-s-i-s-s-i-p-p-i
Mississippi Basin
Mississippi Boat Race
Mississippi Boat Song
Mississippi Cabaret
Mississippi Dream Boat
Mississippi Flood
Mississippi Mud
Mississippi River Blues
Mississippi River (Keep on Croonin')
Mississippi Shore
Mississippi Stoker
Mississippi Valley Blues
Miss the Mississippi and You
The Moon Fell in the River
Moonlight Bay
Moonlight on the Mississippi
Moonlight on the River
Moon on the River
Moon River
Moon River Rapids
My Mississippi Missus Misses Me
My River Home

The Natchez and the Robert E. Lee
Natchez Ball
New Orleans
New Orlean Blues
New Orleans Bump
New Orleans Hop-Scop Blues
New Orleans Low-Down
New Orleans Medley
New Orleans Parade
New Orleans Shags
New Orleans Shuffle

New Orleans Stomp
New Orleans Twist
New Orleans Wiggle
New River Train
No More Rivers to Cross

O'er the River
Oh, Bury Me Down by the River's Side
Oh, Mystical River!
Ol' Man River
Old Mississippi River
Old St. Louis Blues
On the Banks of the Great Mississippi
On the Banks of the Wabash, Far Away
On the Levee, by the River Side
On the Mississippi
On the Wild, Wide Mississippi
On the River
Our Dream by the River
Our Home by the River of Life
Out on the Moon-lit River

Papa, Come Help Me Across the Dark River
Peaceful as a River's Flow
Pittsburgh, Pa.

Rainbow on the River
Rainbow River
Ready for the River
Red River Blues
Red River Valley
Red River Valley Mother
Rhythm of the River
Rhythm on the River
Rhythm River
Riding for the River
Riding up the River Road
The River and Me
The River and the Sea
River Bed Blues

River Blues
River Boat
River Boats
Riverboat Shuffle
River, Do You Remember?
River Girl
River God
River Home
River in the Valley
The River Is Free
River Man
River Night
River of Life
River of No Return
River of Romance
River of Smoke
River of Sorrow
River of Tears
River Pays Me No Mind
River Reverie
River, River
River Road
River's Edge
Riverside Blues
River Sings a Song
Rivers of Living Water
River Song
The River's Takin' Care of Me Now
River, Stay Away from My Door
Rock-a-Bye River
Rogue River Valley
Rollin' Down the River
Roll, Jordan, Roll
Roll on, Mississippi
Roll on, Mississippi, Roll On
Roustabout

Sailing on the Robert E. Lee
St. Louis Blues
St. Louis Breakdown

St. Louis Gal

St. Louis Holiday

St. Louis Serenade

St. Louis Shuffle

St. Louis Tickle

St. Louis Wiggle Rhythm

St. Louis Woman

Selections from *Show Boat*

Shanty Boat on the Mississippi

Showboat

Showboat Shuffle

Shreveport Stomp

Silver River

Sleepy Ol' River

Sleepy River

Slow River

Song of the 1927 Mississippi Flood

Song of the River

Southbound Water

Star Light on the River

Steamboat Bill

Steamboat Blues

Steamboat Man Blues

Steamboat Mississippi

Steamboat Rag

Steamboat Stomp

Steamin' and Beamin'

Stevedore Stomp

Stevedore's Serenade

Summer Night on the River

Sunny River

Swanee River

Swan River Polka

Sweet Mississippi

Take Me to the River

That's Where the South Begins

There Is Peace Beyond the River

They Call It the Dixie Blues

They've Sold Me Down the River

Underneath the Cotton Moon
Up the River

Wabash Blues
Wabash Moon
Wabash Stomp
Waitin' for the *Robert E. Lee*
Waiting Down by the Mississippi Shore
Walkin' by the River
Wanderer's Dream
Way Down upon the Swanee River
Way Down Yonder in New Orleans
Weary River
We're Afloat on the River
We Sat by the River, You and I
When It's Sleepy Time Down South
When the Steamboats on the Swanee Whistle Ragtime
When We Meet Beyond the River
Where the Lazy Mississippi Flows
Where the Lazy River Goes By
Wild River

Notes

Introduction

    1. William Ivy Hair, *Carnival of Fury: Robert Charles and the New Orleans Race Riot of 1900* (Baton Rouge: Louisiana State University Press, 1986), 70.

    2. I take this phrase from Gaston Bachelard, who likens this psychological state to staring at a log fire in a fireplace. Bachelard, *The Psychoanalysis of Fire*, trans. Alan C. M. Ross (Boston: Beacon Press, 1964), 3.

    3. Norbury L. Wayman, *Life on the River: A Pictorial History of the Mississippi, the Missouri, and the Western River System* (New York: Crown Publishers, 1971), chap. 2.

    4. Alev Lytle Croutier, *Taking the Waters: Spirit, Art, Sensuality* (New York: Abbeville Press, 1992), 51, 61.

    5. Philip Dray, *At the Hands of Persons Unknown: The Lynching of Black America* (New York: Random House, 2002), 254.

    6. This way of explaining the cultural positioning of jazz musicians on the river begins with Homi Bhabha's use of the word "interstice" to describe the cultural position of an immigrant still at the traveling stage. Such a person lives somewhere between his point of departure and the viewpoint of his host country. Bhabha emphasizes the originality in this intermediate cultural position that allows the migrant to creatively juxtapose elements from past and present cultures. For the excursion boat audiences, my terminology derives from the work of Victor Turner, who uses the adjective "liminal" to describe the emotional power of music and dance to those who feel adrift between opposing factions in times of radical social change. Such individuals symbolically reaffirm social order in music and dance. Liminality is a "threshold" experience in the sense that one anticipates what is emerging without yet knowing it well. Homi Bhabha, "Unpacking My Library . . . Again," in *The Post-colonial Question: Common Skies, Divided Horizons*, ed. Iain Chambers and Lidia Curti (New York: Routledge, 1996), 199–212; Victor Turner, *Dramas, Fields, and Metaphors: Symbolic Action in Human Society* (Ithaca: Cornell University Press, 1974), 29–56, 272–286; Turner, *From Ritual to Theater: The Human Seriousness of Play* (New York: PAJ Publications,

1982), 20–60. According to these theories, jazz flourishes in interstitial locations where audiences feel liberated from their workaday identities and poised on the brink of some exciting new identity.

7. Jonathan Raban, *Old Glory: An American Voyage* (New York: Simon and Shuster, 1981).

8. Zuckerkandl is quoted in Nathaniel Mackey, "Sound and Sentiment, Sound and Symbol," in *The Jazz Cadence of American Culture*, ed. Robert O'Meally (New York: Columbia University Press, 1998), 626.

9. Walter Donaldson, *Changes* (New York: Leo Feist, 1927).

10. Victor Zuckerkandl, *Sound and Symbol: Music and the External World* (Princeton: Princeton University Press, 1969), 169–174, explains the tension between meter and rhythm as an opposition between machine and human life.

11. Edna Ferber, *Show Boat* (Garden City, N.Y.: Doubleday, Page, 1926).

12. John M. Barry, *Rising Tide: The Great Mississippi River Flood of 1927 and How It Changed America* (New York: Touchstone Books, 1998); Pete Daniel, *Deep'n As It Come: The 1927 Mississippi River Flood* (New York: Oxford University Press, 1977).

13. Ferber is quoted in Juda Bennett, *The Passing Figure: Racial Confusion in Modern American Literature* (New York: Peter Lang, 1996), 74–75.

14. Robin Breon, "*Show Boat:* The Revival, the Racism," *Theater and Drama Review* 39, no. 2 (Summer 1995): 86–105; Breon, "Show Boat: The Past Revisits the Present," *Canadian Theatre Review* 79–80 (Fall 1994): 70–79; Lauren Berlant, "*Pax Americana:* The Case of *Show Boat*," in *Cultural Institutions of the Novel*, ed. Diedre Lynch and William B. Warner (Durham, N.C.: Duke University Press, 1996), 399–422.

15. This praise was uniform and plentiful; see Philip R. Evans and Linda K. Evans, *Bix: The Leon Bix Beiderbecke Story* (Bakersfield, Calif.: Prelike Press, 1998), 70; John Knoepfle, interview with Sid Dawson, n.d., Inland Waterways Collection, Cincinnati Public Library; Peg Meyer, *Backwoods Jazz in the Twenties* (Cape Girardeau: Southeast Missouri State University Press, 1989), 53; Alan Bates and Clarke Hawley, *Moonlight at 8:30: The Excursion Boat Story* (Louisville, Ky.: Alan Bates and Clarke Hawley, 1994).

16. John Russell David, "Tragedy in Ragtime: Black Folktales from St. Louis" (Ph.D. diss., St. Louis University, 1976, 87–92); Cecil Brown, *Stagolee Shot Billy* (Cambridge: Harvard University Press, 2003), chap. 11.

17. Peter Linebaugh and Marcus Redicker write of the "organization of many thousands of workers into transatlantic circuits of commodity exchange" in their impressive article "The Many-Headed Hydra: Sailors, Slaves, and the Atlantic Working Class in the Eighteenth Century," *Journal of Historical Sociology* 3, no. 3 (September 1990): 226. See also David Chevan, "Riverboat Music from St. Louis and the Streckfus Steamboat Line," *Black Music Research Journal* 9, no. 2 (Fall 1989): 153–180.

18. Gerald Early, introduction to *Black Heartland: African American Life, the Middle West, and the Meaning of American Regionalism*, African and Afro-American Studies Occasional Papers, vol. 1, no. 2 (xxxx), 1–3.

19. James C. Scott, *Domination and the Arts of Resistance: Hidden Transcripts* (New Haven: Yale University Press, 1990), 58.

Chapter One

1. Frederick Way, *The Log of the Betsy Ann* (New York: McBride, 1933), 3.

2. "Rhine and Mississippi," *Waterways Journal*, September 28, 1918, 1–2.

3. Ibid.

4. Manuscript journal of Margaret Ann Streckfus (1880–1965), William Carroll/Streckfus Family Papers, Maritime Library, University of Missouri at St. Louis.

5. *St. Louis Globe-Democrat*, April 12, 1945; "Streckfus Quit Grocery for Boating," *Quad-City Times*, March 23, 1980, 1C, 4C.

6. *Waterways Journal*, December 22, 1894, 8; April 20, 1895, 8; October 26, 1895, 4.

7. *Waterways Journal*, May 12, 1900, 4.

8. "A Fine River Packet," *Waterways Journal*, January 5, 1901, 12.

9. *Waterways Journal*, December 8, 1900, 10.

10. *Waterways Journal*, July 26, 1902.

11. *Waterways Journal*, April 20, 1895, 8.

12. "Masters of the River: The Story of the Streckfus Fleet and the Men Who Built It," photocopy of unidentified article from *Streckfus Steamers Magazine*, St. Louis Mercantile Library.

13. *Waterways Journal*, December 17, 1910, 9.

14. *Waterways Journal*, February 11, 1911, 9; Streckfus Steamers, Inc., St. Louis 2, Missouri, Application for Relief under section 722 of the Internal Revenue Code for the Calendar Year 1942, TS, Capt. William Carroll, Streckfus Steamers, box 46, St. Louis Mercantile Library.

15. Ibid.

16. *St. Louis Argus*, July 27, 1921, 5.

17. "Bad Crossing Blamed," *Waterways Journal*, September 28, 1918, 4.

18. Streckfus Line Magazine (1924), 24–25.

19. Ibid., 24.

20. Alan Bates and Clarke Hawley, *Moonlight at 8:30: The Excursion Boat Story* (Louisville, Ky.: Alan Bates and Clarke Hawley, 1994), 151–152.

21. Streckfus Steamers, Inc., By-Laws and Minutes, March 2, 1926–December 31, 1935, William Carroll Collection, Streckfus Papers, Maritime Collection, University of Missouri at St. Louis.

22. Ibid.

23. Ibid.

24. William Carroll, interview, St. Louis, Missouri, January 20, 2000.

25. "Scenic St. Louis Cruises," in Streckfus Steamers, *On the Enchanting Mississippi* (1926), archives of the Putnam Museum of History and Natural Sciences, Davenport, Iowa, 2.

26. Bates and Hawley, *Moonlight at 8:30*, 1–2.

27. Ibid., 41.

28. Dolores Jane Meyer, "Excursion Steamboating on the Mississippi with Streckfus Steamers, Inc." (Ph.D. diss., St. Louis University, 1967), 45, 49.

29. "Masters of the River," 4; Norbury L. Wayman, *Life on the River: A Pictorial History of the Mississippi, the Missouri, and the Western River System* (New York: Crown Publishers, 1971), 154.

30. See Mary Ryan, "The American Parade: Representations of the Nineteenth-Century Social Order," in *The New Cultural History*, ed. Lynn Hunt (Berkeley: University of California Press, 1989), 132–133.

31. Bates and Hawley, *Moonlight at 8:30*, chap. 3.

32. See the social history of St. Louis in Ernest Kirschten, *Catfish and Crystal* (Garden City, N.Y.: Doubleday, 1960).

33. Meyer, "Excursion Steamboating," 62.

34. Bates and Hawley, *Moonlight at 8:30*, 37.

35. Streckfus Steamboat Line, "Fun with the Roustabouts," *Vacation Trips on the Upper Mississippi*, n.d., archives of the Putnam Museum of History and Natural Sciences, Davenport, Iowa.

36. Conrad Freeric, "Millennium's Luck," *Streckfus Steamers Magazine* (1932–33), 20–24, 53–58.

37. "Streckfus Mississippi Bubbles," *Streckfus Steamers Magazine*, Bicentennial Edition (1976), 23.

38. Gaston Bachelard, *Air and Dreams: An Essay on the Imagination of Movement*, trans. Edith R. Farrell and C. Frederick Farrell (Dallas: Dallas Institute of Humanities and Culture, 1988), 2–3.

39. Gaston Bachelard, *The Psychoanalysis of Fire*, trans. Alan C. M. Ross (Boston: Beacon Press, 1964), 16, 22–23.

40. Bachelard, *Air and Dreams*, 16–29.

41. Ibid., 10, 42–43.

42. Ibid., 50, 84–86.

43. Ibid., 49.

44. Gaston Bachelard, "*Air and Dreams:* An Annotated Translation with an Introduction by Edith Rogers Farrell" (Ph.D. diss., State University of Iowa, 1965), 419–433.

45. Roger Kinkle, *The Complete Encyclopedia of Popular Music and Jazz, 1900–1950* (New Rochelle, N.Y.: Arlington House, 1974), 2:551.

46. Paul Whiteman Orchestra, "Mississippi Mud," Victor 25366/21274 (New York City, February 18, 1928), Tom Lord, *The Jazz Discography*, CD-ROM, version 3.3.

47. Joseph Streckfus, interview, February 20 and March 18, 1958, TS, Hogan Jazz Archive vertical file, Tulane University, New Orleans.

Chapter Two

1. Oliver W. Johnson to Elmer George Hoefer, TS, February 9, 1947, vertical file, Institute of Jazz Studies, Rutgers, University, Newark, New Jersey.

2. David Chevan, "Riverboat Music from St. Louis and the Streckfus Steamboat Line," *Black Music Research Journal* 9, no. 2 (Fall 1989): 153–180.

3. Paul Allen Anderson, *Deep River: Music and Memory in Harlem Renaissance Thought* (Durham, N.C.: Duke University Press, 2001), chap. 3.

4. See Ronald Radano, "Soul Texts and the Blackness of the Folk," *Modernism/Modernity* 2, no. 1 (1995): 71–95.

5. Wilma Dobie (a newspaper reporter and friend of Marable), telephone interview with the author, September 19, 2001. I thank Dan Morgenstern and Tad Hershorn of the Institute of Jazz Studies for putting me in contact with Ms. Dobie.

6. Wilma Dobie, "Remembering Fate Marable," *Storyville* 38 (December 1971), 44–49.

7. Isadora Marable Sandidge, telephone interview with the author, February 13, 2001.

8. Homi K. Bhabha, "Unpacking My Library . . . Again," in *The Post-colonial Question*, ed. Iain Chambers and Lidia Curti (London: Routledge, 1996), 199–211.

9. Isadora Marable Sandidge and Fate C. Marable Jr., Fate Marable's son and daughter, telephone interview with the author, December 27, 2000.

10. Sinbad Condelucci quoted in John Chilton, *Ride, Red, Ride: The Life of Henry "Red" Allen* (London: Cassell, 1999), 29.

11. Bhabha, "Unpacking," 206.

12. Fate Marable Jr. and Isadora Marable Sandidge, interview with Philip Cartwright and the author, October 6, 1999, Pittsburgh, Pennsylvania.

13. Clarence Elder, "Fate Marable," *S&D Reflector*, June 1968, 16.

14. Leslie C. Swanson, *Steamboat Calliopes* (Moline, Ill.: L. C. Swanson, 1983).

15. Alan Bates and Clarke Hawley, *Moonlight at 8:30: The Excursion Boat Story* (Louisville, Ky.: Alan Bates and Clarke Hawley, 1994), 53–54.

16. Ibid., 53.

17. Marable is quoted in Beulah Schacht, "Riverboat Jazz," *St. Louis Globe-Democrat*, July 22, 1945.

18. Bates and Hawley, *Moonlight at 8:30*, 53.

19. Verne Streckfus, interview digest, September 22, 1960, Hogan Jazz Archive, Tulane University, New Orleans. He also declares that Mills "toured foreign countries, playing a command performance for the King of England, died in Chicago and was buried with honors in Quincy."

20. "Riverboat Jazz," *St. Louis Globe-Democrat*, July 22, 1945.

21. "Excursion Steamer *J.S.* Burns," *Waterways Journal*, July 2, 1910, 3; Fate Marable, MS autobiography in the private collection of Wilma Dobie, quoted in Chevan, "Riverboat Music from St. Louis," 160–161.

22. De Soto (Wisconsin) *Argus*, June 25, 1910, as reprinted in *S&D Reflector*, March 1965, 4–5.

23. Peter Bocage, interview transcript, January 29, 1959, Hogan Jazz Archive, Tulane University, New Orleans.

24. Louis Armstrong, *Satchmo: My Life in New Orleans* (New York: Prentice-Hall, 1954), 183.

25. Marable is quoted in Beulah Schacht, "Story of Fate Marable," *Jazz Record* (March 1946), 5.

26. Verne Streckfus interview.

27. James Ault, interview with John Knoepfle, August 1, 1956, Sangamon State University, photocopy, Inland Waterways Collection, Cincinnati Public Library.

28. Verne Streckfus interview.

29. Raymond F. Meyer, *Backwoods Jazz in the Twenties* (Cape Girardeau: Southeast Missouri State University Press, 1989), 65–66.

30. Joseph Streckfus, interview, March 18, 1958, TS, vertical file, Hogan Jazz Archive, Tulane University, New Orleans.

31. Ibid.

32. Joseph Streckfus, digest of interview, February 20, 1958, TS, Hogan Jazz Archive, Tulane University, New Orleans.

33. Louis Armstrong, *Swing That Music* (New York: Da Capo Press, 1993), 51.

34. Les Tomkins, "Henry 'Red' Allen," *Crescendo*, February 1966, 16–17; Chilton, *Ride, Red, Ride*, 28–36.

35. Schacht, "Story of Fate Marable," 5–6, 14.

36. Barker is quoted in Nat Shapiro and Nat Hentoff, eds., *Hear Me Talkin' to Ya* (New York: Dover, 1955), 75.

37. The best scholarly description of the roustabouts is Eric Arnesen, *Waterfront Workers of New Orleans: Race, Class, and Politics, 1863–1923* (Urbana: University of Illinois Press, 1994), 38–39, 103–106.

38. Meyer, *Backwoods Jazz in the Twenties*, 76.

39. Nathan B. Young, "Steamboat Era," in *Ain't But a Place: An Anthology of African American Writings About St. Louis*, ed. Gerald Early (St. Louis: Missouri Historical Society Press, 1998), 340.

40. Arnesen, *Waterfront Workers*, 39–40, 104; "Memphis Rousters Return to Work After Winning Union Agreement," *Pittsburgh Courier*, July 24, 1937, 5.

41. Julian Ralph, "The Old Way to Dixie," *Harper's New Monthly Magazine*, January 1893, 175; "Roustabouts of the Mississippi," *New Orleans Republican*, August 2, 1874, 5.

42. Bhabha, "Unpacking," 204–205.

43. Robin D. G. Kelley, "We Are Not What We Seem," in Kenneth W. Goings and Raymond A. Mohl, *The New African American Urban History* (Thousand Oaks, Calif.: Sage Publications, 1996), 196–197.

44. Young, "Steamboat Era," 341.

45. Mary Wheeler, *Steamboatin' Days: Folk Songs of the River Packet Era* (Freeport, N.Y.: Books for Libraries, 1944), 92.

46. See also Jelly Roll Morton's fine description of the roustabouts in Rudi Blesh and Harriet Janis, *They All Played Ragtime* (New York: Oak Publications, 1971), 39.

47. Irvin S. Cobb, introduction to *Roustabout Songs: A Collection of Ohio River Valley Songs* (New York: Remick Music, 1939), 4.

48. Ibid.

49. Meyer, *Backwoods Jazz*, 77. In the 1890s, further north, near Moline, passengers enjoyed showering roustabouts on the lower deck with pennies. See the memoir of Moline's Alice Paddock Wright, *One Fifth Avenue* (New York: Paddock Press, 1954), 7.

50. Warren Dodds, interview with Larry Gara, May 2, 1953, TS, 62, Russell Collection, Williams Research Center, New Orleans, Louisiana. This is a typescript draft of what ulti-

mately became *The Baby Dodds Story as Told to Larry Gara* (Los Angeles: Contemporary Press, 1959).

51. Dodds, *Baby Dodds Story*, 28; Dodds interview, 62.

52. Clarence Elder, "Music on the River," *S&D Reflector*, September 1965, 6–7.

53. Armstrong, *Swing That Music*, 49.

54. Armstrong to Shaw, TS photocopy, July 27, 1936, kindly furnished by St. Louis reedman and bandleader Eric Sager.

55. Dodds interview, 58.

56. Dobie, "Remembering Fate Marable," 44.

57. Doug Ramsey, *Jazz Matters: Reflections on the Music and Some of Its Makers* (Fayetteville: University of Alabama Press, 1989), 37.

58. Daniel F. Havens, "Fate Marable: A Jazz Life on the Mississippi," *Popular Music and Society* 12, no. 2 (Summer 1988): 55–62.

59. King is quoted in J. Lee Anderson, "Riverboats, Fate Marable, and the Streckfus Family Matters," *Mississippi Rag*, July 1994, 11.

60. Vertna Saunders, interview, April 5, 1982, National Ragtime and Jazz Archive, Lovejoy Library, Southern Illinois University Library, Edwardsville.

61. Bob Rusch, "Floyd Campbell: Interview," *Cadence*, March 1981, 5–7, 27.

62. Dobie, "Remembering Fate Marable," 45.

63. Armstrong, *Satchmo*, 161.

64. Ibid., 188–189.

65. Marable, as quoted by Wilma Dobie. Interview with Dobie, September 19, 2001.

66. Al Morgan as quoted in Nat Hentoff, "Al Morgan—Riverboat Bass," *Jazz Record*, February 1946, 11–13.

67. Rusch, "Floyd Campbell: Interview," 5–9, 26.

68. For a lucid description of additive rhythms, see Martha Bayles, *Hole in Our Soul: The Loss of Beauty and Meaning in American Popular Music* (Chicago: University of Chicago Press, 1994), 20–21; David Chevan, "The Hands of Fate: Fate Marable and the Development of Early Jazz," unpublished paper kindly furnished by Fate C. Marable Jr. and Isadora Marable Sandidge.

69. Druie Bess, interview with Peter Etzkorn, Irene Cortinovis, and Leonard Licata, TS, November 5, 1971, University of Missouri at St. Louis, Archive and Manuscript Division.

70. Verne Streckfus, interview with Richard Allen and Paul R. Crawford, TS, September 22, 1960, Hogan Jazz Archive, Tulane University, New Orleans.

71. Gunther Schuller, *The Swing Era: The Development of Jazz, 1930–945* (New York: Oxford University Press, 1989), 786n. See Paul Berliner, "Give and Take: The Collective Conversation of Jazz Performance," in *Creativity in Performance*, ed. R. Keith Sawyer (Greenwich, Conn.: Ablex, 1997), chap. 2.

72. In 1943, the Brunswick label brought out an album of four 10-inch 78 r.p.m. records under the title *Riverboat Jazz: New Orleans to Chicago*. Despite its claim to be music "as played by famous jazzmen on the Mississippi," only one of the bands—Dewey Jackson's Peacock Orchestra—ever played on the river. One of the other bands—King Oliver's Dixie Syncopa-

tors—did include the St. Louis trumpeter Bob Shoffner, who had, indeed, played on the riverboats.

73. Dodds interview.

74. Clarence Thornton, interview, New Orleans, January 16, 1999.

75. Fate Marable Jr. and Isadora Marable Sandidge, interview, Pittsburgh, Oct. 6, 1999.

Chapter Three

1. Paul Gilroy, *The Black Atlantic: Modernity and Double Consciousness* (Cambridge: Harvard University Press, 1993); James R. Grossman, *Land of Hope: Chicago, Black Southerners, and the Great Migration* (Chicago: University of Chicago Press, 1989).

2. Florette Henri, *Black Migration: Movement North, 1900–1920* (Garden City, N.Y.: Anchor Books, 1976), 191–192.

3. Peter Gottlieb, *Making Their Own Way: Southern Blacks' Migration to Pittsburgh, 1916–30* (Urbana: University of Illinois Press, 1987).

4. Louis Armstrong, *Satchmo: My Life in New Orleans* (New York: Da Capo, 1986), 191.

5. Louis Armstrong, *Swing That Music* (New York: Da Capo, 1993), 53–54.

6. Scott Deveaux, *The Birth of Bebop: A Social and Musical History*, 236–260, as quoted in Ingrid Monson, ed., *The African Diaspora: A Musical Perspective* (New York: Garland, 2000), 8.

7. The Louis Armstrong Companion: Eight Decades of Commentary, ed. Joshua Berrett (New York: Schirmer Books, 1999), 88–89.

8. Laurence Bergreen, *Louis Armstrong: An Extravagant Life* (New York: Broadway Books, 1997); Homi Bhabha, "Unpacking My Library . . . Again," in *The Post-Colonial Question: Common Skies, Divided Horizons*, ed. Iain Chambers and Lidia Curti (London: Routledge, 1996).

9. Bergreen, *Louis Armstrong*, 1–6, 21.

10. Nathaniel Mackey, "Sound and Sentiment, Sound and Symbol," in *The Jazz Cadence of American Culture*, ed. Robert O'Meally (New York: Columbia University Press, 1998), 602–628.

11. Mackey is quoted in Brent Hayes Edwards, "Louis Armstrong and the Syntax of Scat," in *Playing Changes: New Jazz Studies*, ed. Robert Walser (Durham, N.C.: Duke University Press, forthcoming).

12. George Lipsitz, "Music, Migration, and Myth: The California Connection," in *Reading California: Art, Image, and Identity, 1900–2000*, ed. Stephanie Baron, Sheri Bernstein, and Ilene Susan Fort (Berkeley: University of California Press, 2000), 153–169.

13. Charles Chamberlain, "Searching for 'The Gulf Coast Circuit': Mobility and Cultural Diffusion in the Age of Jim Crow, 1900–930," *Jazz Archivist* 14 (2000): 1–18.

14. Christopher Wilkinson, *Jazz on the Road: Don Albert's Musical Life* (Berkeley: University of California Press for the Center for Black Music Research, 2001), chap. 2.

15. Edward "Kid" Ory, interview with Neshui Ertegun, Hogan Jazz Archive, Tulane University, New Orleans.

16. William Howland Kenney III, "'Going to Meet the Man': Louis Armstrong's Autobiographies," *Melus* 15, no. 2 (Summer 1988): 27–46.

17. Ibid., 32.

18. W. T. Lhamon Jr., *Raising Cain: Blackface Performance from Jim Crow to Hip Hop* (Cambridge: Harvard University Press, 1998), chap. 2.

19. Victor Zuckerkandl, *Sound and Symbol: Music and the External World* (Princeton: Princeton University Press, 1956), as quoted in Mackey, "Sound and Sentiment," 626.

20. James Clifford, *Routes: Travel and Translation in the Late Twentieth Century* (Cambridge: Harvard University Press, 1997), chaps. 1, 10.

21. W. Jeffrey Bolster, *Black Jacks: African American Seamen in the Age of Sail* (Cambridge: Harvard University Press, 1997), 62–66.

22. Herskovits is quoted in ibid., 64.

23. Sterling Stucky, *Slave Culture: Nationalist Theory and Foundations of Black America* (New York: Oxford University Press, 1987), chap. 1.

24. These can be found in *Lift Every Voice and Sing II: An African American Hymnal* (New York: Church Publishing, 1993).

25. Samuel A. Floyd Jr., "Ring Shout! Literary Studies, Historical Studies, and Black Music Inquiry," in *Signifyin(g), Sanctifyin', and Slam Dunking: A Reader in African American Expressive Culture*, ed. Gena Dagel Caponi (Amherst: University of Massachusetts Press, 1999), 135–156.

26. Tom Buchanan, "The Slave Mississippi: African-American Steamboat Workers, Networks of Resistance, and the Commercial World of the Western Rivers, 1811–1880" (Ph.D. diss., Carnegie-Mellon University, 1998).

27. Ibid., chap. 2.

28. Armstrong is quoted in James Lincoln Collier, *Louis Armstrong: An American Genius* (New York: Oxford University Press, 1983), 124–125, and Bergreen, *Louis Armstrong*, 245.

29. Ibid.

30. Walter Ong, *Orality and Literacy: The Technologizing of the Word* (New York: Routledge, 2000), 80, 101.

31. Ibid., 78–79.

32. Ibid.

33. "Glossary of Swing Terms," in Armstrong, *Swing That Music*, 135–136.

34. John Chilton, *Ride, Red, Ride: The Life of Henry "Red" Allen* (London: Cassell, 1999), 10.

35. Jacques Attali, *Noise: The Political Economy of Music*, trans. Brian Massumi (Minneapolis: University of Minnesota Press, 1985).

36. Attali should be read in conjunction with Ronald Radano, "Black Noise/White Mastery," in *Decomposition: Post-disciplinary Performance*, ed. Sue-Ellen Case, Philip Brett, and Susan Leigh Foster (Bloomington: Indiana University Press, 2000), 39–49.

37. Charles Hiroshi Garrett, "Louis Armstrong and the Sound of Migration," unpublished paper kindly shared with me by its author; Bergreen, *Louis Armstrong*, 168–169; Warren Dodds, *The Baby Dodds Story as Told to Larry Gara* (Los Angeles: Contemporary Press, 1959), 26; Joseph Streckfus, "Louis Armstrong—Fate Marable," TS, vertical file, Hogan Jazz Archive, Tulane University, New Orleans.

38. Wayne D. Shirley, "The Coming of Deep River," *American Music* 15, no. 4 (Winter 1997): 493–534.

39. My thanks to Bruce Boyd Raeburn for pointing out the New Orleans inspiration for this particular arrangement.

40. Paul Allen Anderson, *Deep River: Music and Memory in Harlem Renaissance Thought* (Durham, N.C.: Duke University Press, 2001), chaps. 1–2.

41. Lawrence W. Levine, "Jazz and American Culture," in *The Jazz Cadence of American Culture*, ed. Robert G. O'Meally (New York: Columbia University Press, 1998), chap. 24.

42. Homi K. Bhabha, *The Location of Culture* (London: Routledge, 1994), 225–226.

43. Darrell K. Fennell, "List of Recordings," in Bergreen, *Louis Armstrong*, 499–518.

44. Richard Runsiman Terry, ed., *The Shanty Book, Part I* (London: J. Curwen and Sons, 1921), v–vi.

45. Peter Linebaugh and Marcus Redicker, "The Many-Headed Hydra: Sailors, Slaves, and the Atlantic Working Class in the Eighteenth Century," *Journal of Historical Sociology* 3, no. 3 (September 1990): 225–252.

46. Miles Davis with Quincy Troupe, *Miles, the Autobiography* (New York: Simon and Schuster, 1989), fig. 5 caption; see also figs. 6, 7, and 8.

47. Armstrong, *Swing That Music*, 57–58; Kenney, "'Going to Meet the Man,'" 33.

48. Collier, *Louis Armstrong*.

49. Charles Hersch, "Poisoning Their Coffee: Louis Armstrong and Civil Rights," *Polity* 34, no. 3 (Spring 2002): 371–392.

Chapter Four

1. Norbury L. Wayman, *Life on the River: A Pictorial History of the Mississippi, the Missouri, and the Western River System* (New York: Crown Publishers, 1971), 94–95.

2. Gloria Brown Melton, "Blacks in Memphis, Tennessee, 1920–1955" (Ph.D. diss., Washington State University, 1982), 2; Fred J. Hay, *Goin' "Back to Sweet Memphis": Conversations with the Blues* (Athens: University of Georgia Press, 2001), xvii–xxxviii.

3. Margaret McKee and Fred Chisenhall, *Beale Black and Blue* (Baton Rouge: Louisiana State University Press, 1981), 16.

4. Hay, *Goin' Back*, xix.

5. George W. Lee, "Beale Street and the Blues," Speech delivered on April 23, 1967, audiotaped and transcribed by F. Jack Hurley, Oral History Research Office, Memphis State University, 5.

6. Ibid., 6–7, 8

7. Ibid., 5.

8. Ibid.

9. Melton, "Blacks in Memphis"; Michael J. Honey, *Southern Labor and Black Civil Rights* (Urbana: University of Illinois Press, 1993), 18.

10. James H. Robinson, "A Social History of the Negro in Memphis and in Shelby County" (Ph.D. diss., Yale University, 1934), 44; William S. Worley, *Beale St.: Crossroads of America's Music* (Lemexa, Kans.: Addax Press, 1998), 17.

11. "'S.S. Brown,' 'Rees Lee,' 'Majestic,'" *S&D Reflector*, June 1972, 24.

12. Frederick Way Jr., *Way's Packet Directory, 1848–1994* (Athens: Ohio University Press, 1983), 222.

13. W. C. Handy, *Father of the Blues: An Autobiography* (New York: Macmillan, 1947).

14. Buster Bailey is quoted in Nat Shapiro and Nat Hentoff, eds., *Hear Me Talkin' to Ya: The Story of Jazz as Told by the Men Who Made It* (New York: Dover, 1955), 77–78.

15. Larry Nager, *Memphis Beat: The Lives and Times of America's Musical Crossroads* (New York: St. Martin's, 1998), 86–87.

16. Adam Gussow, "Racial Violence, 'Primitive Music,' and the Blues Entrepreneur: W. C. Handy's Mississippi Problem," *Southern Cultures* 8, no. 3 (Fall 2002): 65–77.

17. Handy, *Father of the Blues*, as quoted in ibid., 67.

18. Lee, "Beale Street and the Blues," 4.

19. Robert A. Sigafoos, *Cotton Row to Beale Street: A Business History of Memphis* (Memphis: Memphis State University Press, 1979), 138–140.

20. James Neal Primm, *Lion of the Valley: St. Louis, Missouri* (Boulder, Colo.: Pruett, 1981), 458.

21. Florence Rebekah Beatty-Brown, "The Negro as Portrayed by the *St. Louis Post-Dispatch* from 1920 to 1950" (Ph.D diss., University of Illinois, 1951), 17.

22. Katherine T. Corbett and Mary E. Seematter, "No Crystal Stair: Black St. Louis, 1920–1940," *Gateway Heritage* 8, no. 2 (Fall 1987): 9.

23. "Statistics Are Given on the Negro in St. Louis," *St. Louis Argus*, March 1, 1935.

24. Beatty-Brown, "Negro as Portrayed by the *St. Louis Post-Dispatch*," 17.

25. Lawrence Oland Christensen, "Black St. Louis: A Study in Race Relations, 1865–1916" (Ph.D. diss., University of Missouri, Columbia, 1972), 52–58.

26. Corbett and Seematter, "No Crystal Stair," 8–15.

27. George Lipsitz, *A Life in the Struggle: Ivory Perry and the Culture of Opposition* (Philadelphia: Temple University Press, 1988), 65.

28. Miles Davis with Quincy Troupe, *Miles: The Autobiography* (New York: Simon and Shuster, 1989), 38.

29. "Statistics Are Given on the Negro."

30. *Pittsburgh Courier*, August 6, 1938, 4, and August 20, 1938, 20; Corbett and Seematter, "No Crystal Stair," 10–11.

31. George Lipsitz, *Sidewalks of St. Louis: People, Places, and Politics in an American City* (Columbia: University of Missouri Press, 1991), 52–53.

32. "Statistics Are Given on the Negro."

33. John Russell David, "Tragedy in Ragtime: Black Folktales from St. Louis" (Ph.D. diss., St. Louis University, 1976), 62.

34. Ibid., 389.

35. John Russell David, "The Rise and Decline of the Variety Theater in St. Louis, 1867–1896" (master's thesis, Southern Illinois University, Edwardsville, 1969), 67.

36. John A. Wright, "The Castle Club," in Wright, *Discovering African American St. Louis: A Guide to Historical Sites* (St. Louis: Missouri Historical Society Press, 2002), 11.

37. David, "Tragedy in Ragtime," 87–92; Angela de Silva, "Babe Conners and the Castle Club," in de Silva, *St. Louis Attitude*, galley proofs in the archives of St. Louis University.

38. Nancy Grant, "From Showboat to Symphony: A Study of Black Classical Musicians in St. Louis, 1920–1980," in *Ain't But a Place: An Anthology of African American Writings About St. Louis*, ed. Gerald Early (St. Louis: Missouri Historical Society Press, 1998), 402–412.

39. http://stlouis.missouri.org/government/heritage/history/afriamer.htm.

40. "'Madam Babe': St. Louis' Golden Bordello Idyllic," TS, Judge Nathan B. Young Papers, Archives, St. Louis University.

41. Rudi Blesh and Harriet Janis, *They All Played Ragtime* (New York: Oak Publications, 1971), 52.

42. Ibid., 56–57.

43. *St. Louis Argus*, January 21, 1916, 4.

44. *St. Louis Argus*, April 14, 1916, 1.

45. *St. Louis Argus*, June 27, 1919, 4; August 15, 1919, 1.

46. *St. Louis Argus*, July 2, 1920, 5.

47. Christensen, "Black St. Louis," 97.

48. John Chilton, *Roy Eldridge: Little Jazz Giant* (London: Continuum, 2002), 40.

49. John Cotter, "The Negro in Music in St. Louis," TS, 326–327, National Ragtime and Jazz Archive, Southern Illinois University, Edwardsville.

50. Sammy Long, interview with Irene Cortinovis, April 18, 1973, TS, University of Missouri, St. Louis.

51. *St. Louis Argus*, March 19, 1915, 4.

52. *St. Louis Argus*, April 21, 1916, 3.

53. *St. Louis Argus*, August, 15, 1919, 1; December 5, 1919, 4; July 2, 1920, 5.

54. *St. Louis Argus*, October 13, 1922, 3; February 23, 1923, 3.

55. The twelve sides cut by the Jazz-O-Maniacs have been reissued on the CD *Jazz in Saint Louis, 1924–1927*, Timeless Records CBC 1-036 Jazz. They can also be heard on the World Wide Web at www.redhotjazz.com/maniacs.html.

56. George "Pops" Foster with Tom Stoddard, *The Autobiography of a New Orleans Jazzman* (Berkley: University of California Press, 1971), 127.

57. Eddie Johnson (as well as Shaw, Finney, and Randle), interview with Irene Cortinovis, MS, August 20, 1971, University of Missouri, St. Louis.

58. *St. Louis Argus*, June 23, July 7, July 21, 1916.

59. *St. Louis Argus*, June 4, 1920, 5.

60. *St. Louis Argus*, June 18, 1920, 2.

61. *St. Louis Argus*, July 23, 1922, 3, 12; includes a photo of the boat.

62. *St. Louis Argus*, June 4, 1926, 6; includes a photo of the boat.

63. Way, *Way's Packet Directory*, 90, 304.

64. Johnson, Shaw, Finney, Randle interview, 51.

65. John W. Randolph, "Dewey Jackson: King of the Riverboat Trumpets," *Jazz Report* 6, no. 4 (May 1958): 7–8, 10.

66. Martin Luther MacKay interview with Irene Cortinovis, May 21, 1971, TS, University of Missouri, St. Louis.

67. Cotter, "Negro in Music in St. Louis," 334–338.

68. *St. Louis Argus*, January 27, 1928, 3.

69. "The Floyd Campbell Story," as told to Bertrand Demeusy, TS, National Ragtime and Jazz Archive, Southern Illinois University, Edwardsville.

70. Eddie Randle interview.

71. Elijah Shaw, interview with Irene Cortinovis, August 20, 1971, TS, University of Missouri at St. Louis.

72. Ibid.

73. *St. Louis Argus*, February 26, 1932, 5.

74. *St. Louis Argus*, May 13, 1932, 5.

75. *St. Louis Argus*, September 21, 1934, 1.

76. *St. Louis Argus*, September 9, 1932, 5. According to Primm, *Lion of the Valley*, 442, "black members were allowed to form a subsidiary totally dominated by the white organization."

77. Ben Thomas, "Musicians' Local and Non-Union Bands Air Their 3 Year Conflict," *St. Louis Argus*, October 29, 1937, 5.

78. Cotter, "Negro in Music in St. Louis," 341.

79. "Jazz Benefit for Norman Mason, Goldenrod Showboat" April 15, 1970, TS, kindly supplied by Diane Faulhaber, whose father Bert Bailey played saxophones in the Marable orchestra.

80. Cotter, "Negro in Music in St. Louis," 324–326.

81. D. Crowder and A. F. Niemoeller, "Norman Mason, Riverboat Jazzman," *Record Changer*, February 1952, 8, 19.

82. Cotter, "Negro in Music in St. Louis," 324–326.

83. I have based the factual narrative of Campbell's life on Bertrand Demeusy, "The Floyd Campbell Story," TS, archives, University of Missouri, St. Louis, and Bob Rusch, "Floyd Campbell: Interview," *Cadence*, March 1981, 5–9, 26.

84. Demeusy, "Floyd Campbell Story."

85. Gus Perryman, interview with Irene Cortinovis, TS, Archive and Manuscript Division, University of Missouri, St. Louis.

86. Rusch, "Floyd Campbell," 6.

87. *St. Louis Argus*, September 28, 1928, 5.

88. Rusch, "Floyd Campbell," 7–8.

Chapter Five

1. Joseph Streckfus's list of bandleaders includes for some the number of seasons they played. Ralph Williams played for three seasons; Jules Buffano and Wayne King, Burke and Leins, two seasons; Tony Catalano, eight seasons; Gene Rodemich and Al Roth, one season; Dick Little and Herzog, two seasons; John Polzin, six seasons; Hal Havird, ten seasons; Johnny Lyons, Doc Wrixon, Carlisle Evans, Bonnie Ross, and Tommy Trigg, two seasons each. Joseph Streckfus, "Music on the Mississippi River Excursion Steamers," Feb. 20, 1958, TS, vertical file, Hogan Jazz Archive, Tulane University, New Orleans.

2. Alan Bates and Clarke Hawley, *Moonlight at 8:30: The Excursion Boat Story* (Louisville, Ky.: Alan Bates and Clarke Hawley, 1994).

3. Antoine Hennion, "For a Pragmatics of Taste," TS kindly supplied by its author.

4. This is how Nathaniel Mackey, "Sound and Sentiment, Sound and Symbol," in *The Jazz Cadence of American Culture*, ed. Robert G. O'Meally (New York: Columbia University Press, 1998), 602–628 expresses it. His article makes reference to the black diaspora in particular, but the process that he describes involves a shared human experience that is not necessarily dependent on racial identity. Rather, racism and poverty created a horrifying number of complications in family life.

5. Richard M. Sudhalter and Philip R. Evans with William Dean-Myatt, *Bix: Man and Legend* (New Rochelle, N.Y.: Arlington House, 1974), 17–19.

6. Eunice J. Schlichting to the author, May 3, 2002, with photocopied research notes. See also Schlichting, "Music in the Quad Cities Research Report," TS, 1991, Archives, Putnam Museum of History and Natural Sciences, Davenport, Iowa.

7. Spurrier is quoted in Sudhalter and Evans, *Bix*, 48.

8. *Davenport Democrat and Leader*, April 27, 1914, 11; April 29, 1914, 11.

9. *Davenport Democrat and Leader*, March 17, 1914, 6.

10. Roald D. Tweet, *History of Transportation on the Upper Mississippi and Illinois Rivers* (http://mts.tamug.tamu.edu/History-Links/upmiss.html) (U.S. Army Engineers Water Resources Support Center, 1983), 35.

11. http://www.americatravelling.net/usa/iowa/davenport/davenport_history.htm.

12. Tweet, *History*, 62. Between 1890 and 1908 the Illinois and Mississippi Canal, a feeder for the Illinois and Michigan Canal, was added. Eunice Schlichting, e-mail message to author, February 9, 2004.

13. *Davenport Democrat and Leader*, April 27, 1914, 11; May 5, 1914, 17.

14. Tweet, *History of Transportation*, 65–74.

15. Sudhalter and Evans, *Bix*, 27–28.

16. Ibid., 19.

17. According to Philip R. Evans and Linda K. Evans in *Bix: The Leon Bix Beiderbecke Story* (Bakersfield, Calif.: Prelike Press, 1998), 47–48, Armstrong himself mentions hearing Bix "blowing a lot of pretty cornet" in 1920. The *Capitol* worked its way up the river for the first time as a Streckfus steamer that year, when Bix was still a neophyte. In his autobiographies Armstrong remains vague about the dates of these encounters.

18. Armstrong is quoted in William Howland Kenney III, "'Going to Meet the Man': Louis Armstrong's Autobiographies," *Melus* 15, no. 2 (Summer 1988): 38.

19. Evans and Evans, *Bix*, 69–70.

20. Ibid., 61.

21. George Lipsitz, *The Possessive Investment in Whiteness: How White People Profit from Identity Politics* (Philadelphia: Temple University Press, 1998), 119–123.

22. Works Progress Administration, "The Negro in Pittsburgh," Works Progress Administration Ethnic Survey, job 64, roll 1 (microfilm).

23. Sudhalter and Evans, *Bix*, 35.

24. Ibid., chap. 3.

25. "Days When Musicians Couldn't Read a Note," *Down Beat*, May 1938, 7; Duncan Schiedt, *The Jazz State of Indiana* (Pittsboro, Ind.: Scheidt, 1977), 3–4.

26. Brian Harker, "The Early Musical Development of Louis Armstrong, 1901–1928" (Ph.D. diss., Columbia University, 1997), 53–60.

27. Frederick Way Jr., *Way's Packet Directory, 1848–1994* (Athens: Ohio University Press, 1983), 304; *S&D Reflector,* June 1972, 23–32.

28. Sudhalter and Evans, *Bix*, 47, 57.

29. Trumbauer is quoted in Philip R. Evans and Larry F. Kiner with William Trumbauer, *Tram: The Frank Trumbauer Story* (Metuchen, N.J.: Scarecrow Press, 1994), 54.

30. Richard Sudhalter, *Lost Chords: White Musicians and Their Contribution to Jazz, 1915–1945* (New York: Oxford University Press, 1999), 802–803, n. 31.

31. Davenport Sunday Democrat, February 10, 1929, as quoted in Sudhalter and Evans, *Bix*, 268–269.

32. Robert Hilbert, *Pee Wee Russell: The Life of a Jazzman* (New York: Oxford University Press, 1993), 15–16.

33. Sudhalter and Evans, *Bix*, chaps. 10–11

34. Lincoln Allison, *Amateurism in Sport* (London: Frank Cass, 2001), 3.

35. I have culled this summary of the pianist's early life from the following sources: Derek Coller, *Jess Stacy: The Quiet Man of Jazz* (New Orleans: Jazzology Press, 1997); Peg Meyer, *Backwoods Jazz in the Twenties*, intro. Frank Nickell (Cape Girardeau: Center for Regional History, Southeast Missouri State University, 1989); Frank Nickell, interview with the author, Cape Girardeau, Missouri, May 22, 2001; Whitney Balliett, "Profiles: Back from Valhalla," *New Yorker,* August 18, 1975, 32–37; Otis Ferguson, "Piano in the Band," *New Republic,* November 24, 1937, 68–70.

36. Nickell is quoted in the introduction to Meyer, *Backwoods Jazz.*

37. Meyer and Stacy are quoted in Coller, *Jess Stacy,* 17, 20.

38. Stacy is quoted in ibid., 21.

39. Ed Crowder and A. F. Niemoeller, "White Musicians of St. Louis," *Record Changer,* n.d., vertical file, Institute of Jazz Studies, Rutgers University, Newark, New Jersey.

40. Balliett, "Back from Valhalla," 35.

41. Coller, *Jess Stacy,* 25–27.

42. http://findusat309.com/articles/_TomPletcher_2003_Bix_Fest.html.

Chapter Six

1. Darrel E. Bigham, "River of Opportunity: Economic Consequences of the Ohio," in *Always a River: The Ohio River and the American Experience*, ed. Robert L. Reid (Bloomington: Indiana University Press, 1991), 164.

2. Leland R. Johnson, "Engineering the Ohio," in *Always a River: The Ohio River and the American Experience*, ed. Robert L. Reid (Bloomington: Indiana University Press, 1991), 180–209.

3. Patrick H. Carigan, "How Green Is Your Valley?" in *The River Book: Cincinnati and the Ohio*, ed. Joyce V. B. Cauffield and Carolyn E. Banfield (Cincinnati: Program for Cincinnati, 1981), 178.

4. James Ault, interview with John Knoepfle, 1988, Sagamon State University, Springfield, Illinois.

5. http://www.cincinnati.com/tallstacks/history_2centuries.html.

6. Alan L. Bates, "Shipbuilding," in *The River Book: Cincinnati and the Ohio*, ed. Joyce V. B. Cauffield and Carolyn E. Banfield (Cincinnati: Program for Cincinnati, 1981), 150–155.

7. O. W. Frost, introduction to *Children of the Levee*, by Lafcadio Hearn (Lexington: University of Kentucky Press, 1957), 6.

8. Lafcadio Hearn, *Children of the Levee* (Lexington: University of Kentucky Press, 1957), 75.

9. Ibid., 76–77.

10. Joe William Trotter Jr., *River Jordan: African American Urban Life in the Ohio Valley* (Lexington: University of Kentucky Press, 1998), 75; Lyle Koehler, *Cincinnati's Black Peoples: A Chronology and Bibliography, 1787–1982* (Cincinnati: Neighborhood and Community Studies, 1986), 115–118.

11. *Cincinnati Union*, September 14, 1920, 2.

12. Lynn Driggs Cunningham and Jimmy Jones, eds., *Sweet, Hot, and Blue: St. Louis' Musical Heritage* (Jefferson, N.C.: McFarland Press, 1989), 153.

13. Gene Sedric vertical file, Institute of Jazz Studies, Rutgers University, Newark, New Jersey.

14. Len Kunstadt, "Eugene Sedric—Gentleman Musician," *Record Research* 55 (September 1963): n.p.

15. http://enquirer.com/editions/2001/01/08/tem/cincinnati_has_jazz.html.

16. Bill Coleman, *Trumpet Story* (Boston: Northeastern University Press, 1991), 4.

17. Steven C. Tracy, *Goin' to Cincinnati: A History of the Blues in the Queen City* (Urbana: University of Illinois Press, 1993), 88–89.

18. Coleman, *Trumpet Story*, 37, 39.

19. http://www.cincinnati.com/tallstacks/history_2centuries.html.

20. James Ault, interview with John Knoepfle, August 1, 1956. Inland Rivers Collection, Cincinnati Public Library.

21. Ault interview.

22. Tracy, *Goin' to Cincinnati*, 88; John Chilton, *Who's Who of Jazz: Storyville to Swing Street* (New York: Time-Life Books, 1978).

23. John H. White and Robert J. White, *The Island Queen: Cincinnati's Excursion Steamer* (Akron, Ohio: University of Akron Press, 1998); Frederick Way Jr., *Way's Packet Directory, 1848–1983* (Athens: Ohio University Press, 1983).

24. Works Progress Administration, "The Negro in Pittsburgh," Works Progress Administration Ethnic Survey, job 64, roll 1 (microfilm), 66–74, as quoted in Curtis Miner, *Pittsburgh Rhythms: The Music of a Changing City, 1840–1930* (Pittsburgh: Historical Society of Western Pennsylvania, 1991), 29–32.

25. "History of Streckfus Steamers, Incorporated and Its Wholly-Owned Subsidiary, Steamer Service Co.," 8–47, TS, Carroll Papers, box 46, St. Louis Mercantile Library.

26. Sharon A. Pease, "Fats Pichon a Video Star Now," *Down Beat*, n.d., Pichon Vertical File, Institute of Jazz Studies, Rutgers University, Newark, New Jersey.

27. New Orleans *States-Item*, February 27, 1967.

28. Singleton Palmer, interview with Irene Cortinovis, November 9, 1971, TS, Archives and Manuscripts Division, University of Missouri, St. Louis.

29. "Eddie Johnson Takes Pittsburgh by Storm," *Pittsburgh Courier*, December 31, 1932.

30. Works Progress Administration, "Negro in Pittsburgh."

31. John Bodnar, Roger Simon, and Michael P. Weber, *Lives of Their Own: Blacks, Italians, and Poles in Pittsburgh, 1900–1960* (Champaign: University of Illinois Press, 1982), 71.

32. Peter Gottlieb, *Making Their Own Way: Southern Blacks' Migration to Pittsburgh, 1916–30* (Urbana: University of Illinois Press, 1987), 66–67.

33. http://www.cmh.pitt.edu/newsenclave.htm.

34. Charles F. Danver, "Pittsburghesque," *Pittsburgh Post-Gazette*, August 2, 1932.

35. Works Progress Administration, "Negro in Pittsburgh," 65.

36. Michelle Fanzo, "The History of the Hill District," *Observer*, June1995; http://www.northbysouth.org/2000/Beauty/Crawford.htm; Sandy Hamm, "Hill District Jazz Culture Revisited," *New Pittsburgh Courier*, June 9, 1993, B1.

37. Works Progress Administration, "Negro in Pittsburgh," 67–69.

38. Ibid.

39. Ibid.

40. Ibid., 68–71.

41. *Pittsburgh Courier*, September 1, 1923, 5, and September 15, 1923, 11.

42. *Pittsburgh Courier*, December 1, 1923, 9.

43. Stanley Dance, "Lois P. Deppe," in Dance, *The World of Earl Hines* (New York: Scribner's, 1977), 130–141.

44. Works Progress Administration, "Negro in Pittsburgh," 66.

45. Ibid., 67.

46. Dance, *World of Earl Hines*.

47. Ibid., 16.

48. Ibid., 16–18.

49. *Pittsburgh Courier*, December 1, 1923; August 9, 1924, 5.

50. Linda Dahl, *Morning Glory: A Biography of Mary Lou Williams* (New York: Pantheon Books, 1999), 5

51. Ibid., 22.

52. Ibid., 21.

53. Ahmad Jamal as quoted in David Hajdu, *Lush Life: A Biography of Billy Strayhorn* (New York: North Point Press, 1996), 14.

54. Dahl, *Morning Glory*, 31.

55. http://www.ratical.org/MaryLouWilliams/MMiview1954.html: "In her own words"; "Mary Lou Williams Interview," *Melody Maker* (April–June 1954).

56. Hajdu, *Lush Life*, 6–7.

57. Ibid., 14.

58. Ibid., 15.

59. James M. Doran, *Erroll Garner: The Most Happy Piano* (Metuchen, N.J.: Scarecrow Press, 1985), 31–33.

60. Whitney Balliett, "Jazz: Being a Genius," *New Yorker*, February 22, 1982, 59–72.

61. Doran, *Erroll Garner*, 31–32.

62. Ruth Garner Moore, Erroll's sister, and Erroll's close friend Allen "Licorice" Carter are quoted in Doran, *Erroll Garner*, 18, 29.

63. *Pittsburgh Courier*, July 3, 1926, 1.

64. *Pittsburgh Courier*, May 9, 1931, 1.

65. Carter is quoted in Doran, *Erroll Garner*, 29.

66. Vertna Saunders, interview with Dan Havens, St. Louis, April 5, 1982, National Ragtime and Jazz Archive, Lovejoy Library, Southern Illinois University, Edwardsville, Illinois.

67. Kim Pereira, *August Wilson and the African-American Odyssey* (Urbana: University of Illinois Press, 1995), 2.

68. August Wilson, *The Piano Lesson* (New York: Plume, 1990), xiii.

69. *Pittsburgh Courier*, March 13, 1926, 3.

70. *Pittsburgh Courier*, March 6, 1926, 3.

71. "Prejudice, Trickery Used, Rumor," *Pittsburgh Courier* October 23, 1926, 10.

72. John W. Fountain, "Men and Music of Another Time and Another War," *New York Times*, April 9, 2003.

73. Ingrid Monson, "Art Blakey's African Diaspora," in *The African Diaspora: A Musical Perspective*, ed. Ingrid Monson (New York: Garland, 2000), 330–333.

74. Richard Brent Turner, *Islam in the African-American Experience* (Bloomington: Indiana University Press, 1997), 139

75. Wylie Avenue Days, VHS, produced by Doug Bolin and Christopher Moore (Pittsburgh: QED Communications, 1991).

76. Fanzo, *History of the Hill District*.

Epilogue

1. Joe Wiley Jr., "Fate Marable off River for the First Time in 22 Years," *Down Beat*, October 15, 1941, 21.

2. "Benefit Dance for Marable," *Down Beat*, February 1, 1941, 2.

3. http://www.rmstitanichistory.com/morro/morro.html.

4. Extracts from yearly minutes of the Board of Directors, Streckfus Steamers, Inc., for 1934 and 1937 in "History of Streckfus Steamers, Incorporated and Its Wholly-Owned Subsidiary, Streckfus Service Co.," TS, Capt. William Carroll/Streckfus Steamers Collection, Western Manuscript Archive, University of Missouri, St. Louis.

5. Joseph Streckfus to Roy Streckfus, October 12, 1943, William Carroll/Streckfus Steamers, box 46, Western Manuscripts Collection, University of Missouri, St. Louis.

6. Ibid.

7. Ibid.

8. Ibid.

9. William Carroll, interview with the author, St. Louis, Missouri, May 17, 2000.

10. Mary Kimbrough and Margaret W. Dagen, *Victory without Violence: The First Ten Years of the St. Louis Committee of Racial Equality* (Columbia: University of Missouri Press, 2000).

11. Richard Dudman, "Commentary: St. Louis' Silent Racial Revolution, Newspapers Did Not Cover Campaign to Integrate Lunch Counters," *St. Louis Post-Dispatch*, June 11, 1990.

12. "Suit Attacking Anti-Bias Law's Validity Filed," *St. Louis Post-Dispatch*, June 29, 1961, 1, 9.

13. *St. Louis Post-Dispatch*, June 30, 1961, 3A.

14. *St. Louis Post-Dispatch*, July 9, 1961, 3A.

15. *St. Louis Post-Dispatch*, August 17, 1961, 3A.

16. *St. Louis Post-Dispatch*, April 23, 1962, 3A.

17. *St. Louis Post-Dispatch*, February 21, 1980; February 22, 1980.

18. Ralph Ellison, *Invisible Man* (New York: Vintage Books, 1980), 54–56.

19. Ibid., *Invisible Man*, 56.

Index

Italicized page numbers indicate illustrations.

A. P. Griggs Piano Company, 120
Acme Packet Company, 16
Admiral: air conditioning of, 172, 174–75; construction of, 26, 173; as ghost, 171; photograph of, *26;* racial integration of, 175–76
advance men, 27
Africa, political movements in, 168–70
African Americans: as authentic riverboat jazz musicians, 9–10, 70, 124; immigrant conflicts with, 153–54, 159, 161; political movements of, 168–70, 175–76; response to *Show Boat* (musical), 8–9; segregated cruises for, 58, 102–3, 163. *See also* Great Migration; roustabouts
Agony Four, 130, 137
Ahmadiyya movement, 169
air conditioning, 23, 171–72
Albatross, 173
Albert, Don, 69
alcohol: Beiderbecke's use of, 117, 124, 128–29, 132, 140; glamorized use of, 129; Jive for, 155; limits on, 28; Marable's use of, 56, 157; passengers' provision of, 17–18; in Prohibition, 89, 112; in variety saloons and theaters, 96–97; wages provided in, 155

Alexander, Charles, 85–86, 148
Alexander, Jane Patton, 160, 161
Allen, Edward C., 99, 100, 109, 111, 145
Allen, Henry "Red": benefit played by, 171; influences on, 38; mentioned, 3–4; photograph of, *65;* recordings of, 83, 150; wages of, 79
amateur, concept of, 117, 134, 140
American Federation of Musicians: benefits of, 55; Davenport Local 67, 126–27; Pittsburgh Local 471, 154, 166–67; St. Louis Local 44, 107–8. *See also* unionism
amplification, sound, 46–47
anticolonialism, 168–70
arcade games, 29, 172
Arcadia Ballroom (Chicago), 139
Arcadia Ballroom (Pittsburgh), 160
Arcadia Ballroom (St. Louis), 131–32
Argand, 147
Arkansas River, excursion boats on, 132
Armenia, 41
Armstrong, Louis: aspirations of, 81–82; associates of, 113–14, 161; aural worldview of, 77–79; background of, 68–69, 78, 118, 129; on Beiderbecke, 123, 124, 206n17; death of, 171; departure from riverboat jobs, 58–59, 60–61, 62–63, 66;

Armstrong, Louis (*continued*)
    improvisation of, 75, 77–79; influences
    on, 73–75, 82, 110; on Marable, 45, 55,
    56, 57, 58; Mason compared with, 110;
    musical literacy of, 75–77, 127; persona
    constructed by, 67–68; photographs of,
    46, 65, 76; playing style of, 47, 49–50,
    126; on popular songs, 48; recordings of,
    72–73, 82–86, 114; reputation of, 3–4;
    resiliency/silences of, 86–87, 168; river-
    boat jobs of, 64–66; Stacy on, 137; as
    traveling musician, 64, 66–67, 71–72,
    73, 122
arranged popular dance music, 39, 47–49, 60
Arthur, Julian, 145–46
Atkins, Boyd, 4, 59, *76,* 103
Attali, Jacques, 81
Augustana Conservatory of music, 120
Ault, John, 147, 148
authenticity, 9–10, 70, 124
automobiles, 21, 172
Avakian, George, 139

Bachelard, Gaston: on air and light, 12; on
    earth and water, 34; on imagination, 30,
    32; on psychological experience of jazz,
    193n2; on swan complex, 32–34; on
    water, 1
Bailey, Bernice, 111
Bailey, Bert, *61,* 111, 205n79
Baker, Harold "Shorty," 4, 99, 105, 151
Baker, Josephine, 99
Baker, Winfield, 105
Balliett, Whitney, 137, 162–63
Bargy, Roy, 61–62
Barker, Danny, 51, 53
Barnum, P. T., 41
Barris, Harry, 34
Bartemeier, Theresa (later Streckfus), 15, 119
Basie, Count, 38, 113
Baskerville, William "Bede," 105
Baskette, Billy, 84
Bates, Alan, 24, 27, 28–29
battle of the bands: concept of, 106–7, 113;
    in Pittsburgh, 152; in St. Louis, 100–
    101, 106–7; with trumpets, 114
Baxter Piano Company, 120

Beale Street (Memphis): blues styles of, 90;
    closing of, 93; description of, 88; reputa-
    tion of, 89
Bechet, Sidney, 69, 77, 126
Beiderbecke, Agatha (mother), 122, 127
Beiderbecke, Charles (brother), 124–25
Beiderbecke, Charles (father), 120, 122, 128
Beiderbecke, Leon "Bix": alcohol use of,
    117, 124, 128–29, 132, 140; background
    of, 117–18, 119–20, 128, 129; Cincinnati
    jobs of, 146; influences on, 114, 116–17,
    122–23, 125, 129–30, 134; jazz as defined
    by, 130–31; legacy of, 139–40; musical
    sensibility of, 118, 126–28; photograph
    of, *133;* playing style of, 123, 124; racial
    stereotypes used by, 123–24; recordings
    of, 34, 118, 130, 131, 132–34; riverboat
    jobs of, 126–27; St. Louis jobs of, 131–
    32; as symbol of riverboat jazz, 4
Bell, Bob, 171
Bell, James "Cool Papa," 154
Benny Goodman Orchestra, 116, 134, 135
Benson, George, 153
Benson Orchestra of Chicago, 61
Bergreen, Laurence, 68
Berland, Lauren, 9
Bess, Druie, 60
Betsy Ann, 12
Bhabha, Homi, 193–94n6
big band: riverboat jazz as precursor of era
    of, 150; use of term, 47
Bingham, George Caleb, 7
Birdlong, Cliff, 113
Bird's Point (Ky.), childhood in, 135
Bix Beiderbecke Memorial Jazz Festival, 140
Black, Louis, 125, *131*
Black and White Review, 146
Black Heartland, use of term, 10, 66
black music: adaptations of, 47–49; aural
    worldview of, 77–79; Beale Street mix-
    tures of, 89; as central to riverboat cul-
    ture, 52–53; commercialized versions of
    (folk), 10; European concert hall music's
    role in, 156; as exotic, 45–46; in-between
    space in, 83–86; popularized in St. Louis,
    95–96; in variety saloons and theaters,
    96–97. *See also* blues; jazz; riverboat jazz

Blakey, Art (Abdullah ibn Buhaina), 141–42, 153, 168

Blanton, James, 4, 38, 109, 150

Blue, Thornton, 4

blue notes, concept of, 50

blues: Beale Street's mix of, 90; in-between space and, 116; Memphis as capital of, 89; recordings of, 101; riverboat jazz influenced by, 89–90; roustabout songs as influence on, 89; as threatening, 81–82

blues singers, 65–66, 113

BobCats, 134

Boehmer, Julia Laughlin, 20

Bolden, Buddy, 70

Bolster, W. Jeffrey, 73

Booker T. Washington Theater (St. Louis), 95, 99

Boppers, 139–40

Bostic, Earl, 4, 150, 171

Bradley, Barnet, *61*

Brandt, J. Clyde, 136, 137

Brashear, Norman, 76

brass bands, 91. *See also* cornet; trumpet

bridges, 6–7

Brown, Ray, 150, *151*, 153

Brown, Red, 113

Brown, Scoville, 84

Brown, Sterling, 39

Brunies, George, 125

Brunswick record label, 199–200n72

Buchanan, Tom, 75

Buckley's Novelty Orchestra, 125

Buescher Musical Instrument Company, 111

Buffano, Jules, 20, 115, 205n1

Buhaina, Abdullah ibn (Art Blakey), 141–42, 153, 168

Bureau of Maritime Inspection and Navigation Service, 172–73

Bureau of Steam Boat Inspection, 172–73

Burke and Leins Orchestra, 205n1

Burleigh, Harry T., 156

Buzzin' Harris and His Hits and Bits, 160–61

Bynum, George, 91

calliopes: as attention getter, 16; playing of, 41–42, 49, 56–57, 139

Calloway, Cab, 38, 106, 109

Campbell, Floyd: background of, 112; band of, 101, 108; Cincinnati jobs of, 146; hiring of, 63; home base of, 109; on Marable, 56, 59; move to Chicago, 114; recordings of, 101; reputation of, 4; as singing drummer, 112–13; as traveling musician, 111–12

canals, 121–22, 206n12

Cape Girardeau, 53, 138, 147

Cape Girardeau (Mo.): excursion boats of, 20, 137; Stacy's time in, 136–37

Capitol: bands on, 21, 76, 101, 105, 111, 113, 125, 126, 138, 150; at Cape Girardeau, 137; at Davenport, 123, 206n17; demise of, 26, 173–74; at New Orleans, 119; origins of, 20; photograph of, 150, *151*; riverboat jazz on, 34; segregated cruises on, 58

Capitol Palace (St. Louis), 106

Capitol Theater (Davenport), 120

Capote, Truman, 27

Carmichael, Hoagy, 85, 132, 140

Carnegie Hall (New York), 135

Carolina Melodists, 111

carriage trade, boats for, 20, 23

Carroll, William, 21, 24, 174

Carruthers, Earl, 38

Carter, Allen, 163

Carter, Benny, 109

Caruso, Enrico, 156

Casimir, Sam, 150, *151*

Casimir, Willie, 150, *151*

casinos, 23, 176

Castle Ballroom (St. Louis), 105

Castle Club (St. Louis), 97

Catalano, Tony: band of, 115, 125, 139, 205n1; Beiderbecke's relationship with, 125–26; black bandleader of, 42; photographs of, *43*, *44*, *131*; playing style of, 130

Catlett, Sidney, 109

Celestin, Oscar, 69

Chambers, Jordan, 109

chanteys, 74–75, 85

Chauvin, Louis, 98

Cheatham, Doc, 139

Chicago: Beiderbecke on bands of, 123–24; clubs and dance halls in, 114, 139; jazz musicians in, 69, 71, 114, 139

Chisenhall, Fred, 89
"Chocolate Kiddies" Review, 146
Christian, Charlie, 109
Christian symbols, 73–74
church music, 120, 162, 163
Church of the Holy Cross (Pittsburgh), 163
Cincinnati: black population of, 145; clubs
    and dance halls in, 144, 146–47; excur-
    sion boats of, 147–50; jazz musicians of,
    146–47, 148; levee culture of, 141, 143–
    44, 146; as major port, 143; Pittsburgh
    compared with, 152
Cincinnati, 21, 23, 150, 173
Cincinnati Enquirer, Hearn's columns in, 143
Cincinnati Union, on black migrants, 145
Citizens' Liberty League (Republican
    Party), 95
City of Cairo, 103, *104*
City of Winona, 16
Clarke, Kenny (Liaqat Ali Salaam), 153, 168
Classic Jazz Band, 140
Clemens, Samuel. *See* Twain, Mark
Clifford, James, 73
Club Alabam Orchestra, 146
Club Riviera (St. Louis), 109
clubs and dance halls: in Chicago, 114, 139;
    in Cincinnati, 144, 146–47; in Daven-
    port, 120; non-union, 108–9; in Pitts-
    burgh, 152–55, 157, 158, 159; racial seg-
    regation of, 66–67, 109; in St. Louis, 97,
    99–102, 105, 108, 109, 111; whites at
    African American, 152–53
Cobb, Oliver, 105
Cochran, Cliff, 113
Coleman, Bill, 146, 147, 148
Coliseum (St. Louis), 106
Collins, Lee, 69
Columbia record label, 134, 139
Committee of Racial Equality (CORE), 175
Condon, Eddie, 117, 128–29, 134, 140
Coney Island (Ohio), 149
Conners, Sarah B. "Babe," 97
Coobus Club (Pittsburgh), 154
coonjine, definitions of, 52–53
Cooper, Jimmy, 145–46
Co-Operative Hall (New Orleans), 45, 71
CORE (Committee of Racial Equality), 175

cornet, role in jazz, 126
Cortinovis, Irene, 151
cotton, transportation of, 90
Cotton Club (Cincinnati), 146
Courance, Edgar "Spider," 148
Cox, Ida, 110
Crackerjacks: excursions played by, 91, 146,
    151–52; personnel changes in, 109;
    recordings of, 105–6
Crawford Grill (Pittsburgh; earlier, Leader
    House), 157, 159
Crawfords (baseball team), 154
Creamer, Henry, 82, 134, 157
Creath, Charles: as authentic, 9; bands of,
    101, 102, 108, 113, 145; in battle of
    bands, 152; on Garner, 164; home base
    of, 109; jazz promotions of, 99–100,
    102–3; reputation of, 4, 99–100
crews: photograph of, *151*; role of, 6–7;
    typhoid fever epidemic among, 19
Crosby, Bing, 34
Crosby, Bob, 134
Crump, Edward Hull, 91, 93
Crusto, Manuel, 150, *151*
Curt, Wilbur, 171

Dagen, Irv, 175
Dagen, Maggie, 175
Dahl, Linda, 159
Daily Times (Davenport), 120
dance: arranged music for, 39, 47–49, 60;
    emotional power of, 193–94n6; interstice
    in, 116. *See also* clubs and dance halls; hot
    dance music
dance band, use of term, 47
Davenport (Iowa): Armstrong's visit to, 123;
    casino in, 23, 176; clubs and dance halls
    in, 120; German immigrant culture in,
    119–20; musical life of, 120–21, 127–28,
    129–30; riverboat culture in, 122–23,
    124–25; river's role in, 121–22; Streck-
    fus business and family ties in, 119–20,
    122, 125
Davenport, Eugene, 175
Davis, Leonard "Ham," 83, 99, 109
Davis, Miles, 86, 94–95, 101, 106
Davison, William "Wild Bill," 139

"Dear Old Southland," 82
Decca record label, 83–84, 105–6
Dedroit's band, 35
"Deep River," 82, 83
Democrat and Leader (Davenport), 120
Denney, Homer, 42
DeParis, Sidney, 146
DeParis, Wilbur, 146
Deppe, Lois P., 142, 148, 156, 157, 159, 160
Desdunes, Clarence, 69
Desvignes, Sidney, 59, *61*, 61–62
Dial, Harry, 83, 103, 171
Diamond Jo Line, 19, 26
Dixie Bell, 45
Dodds, Johnny, *46*, 59
Dodds, Warren "Baby": on Marable, 55–56,
    63; mentioned, 3–4, 86; photographs of,
    46, *76*; playing style of, 45, 47; silences
    of, 168; on whites' curiosity, 54
Donaldson, Walter, 7–8, 130
Douroux, Irving, 150, *151*
Downs, Matt, 91
drugs, Jive for, 155
Du Bois, W. E. B., 39, 82, 83
Dubuque, 19, 20
Dunbar, Paul Laurence, 156
Duncan, Will, 136
"Dusky Stevedore," 83, 84, 132, 134
Dutrey, Sam, 45, 59

Eagle Packet Company, 19
Early, Gerald, 10, 66
East St. Louis, 156
East St. Louis (Ill.): race riot in, 44, 83; role
    in riverboat jazz's development, 93–94
Eaton, Jimmy, 84
Eckstine, Billy, 153, 154, 168
Economy Hall (New Orleans), 71
Eddie Condon Gang, 117, 134
Edison, Harry "Sweets," 109
education, musical, 91–92, 95, 97–98, 100–
    101, 118, 160. *See also* musical literacy
Elder, Clarence, 40–41, 55
Eldridge, Roy, 99–100, 150, 153
11 Aces, 150
Ellington, Duke, 38, 62, 77, 106, 146, 162
Ellison, Ralph, 177

Ertegun, Neshui, 70
Eureka Brass Band, 158
Europe, jazz musicians touring in, 146
European concert hall music: appreciation
    of, 120, 127; black vernacular mixed
    with, 157; as influence, 129–30, 136; role
    in Pittsburgh jazz, 156; trumpet's role in,
    100. *See also* musical literacy
Evans, Carlisle, 115–16, 125, *131*, 205n1
Evans, George E., 169
excursion boats: children on, 28; commer-
    cialization via, 23; concession profits of,
    27; cultural history of, 13–14, 25–27, 75;
    daytime vs. moonlight cruises on, 24–25;
    demise of, 23–24, 171–77; description of,
    16–17, 28; efforts to resurrect, 170;
    emergence of, 1; packets converted to,
    18–21; role of, 6–7; roustabouts' influ-
    ence on, 51–52; show boats compared
    with, 8; sociology of, 147–48; symbols
    and themes associated with, 2–4, 32–34,
    124–25; tediousness of, 28–29. *See also*
    crews; hot dance music; passengers;
    riverboat jazz

Fair Labor Standards Act, 173
Famous Iowans, Catalano's, 125, 139
"fashionable tour," commercialization of,
    25–26
Fate Marable and the Cotton Pickers, 105.
    See also Marable, Fate; Metropolitan Jaz-
    E-Saz Orchestra
femininity, water associated with, 32–33
Ferber, Edna, 8, 28
Fields, John L., 107
Finney, Chick, 58, 101, 103, 105–6
fire: boats destroyed by, 17–18, 43, 103, 126,
    138, 148–49; construction methods to
    prevent, 21, 23, 26, 172–73; dangers of,
    18; smoking bans due to, 19
Fisher, Bernice, 175
Flindt, Emil, 42, 43, *44*, 125
floods, 8, 135
Floyd, Samuel A., Jr., 74
Fontaine, Letitia Lula Agatha "Mama
    Lou," 97
"Forty Thieves, The" (organization), 163

Foster, George "Pops," 45, *46*, 47, 83, 101
Foster, Willie, *61*
Franklin, Earnest, 151
Frank Trumbauer Orchestra, 131–34
Freddie, 15–16
freedom, search for, 71, 164
Frogs (Pittsburgh), 154
Fulton, Robert, 2, 143

Gandhi, Mahatma, 175
gangs, street, 96
Gara, Larry, 55
Garber, Jan, 20, 139
Garner, Erroll: background of, 142, 153, 166;
    bookings for, 167; as intuitive improviser,
    162–63; riverboat jobs of, 163–64
Garner, Ruth, 163
Garrett, Charles, 84
Gaslight Club (St. Louis), 111
German Reformed church, 120
Gershwin, George, 61, 150
Gershwin, Ira, 150
"get-off" music, use of term, 11. *See also* im-
    provisations
Gibbs, A. Harrington, 129
Gibson, Josh, 154
gift shops, 29
Glaser, Joe, 67, 167
Goldkette, Jean, 132, 133
Goodman, Benny, 116, 134, 135
Goodson, Edna, 69
Goodson, Ida, 69
Gordon C. Greene, 147
Graham and Morton Line, 126
Grant, B. David, 12, 37
Great Depression: audience numbers decline
    in, 114; excursions' affordability in, 142,
    148; jobs lost in, 108–9. *See also* Great
    Migration
Greater New Orleans, 23
Greater Pittsburgh, 150
Great Migration: hazards of, expressed in
    music, 73; hopes in, 5, 93, 95; impetus
    for, 37–38; jazz stream in, 3–4, 10–11,
    38, 58, 65–66; keyboard virtuosity linked
    to, 164; Memphis as stop in, 90; Missouri
    as stop in, 136; neighborhood changes

due to, 158; Ohio valley as stop in, 144–
    45, 153; play's depiction of effects of,
    164–66; professionalization in context
    of, 57–58; realities of, 167; as threaten-
    ing, 81–82
Greene, Gordon C., 147
Greene, Mary, 147
Greene, Tom, 147
Greene Line, 147, 176
Greenfield, Jack, 112
Greer, Bill, 125
Grey Eagle, 102, 103
Grieg, Edvard, 161
Gussow, Adam, 92

habitus concept, 73
Hackett, Bobby, 139–40
Hajdu, David, 161
Hall, Edmund, 69
Hammerstein, Oscar, 8
Hampton Institute, 82–83
Handy, John, 69
Handy, W. C. (William Christopher): bands
    of, 89, 91–92, 112; compositions of, 49,
    92; on Malone, 92, 177
Hannibal (Mo.), attitudes toward black mu-
    sicians in, 54
Hardin, Lil, 91
Hardy, Emmet, 125
Harker, Brian, 126
Harlem Globe Trotters team, 114
Harlem Steppers, 152
Havens, Daniel F., 56
Havird, Hal, 205n1
Hawley, Clark, 24, 27, 28–29, 41–42
Hayes, Edgar, 146
Hearn, Lafcadio, 29, 141, 143–44
Helena (Ark.): blues in, 113; river traffic in,
    112
Hemenway (Hemingway), Janie, 103, 113
Henderson, Fletcher: band of, 75–76, 77;
    Cincinnati jobs of, 146; colleagues of,
    62; as influence, 101, 106; St. Louis
    tradition introduced to, 109
Hennion, Antoine, 117
Herskovits, Melville, 73
Hertzog (Herzog), Charlie, 42, 205n1

"He's a Son of the South," 83
Hickman, Art, 47, 48
Hill District. *See* Pittsburgh
Hilliard, Lee, 106
Hilton, Bleigh, 122
Hines, Earl: background of, 142, 153, 156, 158–59, 166; as influence, 161; reputation of, 157, 159, 164
historic sites, 24, 29
homophony, 50
Honey, Michael J., 90
Hopkins, Claude, 106
Horne, Lena, 153
hot dance music: appeal of, 122–23; black and white responses to, 5; decline of, 171–77; evocativeness of, 32–33; impetus for providing, 29; in levee culture, 143; origins of, 97–98; promotion of, 20, 27–28; psychological experience of, 7–8; racial and musical stimulation of, 30, 32; slang of movement in, 72; St. Louis role in, 109–10; Stacy's playing of, 136–37; tempi of, 35, 48–49; use of term, 2. *See also* riverboat jazz
hotels, blacks excluded from, 67. *See also* clubs and dance halls
Howard, Joe, 45, *46*, 59, 109
Huck Finn (boat), 173
Huckleberry Finn (Twain), 8
Hudson, George, 109
Hughes, Langston, 39
Hunter, Alberta, 89
Hurston, Zora Neale, 39
"Hyena Stomp," 72

Idlewild, 91, 105, 108, 151
Illinois and Michigan Canal, 121–22, 206n12
Illinois and Mississippi Canal, 206n12
Illinois River, improvements of, 122
imagination, music's effects on, 30, 32, 33–34
immigrants: African American conflicts with, 153–54, 159, 161; cultural position of, 193–94n6; German, 119–20
improvisations: concept of, 11; controlling amount of, 34–35; defense of, 57; popularity of, 59; slang of, 77; sophistication of, 39; as threatening, 81–82; white mu-

sicians' pursuit of, 118. *See also specific musicians (e.g., Armstrong, Louis)*
Ink Spots, 109, 114
insurance, 13
Internal Revenue Service, 174
International Sweethearts of Rhythm, 106
Interracial Review, 105
Interstate Commerce Commission, 173
interstice concept, 116, 193–94n6
Invisible Man (Ellison), 177
Irwin, May, 97
Islam, 168, 169
Island Queen (three boats), *25*, 116, 147, 148–49

Jackson, Bennie, 151
Jackson, Dewey: as authentic, 9; background of, 103; bands of, 101, 105, 108, 145, 151; in battle of bands, 152; home base of, 109; recordings of, 113, 199–200n72; reputation of, 4, 99–100
Jamal, Ahmad (Fritz Jones), 153, 160, 168, 169
James, Baby, 100
James Rees and Sons, 143
jazz: ambivalence of, 167; "authentic" black, 9–10, 70, 124; cornet's role in, 126; definitions of, 130–31; as habitus, 73; illusion of absence of, in public life, 4–5; movement linked to, 71–72; origins of, 50–51; political activism and, 95; psychological experience of, 193n2; reach of, under surface of public life, 7–8; seductiveness of, 4; as shield of optimism and emotional solace, 118; St. Louis and national styles blended in, 109; trumpet's role in, 99–101; use of term, 23, 44; whites' fascination with, 5. *See also* hot dance music; improvisations; New Orleans jazz; riverboat jazz
jazz jubilee, 120
Jazzland dance hall (St. Louis), 99, 100
jazzmen and jazz musicians: as amateurs, 117, 134, 140; booker for, 101–3, 166–67; as heralds, 1–2, 65–66; migration of, 89–90, 93; networking among, 66, 154–55; role of, 6–7; use of term, 5. *See also* riverboat jazz musicians

Jazz-O-Maniacs, 99, 101, 204n55
Jean Goldkette Orchestra, 132, 133
Jefferson, Eddie, 101
Jeffersonville (Ind.), shipyards of, 143
Jessup, Rex, 42, 43, *44*, 125
Jeter, James, 109
Jeter-Pillars Orchestra, 108, 109, 146
Jive, 155–56
Johnson, Albert "Budd," 84
Johnson, Eddie: as authentic, 9; band of,
    105, 109; excursions played by, 91, 105,
    146, 151; on Jesse Johnson, 103. *See also*
    Crackerjacks
Johnson, J. C., 84
Johnson, J. Rosamond, 156
Johnson, Jesse: battle of the bands concept
    of, 106–7, 113; as jazz booker, 101–3,
    105, 106
Jones, David, 45, *46*, 59, 75, *76*, 110
Jones, Fritz (Ahmad Jamal), 153, 160, 168,
    169
Jones, Jimmie, 171
Jones, Joe, 109
Joplin, Scott, 98
Jordan, Joe, 98, 156
Jordan, Louis, 112
J.S.: bands on, 40–41, 42, 125, 150; burning
    of, 17–18, 43, 149; calliope of, 42; as Jess
    (jazz), 23; photograph of, *18*
J.S. Deluxe: bands on, 113, 115; market for,
    20, 149; musicians on, 131
jukeboxes, 29
Julia Belle Swain, 150

Kate Adams, 112
Kayser, Joe, 139
Kentucky Jazz Band, 44
Kern, Jerome, 8
Keyes, Frances Parkinson, 28
Keystone Jazzers, 100–101
Kid Ory's band, 69–71
Kimball, Henry, *61*, *76*
King, Leon, 56
King, Martin Luther, Jr., 170
King, Vernon, 171
King, Wayne, 20, 115, 205n1
King Oliver's Creole Jazz Band, 66

King Oliver's Dixie Syncopation, 199–
    200n72
Kinkle, Roger, 34
Kirk, Andy, 109, 162
Kittel, Daisy Wilson, 164–66
Kittel, Frederick August (August Wilson),
    164–66
KMOX (radio), 105, 111
Knights of Pythias band, 100, 145
Kratz, George, 16
Ku Klux Klan, 93

L. A. Murray Company, 120
Lake Michigan, excursion boat on, 126
Lala, Peter, 70
Lamont, Jack, 150, *151*
Lane, Eastwood, 129–30
Lang, Harry, 107, 150, *151*
Langford, P. B., 100
Lankford, Harvey, *61*, 152
Laplace (La.), music venue in, 69–70
LaRocca, Nick, 125, 130
"La Veda," 82
Layton, Turner, 82, 134, 157
"Lazy River," 85
"Lazy 'Sippi Steamer," 83, 84, 85
Lee, George W., 88, 89, 93
Lee, Peters, 91
Lee Line, 91
levees, 88, *94*, 121. *See also* roustabout levee
    culture and songs
Lhamon, W. T., Jr., 72
Liberty, 102
Life on the Mississippi (Twain), 8, 26
liminality concept, 193–94n6
Linebaugh, Peter, 194n17
Lipsitz, George, 124
literacy, meanings of, 77. *See also* musical
    literacy
Little, Dick, 205n1
Locke, Alain, 39, 82
locks and dams, 20, 23, 119, 121–22, 142
"Lonesome Road," 85
Long, Sammy, 100, 103, 113
longshoremen, 51, 69. *See also* roustabouts;
    stevedores
lore cycle, 72

Louisiana Purchase Exposition (1904), 98
Lovingood, Burroughs, 4, 56, 150
Lunceford, Jimmie, 38, 89, 106
Luper, Andrew, 103
Lutheran church, 120
lynchings, 37, 83, 92

Mackey, Nathaniel, 68, 73, 206n4
Majestic, 91, 102, 103, 126, 138
Malone, William, 92, 177
Mangan, Carl, *46,* 168
Marable, Elizabeth Lillian (Wharton), 40
Marable, Fate: alcohol use of, 56, 157; Armstrong's relationship with, 64, 82, 83; authoritarian manner of, 55–56; background of, 39–40; bands of, 9, 20–21, 60–62, 77, 105, 111, 145; in battle of bands, 152; Beiderbecke on, 123, 124; calliope playing of, 41–42; Catalano's relationship with, 125; Coleman on, 147; composition of, 43–44; Davenport visit of, 122; death of, 171; as father of school of jazz piano, 157–58; Garner as replacement for, 163–64; home base of, 109, 157; improvisation resisted by, 81; on *J.S.,* 43; musical literacy and professionalism emphasized by, 38–39, 56–60, 75–76, 79, 108; in New Orleans scene, 45; Ohio River scene and, 149, 150; photographs of, 43, *44, 46, 61, 76;* playing style of, 47, 164; racial segregation and, 42–43; recordings of, 60–62; recruitment by, 39, 59, 62–63, 71; restrictions on, 36; role of, 10–11, 38; on roustabout songs, 50–51; silences of, 168; Stacy on, 137. *See also* Metropolitan Jaz-E-Saz Orchestra
Marable, Harold, 40
Marable, James, 40
Marable, Juanita, 40
Marable, Mabel, 40
Marable, Neona, 40
Marietta (Ohio), shipyards of, 143
marine architecture: disadvantages of, 13; fire prevention measures in, 21, 23, 26; innovations in, 16–17; open-air decks in, 28; steamboat gothic style of, 25–26. *See also* fire

Market Street (St. Louis), 97, 99–102
Marshall, Kaiser, 171
Martin, Freddie, 151
Martin, Walter, 151
Mason, Norman, 59, *61, 76,* 109–10, 111
McKay, Claude, 154
McKee, Margaret, 89
McKendrick, Mike, 83–84
McKinney's Cotton Pickers, 114
McPartland, Jimmy, 128–29, 139–40
McPartland, Marion, 137
McVicker, Carl, 160, 161, 162–63
Melody Jazz Band, 125
Melton, Gloria Brown, 90
Memphis: brass bands in, 91; as crossroads, 88–89; economy of, 90; literate black music culture in, 91–92; racial politics in, 92–93; as stop in Great Migration, 90
men, Jive for, 156
Mercantile Library (St. Louis), 172
Metropolitan Jaz-E-Saz Orchestra: competition for, 102–3; Davenport visit of, 122; musicians in, 81–82, 109, 110; playing style of, 47; popularity of, 49–50
Meyer, Henry, 151
Meyer, Joseph, 132–33
Meyer, Raymond F. "Peg," 53, 135, 136–38, 139
Meyers, Henry, 105, 108
Middleton, Velma, 72
Midway Garden band (Chicago), 139
"Mighty River," 83, 84
Miles, Lizzie, 110
Mills, Charlie, 40–41, 42, 197n19
Mills Blue Rhythm Band, 38
Mills Brothers, 109
minstrelsy: black music associated with, 45–46; legacy of, 134; stereotypes of, 9, 29–30, *31,* 67, 84, 123–24
"Mississippi Basin," 83, 84
Mississippi River: Armstrong on, 71, 86; black intercity network along, 75; cultural history of, 13–14; Davenport's development and, 121–22; "fashionable tour" of, 25–26; flood of, 8, 135; Great Swamp of, 135–36; map of, *xi;* musical

Mississippi River (*continued*)
context of, 2; Ohio River compared with, 143; topography of, 5–6; views of, 7, 24; water levels of, 19, 21, 23; winter port on, 119
Missouri, as migration point, 136
Mitchell, Joseph, 95
Moldy Figs, 139–40
moldy figs, use of term, 69
Moline (Ill.), music conservatory in, 120
money, Jive for, 155. *See also* wages
Montmartre Orchestra of Chicago, 20
Morgan, Al, 38, 59
Morgan, Sam, 69
Morgan, Tom, 96
Morning Star, 148
Morro Castle, 172
Morton, Jelly Roll, 72, 111, 147
Mosely, Lawrence "Snub," 83, 109
Moslem Sunrise, focus of, 169
movies, 21
Mozart Comedy Four, 98
mud sill cities, 52
music: as art, 117, 118; changing styles in, 171–77; as complaint and consolation, 68; emotional power of, 193–94n6; innovation in, 81–82; interstice in, between white social dance music and black blues and jazz, 116; Memphis as crossroads of, 89; movement linked to, 71–72. *See also* black music; blues; European concert hall music; hot dance music; jazz; race music; ragtime; riverboat jazz
musical literacy: Armstrong on, 75–77; Beiderbecke's lack of, 116, 126–27; emphasis on, 38–39, 57–60; of Memphis musicians, 91–92; opportunities in St. Louis, 95, 97–98, 100–101; in Pittsburgh's Westinghouse High, 160–62. *See also* sightreading

Natchez, 176
National Association of Negro Musicians, 82–83
National Labor Relations Board, 173
Neal, Myron, *131*
Negro Business League (St. Louis), 99

Negro National League, 154
New Albany (Ind.), shipyards of, 143
New England Conservatory of Music (Boston), 150
New Orleans: Armstrong's departure from, 68–69; Cincinnati compared with, 146; musicians' wages in, 69, 79–80; music venues in and near, 45, 70–71; racial violence in, 68; winter steamers of, 20–21. See also *Capitol*; New Orleans jazz
New Orleans, 143
New Orleans Harmonists, *61*
New Orleans jazz: Beiderbecke on, 122; musicians as emissaries of, 1–2; riverboat jazz as tamed version of, 81–82; roustabouts' music as influence on, 30; tempi and repertoire of, 35
New York Age, on jazzing of spirituals, 82–83
New Yorker, on Garner, 162–63
Nicholas Brothers, 109
Nichols, Lester, 151
Nickell, Frank, 135
Nowland, Ed, 91
Nun, Anna, 144

Odd Fellows Band, 100, 103
Ohio River: boats crushed by ice in, 148; cultural history of, 13–14; improvements of, 142; map of, *xi*; scenic advantages of, 143; topography of, 5–6
Okeh record label, 60–62, 84, 85, 111
Oliver, Joseph "King": bands of, 66, 199–200n72; colleagues of, 62; as influence, 125; move to Chicago, 69, 71; playing style of, 101; recording of, 199–200n72
Ong, Walter, 77–78
Original Dixieland Jazz Band: as influence, 116–17, 130, 132; playing style of, 72; recordings of, 44, 91, 121, 124
Ory, Edward "Kid," 45, 69–71, 79

packet boats: construction of, 143; conversion of, 18–21; cotton transported via, 90; safety regulations on, 172–73; schedules of, 16
packet business: African American role in, 29–30; decline of, 53, 96; elitism in, 147;

making money in, 12–13; roustabouts' role in, 51–52; Streckfus's beginnings in, 15–16

Paducah (Ky.), black musicians' union based in, 54–55

Page, Walter, 109

Paige, Clarence, 146

Paige, Satchel, 154

Palmer, "Bee," 121

Palmer, Singleton, 111, 151, 152

Panico, Louis, 20, 61, 115

Paradise Dance Palace (St. Louis), 106

Parlan, Horace, 153

passengers: dance cards of, 49; excursions' affordability for, 142, 148; musical tastes of, 48–51; release felt by, 33–34; role of, 6–7; segregated cruises for, 58, 102–3, 163; tediousness of, 28–29; voyages of discovery for, 2–4, 8, 13–14, 28, 30, 32

passing for white, 40

Patterson, Pete, 112

Patterson, Sam, 98

Pattona, 91

Paul Whiteman Orchestra, 34, 48, 126, 132, 134

Peacock Orchestra, 199–200n72

Pecci, Buzzi, 156

Perryman, Gus, 112

Persons, Arch, 27

Persons, Ell, 83

Persons, Truman Streckfus, 27

Peterson, Sadie Goodson, 69

Petit, Buddy, 69

Phillips, Homer G., 95

piano, play's depiction of power of, 164–66. *See also* Pittsburgh school of jazz piano

Piano Lesson, The (Wilson), 164–66

Pichon, Walter "Fats," 108, 150–51, *151, 152*

Pierce, Billie, 69

Pilgrim, 102, 103

Pillars, Hayes, 106, 108, 109, 146

Piron, Armand J., 150

Pittsburgh: boat explosion in, 149; clubs and dance halls in, 152–55, 157, 158, 159; description of, 141–42; excursion boats of, 150, 163; jazz musicians of, 156–64,
166–69; jazz scene in, 142, 152–56; play's depiction of, 164–66; "urban renewal" in, 169–70

Pittsburgh Courier: on black unionized musicians, 166–67; on Deppe, 148; on excursion boats, 163; on Hines, 159; offices of, 154

Pittsburgh school of jazz piano: bookings for, 166–67; depth and creativity of, 142; foundations of, 157–58; Garner as exemplar of, 164; Great Migration and, 153; Westinghouse High and, 160–62

Plantation Club (St. Louis), 109

"playing together separately" concept, 60

Pletcher, Tom, 140

Point Pleasant (W.Va.), shipyards of, 143

political activism: African American, 168–70, 175–76; ragtime and jazz linked to, 95

political rallies, 91–92

polyphony, 47, 50, 73

polyrhythm, 73

President: advertisement for, *22;* air conditioning of, 172; bands on, 115, 150, 163–64; as casino, 176; home port of, 173–74; market for, 20; New Orleans cruises of, 119; origins of, 21, 23, 150, 173

primitivism, 39, 130

Princess, 148

professionalism: emphasis on, 38–39, 57–58; historical context of, 50–51; rejection of, 116–17, 134; as reordering social structure, 54–55. *See also* sight-reading; unionism

prostitution, 89, 96, 97, 146

Public Accommodations Law, 175–76

QRS Boys, 150

Quad Cities area: excursion boats of, 20; music conservatory in, 120; Streckfus Block in, 14. *See also* Davenport (Iowa)

Quincy, 19, 20

Quincy (Ill.), groundings near, 20

Raban, Jonathan, 7

Rabbit Foot Minstrels, 110

Rabia, Aliyah (Dakota Staton), 153, 168

race music, meanings of, 39

race relations: avoiding realities of, 6; changes in, 171–77; jazz as window in, 5–6; liminal experiences in, 145; silences about, 86–87, 168

race riots, 44, 83, 170

racial oppression: persistence of, 167–68; piano playing as defense against, 159–60; as subtext, 9, 37–38, 102–3, 162; in theaters, 107–8, 162, 167. *See also* stereotypes; *specific musicians*

racial segregation: of clubs and dance halls, 66–67, 109; in exploitative music business, 165; in housing, 169; increased due to Great Migration, 158; law against, 175–76; in Missouri, 136; in Navy band, 168; promoters' fight against, 102–3; public confidence in, 27; of riverboat cruises, 58, 102–3, 163; of riverboat jazz bands and orchestras, 42–44, 67; spiritual and psychological effects of, 166; in St. Louis, 93; of unions, 38, 44, 55, 106, 166–67

radios, 21

ragtime, 95, 97, 98, 99, 112

railroads: advantages of, 2, 13; canals' demise due to, 122; difficulties of competing with, 19; excursions on, 70; jobs lost to, 53; migration via, 145; schedules of, 16

Rainey, Gertrude "Ma," 110

Rainey, Memphis Ma, 89

Randle, Eddie: as bandleader, 101; dream of, 103; reputation of, 99; sightreading lessons by, 62–63; versatility of, 58; on working hard, 106–7

Randolph, Irving "Mouse," 38, 99, 109, 113, 171

Randolph, Zilner, 83, 84, 112

Ravel, Maurice, 129–30

Razaf, Andy, 83, 84

Redicker, Marcus, 194n17

Red River Hall Gang, 96

Rees, James, 91, 143

Republican Party, 95

Reynolds, Joseph, 19

Rhumboogie Club (Chicago), 114

Rhythm Boys, 34

Ridgley, William "Bebe," 45, *46*, 59

ring shout, 74

riverboat hip, 40

riverboat jazz: Armstrong as figurehead of, 3–4; authenticity of, 9–10, 70, 124; "Blue River" as expression of, 132–33; blues as influence on, 89–90; decline of, 171–77; elements of, 39, 60; evocativeness of, 32–33; innovations of, 2, 111; musical development of, 95–96; origins of, 144–45; precursor of, 150; psychological experience of, 7–8, 193n2; reappearances of, 176–77; role of, 7, 23, 33–34; roustabouts' influence on, 53–54; social dance music compared with, 148; songs of, listed, 184–91; as synthesis of black and white practices, 50; as tamed New Orleans jazz, 81–82; themes of, 2–4, 6, 71; unacknowledged context of, 37–38; use of term, 1. *See also* hot dance music

Riverboat Jazz (album), 199–200n72

riverboat jazz musicians: adjustments of, 49–51; culture of, 11; daily schedule of, 37; dress of, 30; etiquette expected of, 38–39; list of, 179–83; as male, 32–33; recruitment of, 39, 59, 62–63, 71; roustabouts compared with, 52; stereotypes of, 33–34; versatility of, 57–58; white bands of, 20. *See also* professionalism; unionism; *specific musicians*

riverboat jazz orchestras: declining jobs in, 108–9; division of labor in, 77; first saxophone section in, 111; length of performances of, 49, 55, 126; racial segregation of, 42–44, 67. *See also* musical literacy; professionalism; unionism; *specific musicians and bands*

riverboat system: brutal treatment of blacks in, 9–10, 52, 168; demise of, 171–77; disadvantages of, 2, 13; turning point for employment in, 10–11. *See also* crews; fire; packet business; roustabouts; Streckfus Steamers, Inc.; *specific boats*

rivers: cult of, 73–74, 122; decline of, 176; freedom of movement linked to, 74–75; historical themes associated with, 24; jazz's relation to, 1–11, 71–72; people of, 5–6; spiritual power of, 73–74. *See also*

Arkansas River; Illinois River; Mississippi River; Ohio River
Robeson, Paul, 9, 168–69
Robinson, James H., 90
Rock Island (Ill.), Streckfus Block in, 14
Rodemich, Gene, 100–101, 115, 205n1
Rodgers, Bonnie, 168
Roosevelt, Theodore, 42
Roppolo, Leon, 125
Rosebud Café (St. Louis), 98, 99
Ross, Bonnie, 205n1
Roth, Al, 205n1
roustabout levee culture and songs: Armstrong's recordings and, 84; Cincinnati traditions in, 141, 143–44, 146; as influence, 53–54, 89, 122–23; jazz as outgrowth of, 50–51; mud associated with, 34; revisioning of, 53–54; setting of, 37; as show business, 52–53; themes of, 53, 88
roustabouts: appearance of, 144; brutality against, 9–10, 52; jobs lost by, 10–11, 96; sleeping of, 88; stereotypes of, 29–30, 31, 51, 134; work of, 51, 53. See also longshoremen; stevedores
Rushing, Jimmy, 101, 113
Russell, Charles "Pee Wee," 128–29, 132

Sager, Eric, 88
sailors' chanteys, 74–75, 85
Saint James Methodist Episcopal Church (Pittsburgh), 162
Salaam, Liaqat Ali (Kenny Clarke), 153, 168
saloons. See clubs and dance halls; variety saloons and theaters
Samuel Clemens (boat), 173
Sandke, Randy, 140
Saunders, Vertna, 56, 163–64
Sauter's Park (St. Louis), 105
saxophones, first section of, 111
Schaab, Anna Mary (later Streckfus), 14
Schacht, Beulah, 45
Schlichting, Eunice, 120
Schuller, Gunther, 61
Schwartzbach, Elmer, 115
Scott, Shirley, 153
Scottsboro Boys Defense Fund, 105

search for freedom, 71, 164
Sedric, Eugene P. "Honey Bear," 4, 38, 111, 145–46
Sedric, Paul "Con Con," 145
Senator, 20, 60
Sexton, Al, 131
Shaffner, Ruth, 133
Shand, Terry, 84
"Shanty Boat on the Mississippi," 83, 84–85
Shaw, Elijah, 107, 108
Shaw, Leige, 55
Shoffner, Robert Lee, 99, 100, 199–200n72
Show Boat (Ferber), 8, 28
Show Boat (musical): African American response to, 8–9; popularity of, 28; possible revision of, 10; recordings of, 132, 134; Robeson's role in, 168
Sidney: bands on, 34, 46, 64; length of, 19; photograph of, 80; refurbishing of, 21, 150; replacement for, 20
sightreading: emphasis on, 56–57, 120; failure in, 58–59; lessons in, 62–63; memory and, 60; Stacy's ability in, 118, 135, 137; union membership and, 54–55, 126–27; Williams's learning of, 161–62
singing drummer, 112–13
Singing Synco Seven, 113, 146
Singleton, Zutty, 4, 61, 63, 65, 171
slaves: rivers as freedom of movement for, 74–75; swamps as refuge for, 71; water's symbolism for, 73–74
Smith, Jabbo, 114
Smith, Mamie, 110
Smith, Nathan Clark, 98
Smith, Stuff, 106
Smith, Tallmadge "Tab," 4, 38, 109, 150
Snaer, Al, 171
Snowden, Elmer, 150
social dance music, 148
social order, music's function in, 81–82
Society Syncopators, 60–62, 111. See also Metropolitan Jaz-E-Saz Orchestra
"Sometimes I Feel Like a Motherless Child," 82
Sons of Bix, 140
sound amplification, 46–47
Southeastern Missouri State University, 136

Southern Workman, on jazzing of spirituals, 82–83

Spanier, Muggsy, 139

spirituality, water's symbolism in, 73–74

spirituals: jazzing of, 82–83; traditional renderings of, 70

sponsorship and charter system, 28

Spurrier, Esten, 120–21, 127

St. Cyr, John, 45, *46,* 76

St. Louis: Armstrong and, 66, 106; Beiderbecke and, 131–32; black political movements in, 175–76; black population of, 93–95; carriage trade of, 20, 23; "catfish and crystal" elite of, 28; as center of black music, 10, 95–96; clubs and dance halls in, 97, 99–102, 105, 108, 109, 111; hot dance bands in, 109–11; jazz's development in, 93–114; levee in, 88, *94;* musical education in, 95, 97–98, 100–101; opportunities in, 112–13; suburbanization of, 172; variety saloons and theaters in, 96–97. *See also* East St. Louis (Ill.)

St. Louis Argus: advertisements in, 19–20, 103, *104;* on black middle class, 95; on black musicians' union, 107–8; on Marable, 62; on musical education, 100; on ragtime, 99

"St. Louis Blues," 49, 83, 92, 113, 119

St. Louis Chamber of Commerce, 19

St. Louis Peacock Orchestra, 103

St. Louis Post-Dispatch, 175

St. Louis University, 35, 105

St. Paul: bands on, 34, *61,* 105, 106, 113, 150, 152; competition for, 102–3; conversion of, 136; dance floor of, 46–47; dancing on, 35, 49; description of, 19–20; New Orleans cruises of, 119; photograph of, *3;* segregated cruises on, 58

Stacy, Frederick Lee, 135, 136

Stacy, Jesse Alexandria "Jess": background of, 117–19, 129, 135; band of, 130; influences on, 114, 136, 137; legacy of, 139; mentioned, 4; musical sensibility of, 136–37; photograph of, *138;* recordings of, 119; reputation of, 116, 134–35; riverboat jobs of, 137–39

Stacy, Pat, 135

Stacy, Sarah "Vada," 135, 136

Stark, John, 97, 98

Staton, Dakota (Aliyah Rabia), 153, 168

steamboat fever, use of term, 15

steamboats, 2. *See also* excursion boats

stereotypes: of "baad black man," 5; of jazz, 130–31; of minstrelsy, 9, 29–30, *31,* 67, 84, 123–24; of mud and skin color, 34; of riverboat jazz musicians, 33–34; of roustabouts, 29–30, *31,* 51, 134; in *Show Boat,* 8–9

Sterling Hotel (Cincinnati), 146

stevedores, 29–30. *See also* longshoremen; roustabouts

Stewart, Rex, 114, 150

Stocksdale, Harry, 42

Storey, Nathaniel, 38, 113, 150, 171

Storyville: Armstrong's childhood in, 68; closing of, 65, 71; as influence, 82; remembered, 80

Stravinsky, Igor, 129–30

Strayhorn, Billy, 153, 161, 164, 166

Streckfus, Anna Mary (Schaab), 14

Streckfus, Balthazar, 14, 15, 119

Streckfus, Barbara, 14

Streckfus, Catherine, 14

Streckfus, John, Sr.: Armstrong hired by, 64; background of, 14–15; brutality of, 168; excursion boat design of, 16–18; family of, 119, 120; innovation of, 2; musical preferences of, 39, 45, 81, 87, 168; packet boats converted by, 18–21, 43, 136; packet business of, 15–16; photograph of, *15*

Streckfus, John Curran, 174

Streckfus, John Nicholas, Jr., *15,* 23, 86

Streckfus, Joseph Leo: Armstrong's recordings as response to, 83, 84; bandleaders listed by, 115–16, 205n1; company controlled by, 173–74; death of, 171; excursion boats of, 21, 23; family of, 119; musical preferences of, 23, 34–35, 39, 47–51; photograph of, *15;* on safety measures, 172–73; union negotiations and, 107

Streckfus, Michael, 14

Streckfus, Robert, Jr., 176

Streckfus, Robert, Sr., 176

Streckfus, Roy Michael, *15,* 23, 173–76

Streckfus, Steven, 176
Streckfus, Theresa (Bartemeier), 15, 119
Streckfus, Verne Walter, *15*, 23, 60, 173–74
Streckfus, William S., 174
Streckfus Steamers, Inc.: bandleaders of, listed, 115–16, 205n1; calliope playing on, 41–42; competition for, 102–3, 105, 126; cultural interpretation of riverboats by, 25–27; Davenport business and family ties of, 119–20, 122, 125; decline of, 172–76; disdain for, 176–77; dominance of, 14, 19, 23; Ohio River business of, 149–50, 163–64; packets bought by, 19; policy against recording bands of, 82, 151; profits of, 21; riverboat jazz as invention of, 142; rock'n'roll resisted by, 172; roustabouts replaced with dance bands by, 53; segregated cruises of, 58, 102, 103, 163; ticket sales of, 27–28; unionization supported by, 54–55, 127; values embedded in, 9, 27
Streckfus Steamers Magazine: historical themes in, 24; racist stereotypes in, 29–30, 84
strikes, 52
Stuckey, Sterling, 73–74
suburbanization, 172
Sudhalter, Richard, 128, 133, 140
Sullivan, Maxine, 153
swan complex: concept of, 32–34; riverboat jazz as intertwined with, 175; tempi of, 35, 48–49
Swanson, Leslie, 42
Sweatman, Wilbur, 91
syncopation concept, 49

Taft, William Howard, 91
Teagarden, Jack, 45
Tearney, Al, 123, 124
technology, 7, 23, 171–72
television, 21, 172
Telphy, James, 151
tempi: of Armstrong's recordings, 83–84; of swan complex, 35, 48–49
Terrace Gardens (Davenport), 120
Terry, Clark, 4, 56, 58, 99, 150, 168
Teschemacher, Frank, 139
Theater Owners' Booking Association, 161

theaters: black movement in, 156; in Cape Girardeau, 136; in Davenport, 120, 125; racism and sexism in, 107–8, 162, 167; in St. Louis, 95, 99; variety type of, 96–97
"There's a Cabin in the Pines," 83
Thomas, Walter, *61*, 111
Thornton, Clarence "Perch," 63, 150–51, *151*, 168, 176–77
Tom Sawyer (Twain), 86–87
Toomer, Jean, 39
tourism: dreams commercialized by, 14; promoters of, 9. *See also* passengers
Town, Floyd, 139
tramping, concept of, 17
tramp steamer, use of term, 17. *See also* excursion boats
transportation, 2, 13, 171–72. *See also* automobiles; excursion boats; packet boats; railroads
Trask, Clyde, 116
Trent, Alphonso, 106, 113, 147
Trigg, Tommy, 205n1
Trotter, Joe William, Jr., 145
Trumbauer, Frank, 128, 131–34
trumpet, role in jazz, 99–101
Turner, Victor, 193–94n6
Turpin, Charles Udell, 95, 98–99
Turpin, Thomas Million, 98–99, 100
Turrentine, Stanley, 153
Twain, Mark: Ferber's use of, 8; popularization of, 30; river romanticized by, 28, 86–87, 121; on steamboat appearance, 26; youthful rebellion popularized by, 14, 15, 17
Tyler, Jesse Gerald, 97–98

unionism: failures of, 166–67; importance of, 54–55, 107; racial segregation in, 38, 44, 55, 106, 166–67; of roustabouts, 51; sightreading requirements in, 54–55, 126–27; wage negotiations and, 80, 107–8. *See also* American Federation of Musicians
United States: axis of trade in, 13; boat regulations of, 172–73; commercialized idealization of, 11; cultural and technological changes in, 171–72

United States Coast Guard, 26
United States Mail Line, 143
United States Navy band, 168
University of Pittsburgh, 160
urban renewal, 169–70

Vardeman, James Kimble, 92
variety saloons and theaters, 96–97
vaudeville, 96, 121, 167
Vaughan, George, 95
Vaughan, Sarah, 114
Verne Swain, 16, 163
Victor Dance Music Records, 47, 83, 84, 121
Victor Talking Machine Company, 44
Vocalion Records, 103, 113
Von Holtz (teacher), 158
voodoo, 68, 97
voyages of discovery: dreams of, 8, 13–14, 28; imagination and, 30, 32; water's centrality in, 2–4

wages: of bandleaders, 40; of black vs. white bands, 45–46, 55; of New Orleans musicians, 69, 79–80; of Pittsburgh musicians, 154, 155, 166–67; post-WWII, 173; of roustabouts, 52, 53; union negotiations and, 80, 107–8
Walker, Madame C. J., 156
Waller, Thomas "Fats," 38, 106, 145
Warfield, Charlie, 98
Washington, 21, *80*, *149*, 150, 163
Washington, Buck, 82, 161
water and waterways: associations of, 1, 2–3; musical exchange along, 10; popularization of life along, 8; symbolism of, 32, 73–74; transatlantic circuits of exchange along, 194n17. *See also* canals; rivers; voyages of discovery
water pollution, 7
Way, Frederick, 12–13
Webb, Andrew "Big Baby," 100
Webb, Chick, 38
Webb, Speed, 147
welfare state, Jive for, 156
West Africans: political movements of, 168–70; water's symbolism for, 73–74

West Indies, chanteys' origins in, 85
West Memphis Packet Company, 91
Westphal, Frank, 121
Wettling, George, 128–29
WEW (radio), 105
Wharton, Elizabeth Lillian (later Marable), 40
Wheeler, Mary, 37, 88
"When It's Sleepy Time Down South," 85–86
"When the Saints Go Marching In," 70
Whispering Band of Gold, 111
White, Amos, *61*
White, Cecil, 113
Whiteman, Paul, 34, 48, 126, 132, 134, 151
whites: attitudes toward riverboat jobs, 55; at black clubs, 152–53; blacks as mystery to, 67; curiosity of, 5, 54; Great Migration viewed as threat by, 81–82; privileges of, 116–17; venues controlled by, 106–8, 162, 167
Whyte, Zack, 146
Wiley, Arnold, 113
Willett, Jack, *131*
Williams, "Black Benny," 68
Williams, Clarence, 44
Williams, Cootie, 69
Williams, George, 91
Williams, John Overton, 160–61
Williams, Mary Lou: as anticolonialist, 168–69; background of, 153, 159–60, 166; bookings for, 167; jobs of, 160–61; on move to Pittsburgh, 141; playing style of, 164; sightreading learned by, 161–62
Williams, Ralph, 115, 205n1
Williams and Piron Music Publishing Company, 44
WIL (radio), 111
Wilson, August, 164–66
Wilson, Teddy, 83–84, 109
Wisherd, D. W., 91, 126, 137–38
WLW (radio), 145
WOC (radio), 120
Wolverine Orchestra, 132, *133*, 146
women: as jazz pianists, 153; Jive for, 156
Wood, Leo, 129

Wooding, Sam, 146
Works Progress Administration (WPA), 155, 156, 157, 160
World War I, horror of, 116
World War II: effects on excursion boat business, 39–40; racial discrimination in, 167–68
Worley, William S., 90
Wrixon, Albert "Doc," 116, 123, 125, 126, 205n1

Yazoo and Mississippi Valley Railroad Company, 173
Young, Lester, 139
Young, Nathan B., 52, 98

Zebulon Pike, 143
Zuckerkandl, Victor, 7, 194n10